# STORIES FROM THE OLD TESTAMENT

## Volume II

# The Lion Classic Bible Series

*Genesis: The Book of Beginnings*

*Stories from the Old Testament: Volume I*

*Stories from the Old Testament: Volume II*

*The Book of Job: Why Do the Innocent Suffer?*

*The Psalms: Ancient Poetry of the Spirit*

*The Song of Solomon: Love Poetry of the Spirit*

*Sayings of the Wise: The Legacy of King Solomon*

*The Hebrew Prophets: Visionaries of the Ancient World*

*The Great Sayings of Jesus: Proverbs, Parables and Prayers*

*The Gospel of St John: The Story of the Son of God*

*The New Testament Epistles: Early Christian Wisdom*

*Revelation: The Apocalypse of St John*

# STORIES FROM THE
# OLD TESTAMENT

## Volume II

### From King David
### to the Return from Exile

Partially abridged from the text of the
Revised English Bible

Foreword by Morris West
Introduction by Lawrence Boadt

A LION BOOK

Copyright © 1998 Lion Publishing
Arrangement and abridgement copyright
© 1998 Lion Publishing

Published by
**Lion Publishing plc**
Sandy Lane West, Oxford, England
ISBN 0 7459 3889 2

First edition 1998
10 9 8 7 6 5 4 3 2 1 0

Typeset in 10/12 Berkeley Oldstyle
Printed and bound in Great Britain by
Caledonian International Book Manufacturing, Glasgow

# Contents

# ACKNOWLEDGMENTS

The Introduction has been taken from *Reading the Old Testament: An Introduction* by Lawrence Boadt, copyright © 1984 by permission of Paulist Press.

The text of 'Stories from the Old Testament in Literature' has been selected from *A Dictionary of Biblical Tradition in English Literature*, edited by David Lyle Jeffrey, copyright © 1992 by permission of Wm B. Eerdmans Publishing Co.

The abridged text of 'Stories from the Old Testament' (except Jonah and Esther, which are unabridged) has been taken from the Revised English Bible copyright © 1989 by permission of Oxford and Cambridge University Presses.

Robert Frost, 'Masque of Mercy', has been reproduced from *The Poetry of Robert Frost*, edited by Edward Connery Lathem. Copyright © 1947 by Robert Frost, © 1975 by Lesley Frost Ballantine. Published by Jonathan Cape: page 96.

# Foreword

The people of Israel were and are the people to whom their God – the God of Abraham, Isaac and Jacob – was constantly and intimately present. They were in constant discussion, debate and even contention with God.

They understood the commandments of that God, although they were frequently in breach of them. They held to a messianic promise, although the fulfilment of that promise was delayed for generation after generation. They suffered captivities and exiles, but even in the darkest hours God was present to them, a participant in the drama of their lives. Their heroes and heroines, David, Solomon and Esther, were celebrated in the heroic mode. Their delinquencies were recorded on the same epic scale without ever losing their human character.

The element of heroic prophecy is important to the understanding of the Old Testament. It is heroic because it transcends the circumstances of the Jewish people themselves. It is always larger than they are because God is with them, speaking through prophets, heroes and flawed leaders. God is never banished from their personal and national experience. Their cosmos may appear to be in disorder, but the disorder is neither permanent nor radical because of the Creator who made them and who chose them as a particular people.

Islam acknowledged this particular people as the people of the book. The New Testament expresses a different fulfilment of messianic prophecy and attributes other meanings to the characters of the Old Testament. However, Judaic tradition pervades all our Western thought.

This second volume of stories from the Old Testament is an admirable companion to the first. It is a forecourt to the experience of the scriptures themselves because it is not a daunting document but a distillation, not only of the history of a nation but also of its legacy to the world.

*Morris L. West*

# INTRODUCTION

## The Story of David

### David's rise to power

The second half of 1 Samuel (chapters 16–31) traces David's rise to power as Saul's fortunes decline. The prophet Samuel transfers his blessing and anointing from Saul to David; as a result, David is forced to flee. At the same time he begins to build his own power base in the desert areas of Judah, even serving as a mercenary army leader for the Philistine king of Gath. But he does protect the southern tribes from desert raids and from Philistine attacks while making his Philistine overlord think that he is completely loyal to him. Meanwhile Saul wastes his resources and energy searching for David while the Philistines regroup their forces. The end for Saul finally comes in a great battle on Mount Gilboa in the centre of the country. Saul and Jonathan are both killed and the army routed. The era of Saul has ended and that of David has begun.

The book of 2 Samuel centres on the reign of David. It can be divided into two parts. Chapters 1–8 show how he managed to consolidate power in his own hands and to win a large empire for the newly united Israel. Chapters 9–20 record the downfall of many of his hopes as struggles in his own family weaken his reign. It is the story of how his sons fight to become his successor on the throne. Much of the tragic outcome develops from David's own sin.

The rise of David to power showed that he was both a military and a political genius. He defeated his Philistine masters and extended the borders of Israel across all the small states of Syria and Transjordan. He could really be said to rule from the 'river of Egypt to the Euphrates' (Genesis 15:18; Joshua 1:4). Thus the dreams of Israel were fulfilled in David. But even greater than his military conquests was his gift of winning over others to his cause. He had won the loyalty of the South by showering them with benefits while nominally a servant of the Philistines, and was crowned king of Judah at Hebron shortly after Saul's death. He then patiently manoeuvred and waited for the collapse of the badly run remnant of a state set up by Saul's surviving son, Ishbosheth. 2 Samuel 3:1 expresses this period succinctly: 'There followed a long war between the house of Saul and the house of David, in which David grew stronger and the house of Saul weaker.' Finally, Ishbosheth's general, Abner, turned traitor and joined David, Ishbosheth was killed, and the northern tribes came to Hebron and offered to make David their king also. The fact that he became king by *mutual* agreement was very important in the centuries ahead since he took the throne not by right nor by conquest, but by the free consent of these tribes. Later, after the death of Solomon, they would withdraw from his kingdom and form an independent state.

David then accomplished a second brilliant move. He captured the Canaanite city of Jerusalem from a group called the Jebusites. It stood on the border between Judah and the northern tribes and yet was not part of either. David made it his capital, and from then on it was popularly called the city of David. He brought the ark of the covenant into the city to his palace grounds and placed it in a tent, perhaps the very tent that had been used during the desert wanderings in the time of Moses. An oracle by his prophet Nathan prevented him from constructing the magnificent temple he wished, but God did promise him an even greater blessing in 2 Samuel 7, a dynasty that would not end.

This special promise to David forms the high point of the books of Samuel and was celebrated and remembered in the psalms and worship of Judah as the basis of God's special relationship with them. It was looked to as a sign of divine protection in many difficult periods during later centuries (see Isaiah 37:33–35). As a further effort at reconciliation and healing for all segments, David took under his care the last son of Saul, Mephibosheth, and the remaining sons of Eli, the priests of Shiloh who had cared for the ark.

## The dark side of David

Despite the high praises of the Bible, many scholars believe that David was a scheming and calculating war lord who rose to power by less than fully honest means. He may well have played off Saul against the Philistines, bought his loyalties in the south, created an army loyal to no cause but his own person, exploited the deaths of Saul and Jonathan to become king in place of the rightful heir, and perhaps could have arranged the death of Ishbosheth with Abner. While most of this is only hinted at behind the current story, the text does show his bloodthirsty ambition at work when he murders Uriah to get his beautiful wife Bathsheba (2 Samuel 11). The revolts by his own sons and the widespread support they received also suggest that many were unhappy with his despotic rule, especially among the northern tribes (2 Samuel 15–18). His forced labour gangs (2 Samuel 20) and establishment of a military draft after taking a census (2 Samuel 24) became hated elements of the monarchy.

Much of this material is gathered in the second part of 2 Samuel in a single narrative story which many authors today call 'The Court History of David' or 'The Succession Narrative'. It extends from 2 Samuel 9 through 1 Kings 2, with several appendices inserted at 2 Samuel 21–24. The anonymous author dramatically shows how David was able to conquer all external foes and heal the national wounds with the family of Saul, but could not keep peace in his own family. The story begins with a terrible sin by David, the murder of Uriah. When confronted by the prophet Nathan, David repents and does penance (2 Samuel 12). God's judgment through the word of the prophet will not disappear, however: 'Now the sword shall never depart from your house, because you have despised me in taking the wife of Uriah to be your wife. I will bring evil upon you *out of your own house*' (2 Samuel 12:10–11). God will stand by David, but the seeds of his own evil cannot be so easily wiped out.

The Court History is a skilful piece of narrative, filled with dramatic tension as it unfolds the flaws and weaknesses in David while still showing God's constant protection for him and the dynasty which he had founded. David was not perfect, but God's fidelity and promise never wavered. It is one of the best pieces of ancient literature, probably being composed during the reign of Solomon between 960–930BC. It is the fruit of the new culture that David brought to Israel as he established schools in the prosperity of empire.

How did David receive such high praise in the Old Testament tradition when he had so many dubious qualities about him? Key to the biblical portrait is David's blessing from Yahweh and his complete loyalty to Yahweh in return. He sinned, often seriously, but he never forsook this primary loyalty. As a great warrior, he brought the rule of Yahweh to many surrounding nations. As a king he received a promise of divine protection that actually lasted 400 years down to the final end of Judah and Jerusalem at the hands of the Babylonians in 586BC. He established Jerusalem and the central sanctuary of worship for Yahweh and became famous as a composer of psalms and prayers. Israel's memory of David is most influenced by these elements of divine help through which the nation was established soundly. The memory tends to forget or to downplay his weaknesses in 'The Succession Narrative', but it does remember that the primary meaning of both his successes and failures was not that David deserved the praise but God had used the weak king to accomplish his divine purpose.

## Solomon and Israel's Age of Glory

The story of Solomon opens in 1 Kings 2:12, with clear hints of what is to come. 'When Solomon was seated upon the throne of his father David, with his rule firmly established...' Above all, he was *decisive*. He put to death through one excuse or another almost all of the powerful or dangerous rivals from his father's time: Adonijah, his scheming brother; Joab the general who had made most of David's victories possible; the former rebel Shimei. He also exiled the Shiloh priest Abiathar back to his home. Next he cemented his relations with neighbouring kings, entering into a treaty with Hiram of Tyre to the north, and taking a daughter of the pharaoh of Egypt to be his wife. He did more than make peace with Egypt, however. 1 Kings 4 tells how Solomon organized the new empire of Israel along the lines of administration used in Egypt. David had already set up several officials modelled on Egyptian offices (see 2 Samuel 8:16–20; 20:23–26); Solomon added a prime minister, called, as in Egypt itself, the 'one over the house'.

If we had only chapters 3–10 of 1 Kings, Solomon would appear to be an ideal ruler, wise in every respect, lordly in style, pious in his devotion to Yahweh, a king who thought only of the protection of his kingdom, the honour of his God, and the welfare of his people. Even with several passages added in by the Deuteronomic editors that warn the king that prosperity would depend on obedience to God's law and commands (1 Kings 3:14; 9:4–9), the overall picture is one of complete admiration for Solomon's kingship. This praise stems from the central place given to the building of the temple in the history of the Old Testament. Solomon was great because he established Yahweh's house, which was the centre of the nation's worship, faith and hope in their God. Solomon's blessing was understood in the light of God's giving of the temple.

But in chapter 11 a different mood prevails. This chapter shows us another side of Solomon which the tradition condemned. It is also likely to be closer to the real truth about him than the ideal picture drawn in earlier chapters. He becomes a tyrant who outdoes even pagan kings in the luxury of his lifestyle with a thousand wives and concubines. In this, he violated the law of Moses about intermarrying with foreign peoples. But even worse, he built temples for all of their gods as they wished: to Chemosh, god of Moab, and to Moloch, god of Ammon, and to others. In 1 Kings 11:5 it is even recorded that he performed rites for Astarte and Milcom. At the same time, he required vast amounts of supplies to feed and support the large bureaucracy he created, and these had to be obtained by taxing the citizens. Even worse in the eyes of most Israelites were the forced labour gangs he used to build his great projects.

But the major friction created by Solomon's policies came when he transferred rights and privileges from the tribes to the person of the king. Where David had been careful to respect the tribes and their ideals, to win their agreement to him as king, and to avoid favouring one section against another, Solomon aggressively did the opposite. He laid down new boundaries for provinces which split tribes apart, and he seemed to favour the ways of Canaanites and other foreigners over Israel's traditions. He even encouraged religious practices that opposed the worship of Yahweh as the sole God in Israel. He probably was a sincere believer in Yahweh, but he adopted so many pagan practices of ritual and decoration for the temple that he neglected the simple and severe demands of Yahweh's faith that centred on the covenant and the people as a community.

## The Kingdom Divided

Trouble was already brewing when Solomon died after a forty year reign. His great building projects had required heavy taxes and a forced draft of skilled labourers and engineers to build them. Moreover, he needed to maintain a very large and costly army to keep the small neighbouring countries, which David had conquered, under Israel's control. Even worse from many people's standpoint, he disregarded the religious faith and tribal roots that had made Israel what it was. His foreign wives and their pagan gods angered faithful believers, and his redivision of the country to break up the tribes and put all the governors directly under royal control offended the local identity and loyalty of the tribes.

Solomon's son Rehoboam was forced to go to Shechem and discuss the situation with the tribal leaders. When he refused to make any changes in his father's policies, the ten northern tribes broke away from the king and his tribe of Judah, declaring, 'What share have we in David?... To your tents, O Israel! Now look to your own house, O David' (1 Kings 12:16). Rehoboam was forced to flee south to Jerusalem to save his life, while the northern leaders called on Jeroboam, a former chief of Solomon's forced labour gangs who had revolted and fled, to be their king. Now there were two kingdoms: a northern one which called itself Israel, after the old tribal customs, and a southern one, still loyal to the house of David and Solomon, and made up of only the tribe of Judah (and the remnants of Simeon).

Thus began a period of rivalry between the two parts of the Israelite people. The border between the two kingdoms ran only ten miles north of Jerusalem, the southern capital, and the tribal area of Benjamin which lay on the border was constantly being fought over by both nations. Judah had a far smaller population and a more rugged, desert land, but had the advantage of a closer unity among its people, a fierce loyalty to the ruling house of David, and a more isolated and protected geographical location from strong powers to the east. It also possessed the temple in Jerusalem with its ark of the covenant – the two major objects in the worship of Yahweh.

The northern kingdom contained the richer and more fertile part of Palestine, including the lush valley of Esdraelon and the green hills of Galilee. It also had a far greater population. Jeroboam, its first king, set about quickly to create a state with an identity of its own. He named two old and venerated shrine cities as the centres of worship to replace the attraction of Jerusalem: Dan and Bethel. He built two golden calves so that each shrine would have a symbol to counteract the ark of the covenant as Yahweh's seat. The bull-calf was not a pagan god in itself, but rather intended as a throne on which God's invisible presence would reside. He also set about fortifying and repairing Shechem, Bethel and Penuel, the northern cities in which Jacob had lived, so that the people would look back to their older roots in the tribes and forget the more recent Davidic covenant and claims. All in all, Jeroboam was quite successful in this task. Despite the condemnations of much later prophets from Judah, such as Jeremiah and Ezekiel, who lived long after the northern kingdom had been destroyed, no prophet who actually lived or worked in the northern kingdom, such as Elijah, Elisha, Hosea or Amos, ever condemned the shrines as false worship. Only later did Israel look back and see that this was part of the reason for God's punishment and anger against the nation.

The 200 years from 922BC, when Jeroboam began to rule, down to 722, when the northern kingdom fell to the Assyrians, were mostly taken up by war: either battles against Assyria, border disputes with Judah, revolt by subject peoples such as Moab, or the struggle against the growing power of the new Aramean state of Damascus in Syria. The Arameans wanted all the border areas of Israel across the Jordan to the east. Damascus had a number of energetic kings named either Ben hadad or Hazael whose military attacks often posed a grave threat to the very existence of the northern kingdom. But it was above all the age of the rise of Assyria, the great Mesopotamian power. Assyrian ambition was to conquer all the western lands, and it slowly but surely moved against its neighbours in the two centuries after Solomon's death.

## The Books of Kings

The two books of Kings tell the story of the period from David's death to the fall of the southern kingdom of Judah in 586BC before the Babylonians. Thus, in one sense, they can be called the history of David's dynasty, although the picture they present is much larger. It includes the struggles between the northern kingdom and Judah, the rise and flourishing of prophecy, and a religious judgment on everything that happened during these four centuries.

After devoting the first eleven chapters of 1 Kings to the death of David and the reign of Solomon, the rest of the chapters relate the individual reigns of each king in the north and in the south by means of special formulas which begin and end the account of the king. The dates are carefully recorded and compared to the dates of the king in the other kingdom, so that we can gain a good idea of the actual history of the period from these accounts.

The history in 1 and 2 Kings reveals that Judah had a much more stable sense of nationhood. The listing of the queen-mother in each king's dates shows the importance of naming the important families which intermarried with the royal house, and the place of honour and authority given to women at the government's highest level. On the other hand, northern Israel had nineteen kings in just about half the amount of time. Northern prophets and tribal leaders were also much harder on the kings. A large number were assassinated, and often the prophets themselves incited war leaders to kill the king and take over. Such was the case with Jehu in the time of Elisha the prophet, and it even accounts for the original choice of Jeroboam himself, who was picked out by a prophet, Ahijah, in 1 Kings 11. Northern Israel rose and fell in just about 200 years, and most of its life was spent fighting one enemy or another. Judah survived as a kingdom under one dynasty for over 400 years.

### The prophets Elijah and Elisha

About fifty years after Solomon's death, Omri came to the throne of northern Israel, founded a new capital of Samaria and re-established a slipping Israel to power. He cemented relations with the Phoenician kingdom to the north in Lebanon by marrying his son Ahab to a daughter of the king of Tyre, Jezebel. His political sense worked well – even many years later, the Assyrians were still calling the land of Israel by the name 'house of Omri'. But by bringing in a queen who worshipped the pagan god Baal and permitting her to set up a temple to the cult of Baal, Omri stirred up the prophets against his house and began a contest for religious domination that finally brought down his own dynasty in a bloodbath under Jehu some thirty years later.

The central figures in this drama were the prophets Elijah and Elisha. They left no written words like many later prophets, and are found only in the great stories told *about* them in 1 Kings 17–21 and 2 Kings 1–9. Many of these stories are hero-legends, with lots of colour and bravado and great deeds beyond anything performed by ordinary people. For this reason, historians are careful to sort out what probably happened from the great mass of enthusiastic praise and often exaggerated claims in these stories. Miracles make up a large part of their way of acting, and most biblical scholars understand these to be more a means of showing how extraordinary these prophets were, than to be actual events as they are described. It should be noted that we have the words and deeds of many prophets in the years after, and none ever mention such miracles as part of their prophetic mission. No doubt Elijah and Elisha had great psychic and healing powers and did some remarkable things that made a lasting impression on their age, but the present stories have a distinct flavour of the legendary about them.

Elisha, Elijah's disciple, succeeded Elijah as a leading speaker for Yahwistic faith in the northern kingdom. Most readers are familiar with the story of how Elijah was taken to heaven in a fiery chariot and his cloak fell down upon Elisha, who then received the power of Elijah as a prophet (2 Kings 2). But Elisha does *not* work in the style of Elijah – a wild man, wearing a hairy garment and appearing and disappearing suddenly and where least expected. Rather, Elisha seems to be settled down, often associated with a large band of followers, who work themselves into ecstasy with the help of music and dance. Elisha himself is described as a man of miraculous powers, sometimes for the good of those who seek him out and sometimes for harm. He can do all the miracles that Elijah did, raising the dead to life and multiplying food, and much more besides. He brings up heavy metal axes from the bottom of a lake, cleanses the poisoned water of a spring, and calls down bears to maul boys who laugh at him.

But Elisha was more than a wonder-worker. He was a guardian of the true faith in Yahweh. Much more so than Elijah, Elisha directly entered the political world, dealing with officials of the enemy kingdom of Damascus who came to him. These included the traitor Hazael who planned to kill his king, Ben-hadad (2 Kings 8:7–15), and the general Naaman who needed to be cured of leprosy (2 Kings 5:1–27). He anointed Jehu, the Israelite general, to overthrow the dynasty of Ahab and his sons (2 Kings 9:1–37). Elisha was a prophet consulted by the elders, respected for his spirit power and famed for his prophetic word, but he always stood outside the mainstream of Israel's government. Like Elijah he was zealous for fidelity to Yahweh, but unlike Elijah he showed no special moral leadership on behalf of the poor or oppressed. The picture that emerges from the Elisha stories in 2 Kings is a combination of wonder tales about a holy man and reports of momentous political changes brought about by prophetic opposition to royal politics unfaithful to the traditional faith in Yahweh.

## The theology of the books of Kings

Amazingly, the large grouping of stories about the prophets Elijah and Elisha stand as a separate block (1 Kings 17 to 2 Kings 9) within the present books of Kings and have little or none of the moral evaluation found in the formulas that surround the long line of kings, both north and south, everywhere else in the books of Kings. However, stories about the two prophets are mixed together with narratives about the wars between Israel and Damascus in 1 Kings 20 and 22, as well as 2 Kings 3. Apparently, early editors combined the war stories with the lives of the prophets in order to emphasize the control of Yahweh during these desperate times, especially when he spoke through the words of his prophets. They were already written and well known before the author of the books of Kings sat down to compose his history. He simply included them whole in his work.

The one thing that the author of Kings did add was the emphasis on how Elijah and Elisha carried on the role of Moses, the founder of the faith. Just as Moses was a great mediator between Yahweh and Israel, so were these heroes of faith. Elijah goes up to Mount Sinai and experiences God in the rocks as Moses did in Exodus 34; he parts the Jordan as Moses did the Red Sea in Exodus 14; he goes up to heaven in a way seen by no one, as did Moses in Deuteronomy 34; he calls down fire on those who oppose Yahweh as Moses did in Numbers 11. In similar ways, Elisha imitates Moses – he too parts the Jordan, provides water in the desert and bread for the starving, and turns water to blood. For the author or authors of Kings, these two prophets carried on the missions of Moses to defend the covenant and maintain the commandments of Yahweh among a people who constantly murmured against the Lord.

This understanding of Elijah's and Elisha's role fits well into the theology of the larger history of the kings. The books of Kings use old records taken from a number of sources, such as the chronicles of the kings in both Judah and Israel and the legends of the prophets, but fits them into a framework which cares much more about *how faithful* these kings were than how much they *did*. Omri was undoubtedly a great power in his day, but gets barely any mention at all in 1 Kings 16:21–28, while many lesser rulers are treated at length. The only criterion seems to be whether the information will help the reader learn the lessons of history. And for the books of Kings, the lesson above all is that *infidelity to God's covenant given through Moses will lead to disaster and destruction*. Since the last king named is Zedekiah of Judah, who lived at the time of the final fall of the kingdom and the people's exile to Babylon in 586BC, the book's viewpoint looks back from that moment of total defeat and loss to find out why God has allowed it to happen. The answer is given that from the first kings down to the very last, both kingdoms failed to uphold the covenant and its commandments.

## The Books of Chronicles

Because of the changed world of Israel after the exile, the priestly leaders felt the need for an updated version of Israel's history. They took up and rewrote the great Deuteronomic history found in the books of Samuel and Kings from their own perspective. No doubt one important reason to do this was to explain the proper role of the kings over Israel in the past now that they were gone for good. Another was to emphasize the temple for religious worship.

Chronicles often follows the books of Samuel and Kings word for word through whole chapters. But we get a sense of its distinctive message when we compare the many places where it either leaves out matter found in Kings or adds to it new material. In the story of David, for example, it leaves out altogether his terrible sin with Bathsheba, or the revolt of his own son Absalom, and never mentions David's deathbed instructions to kill all his enemies. When Kings reports that David sinned in taking a census, Chronicles adds that it was Satan that tempted him. For the Chronicler, David was a holy and dedicated leader who followed Yahweh faithfully. All his faults are set aside or downplayed. Instead, the Chronicler praises David even more than Kings does. He stresses David's role in composing the psalms and establishing guilds of Levites to serve the temple. And while David never built the temple itself, in Chronicles he gets everything ready and makes all the plans which Solomon only has to carry out (despite the fact that this clearly contradicts the view of the authors of Samuel and Kings that David was forbidden to plan a temple – see 2 Samuel 7). In Chronicles David also prays a lot. In short, David is shown to be totally consumed with zeal for the right worship of Yahweh. He becomes a second lawgiver almost as great as Moses.

This picture of David as the founder of a community centred on the temple becomes the standard by which the Chronicler then judges the rest of Israel's history. For example, he explains the exile and destruction of the nation as the result of the people's failure to perform true worship. The main section of the Chronicler's history (from 1 Chronicles 10 to 2 Chronicles 34) was written soon after the preaching of Haggai and Zechariah and the pitiful rebuilding of the temple in 516BC. It was intended as a blueprint for struggling Judeans just back from exile. Past failures of the people and the true example of David's faith both teach a lesson about how urgent is the need to restore the temple liturgy to its proper ritual, and perhaps even a search for a new king like David who would dedicate his life not to political glory but to the glory of God's worship.

## The Book of Ezra

Ezra can be divided into two major parts: chapters 1–6 and 7–10. Ezra 1–6 gives us some valuable information about the first two groups of returning exiles – those under Sheshbazzar, and those under Zerubbabel. This first part of the Book of Ezra reaches a climax in the rebuilding of the temple in 516BC.

The scene shifts to many years later in chapters 7–10. Under the Persian king Artaxerxes, Ezra, a priest of the highest rank, a descendant of Aaron and Zadok, is sent from Babylon to restore the practice of Israelite faith according to the instructions in the 'law of God' (see Ezra 7:10, 14, 25–26). Ezra faces two major problems. Many Israelites have married Gentiles, and this prevents them from keeping the law. Secondly, there was a general disregard for the regulations about sacrifice, worship, purity and special Jewish customs. He tackled both of these head-on. First, he acted forcefully to invalidate all marriages to pagans. This was not an easy task, for no doubt most of these marriages had been made in good faith and there were children to think of. Ezra called a great assembly of the people and they made public confession of their sins and faults. As a result, the men agreed to give up their foreign wives. They also agreed to observe the weekly sabbath day of rest and to support the temple with a yearly tax.

Ezra followed this policy because any religious reform, especially one which demanded that the people practise the unique requirements of their covenant law at home, would have been impossible if a large part of the people had different faiths and practices in their homes. There was the special stress not only on Israel's election by God as a chosen people, but on the need to be holy and set apart as a community to give witness to other nations. Unity of faith and practice was essential to achieve this goal.

The second problem was to re-establish the whole range of practices that most characterized Israel's special way of life. To this end, Ezra brought out the book of the law of God and had it read to the people in a second great assembly. Once again they celebrated a penance service and a renewal of the promise to obey the covenant in everything. As Ezra read the words, the people wept. At the same time, Levites and priests helped to explain the meaning of each passage to the people. And Ezra himself took the priests and leaders aside and instructed them in the central points of the law. At the conclusion of this ceremony, the people celebrated the seven-day feast of Tabernacles in its pure form as the law had prescribed.

This whole scene is told not in the Book of Ezra but in chapters 8–9 of Nehemiah. It was put there to link Ezra's renewal of the covenant with Nehemiah's completion of the city walls to make Jerusalem a safe home for the temple. It seems almost certain that the law of God that Ezra read was an early version of the present five books of the Torah/Pentateuch. The events described in Nehemiah 8–9 fit very closely the priestly source regulations on the priests, the feast-day observances, and the manner of accepting a covenant found in the Pentateuch, even though Ezra and Nehemiah never quote it directly.

Ezra's role was decisive. Every audience we have seen up to this time showed a Judah with little cohesion, having trouble getting itself together and with dashed hopes of a glorious new day after the exile. Ezra was able to restore the spirit of the people and set the underpinnings for the ideals of holiness, sense of election, and a worship-centred community of faith. He gave a new charter for a new Israel – the authentic traditions of the past were now written down forever in the Pentateuch as a normative guidebook for the future. And most important of all, the final priestly character of the Pentateuch showed a concrete way to put these traditions into daily practice for ordinary believers.

## The Book of Nehemiah

Nehemiah began his work in the twentieth year of King Artaxerxes I – about 445BC. He was a high official in the court despite the lowly-sounding title he bore, 'royal cupbearer'. Nehemiah was a Jew, and had received a heartbreaking letter from his own brother in Palestine describing the terrible conditions that existed there. Since he was an advisor of the king, he had no difficulty in getting the king's ear. He persuaded Artaxerxes to make Judah an independent province, name him its governor, and allow him to rebuild the city walls of Jerusalem. He was skilled enough in political matters to foresee that he would face great obstacles from local officials who did not want any change in the power structure. Nehemiah quickly surveyed the situation and made preparations to start on the walls shortly after his arrival.

But as soon as the project became public, Sanballat, the governor of Samaria, Tobiah, the governor of Ammon, and Geshem, the governor of Edom and the Arab tribes sent troops to stop the fortifications. Nehemiah armed his own workers and finished the basic wall in a rapid fifty-two days. The speed with which he managed to get the work done shows how willing the people were to complete the project. He found, however, that the regulations of the law were being barely obeyed, and he was forced to take measures to re-establish the marriage laws and the sabbath observances. These were the same problems faced by Ezra, and it reveals how difficult was the task of making the reforms take hold permanently among the Jews.

Nehemiah was governor from 445 to 433. When his term ended, he returned to Susa, the capital of Persia. A year or two later he was reappointed and found that the law had again fallen into disuse. This time he took very strong action. He prevented people by force from doing business on the sabbath, broke up marriages with foreigners, arranged permanent sources for the support of the Levites, and even threw out all the furniture of the Ammonite governor Tobiah from an apartment in the temple which the high priest, a relative, had let the governor use.

The Book of Nehemiah is built up around the memoirs of the governor in chapters 1–7 and 11–13. The nature of such an ancient 'autobiography' was to leave a pious record of the leader's achievements. Thus we can expect a rather glowing account of his sense of duty and his success in carrying out his tasks. At the same time, it is an extremely valuable glimpse into the life and thought of a fifth-century Jew. It does not tell us very much about the author's feelings, only his work, but it is perhaps the only first-person story that we actually find in the Old Testament.

## The Book of Jonah

Jonah is found among the prophetic books, but it is totally unlike any other prophetic book. It contains no oracles at all, except the report of Jonah's words to Nineveh in Jonah 3:5. It is a story *about* a prophet, and right from the beginning we are warned to take this prophet with a grain of salt. The author has a great sense of literary style, full of abrupt changes of direction in thought, humorous touches, and unexpected twists in the plot.

Its major literary style is that of irony. Jonah does everything a good prophet should not; from fleeing, to refusing to speak, to complaining that God does not fulfil all the threats of doom that he made Jonah preach. But it is also set up in a number of clever panels, so that the prayer in chapter 2 parallels exactly the dialogue found in chapter 4, although one is praise, the other complaint.

The hero of the story is himself a kind of ironic note. Jonah ben Amittai is mentioned in 2 Kings 14:25 as a prophet who predicts that King Jeroboam II will be able to expand his kingdom to take over the pagan nations. Here Jonah is summoned to preach the opposite – that God will bless these pagan nations. The book really addresses two major questions: (1)What is the relation of Israel and her God to other nations? (2) What is the meaning of divine justice? Jonah becomes a perfect character for the discussion of whether God can in fact use a prophet to bring good news to pagan nations. Certainly the lesson is clear: God's mercy is more powerful than his judgments, and his plan will not be thwarted even by the negative 'righteousness' of his prophet. Along the way the author makes use of several major prophetic stories from earlier books of the Bible. The prayer of Jonah in the belly of the fish resembles the prayer of King Hezekiah during his illness in Isaiah 38:10–20. Jonah's stay under the leafy plant is built on a similar incident from the life of Elijah – only Elijah proved obedient (1 Kings 19). Nineveh finds faith as a divine gift, as Abraham did in Genesis 15:6. Above all, Jonah echoes expressions taken from Jeremiah, such as his use of 'man and beast' to stand for everything that lives in the land (Jonah 3:7–8), found in Jeremiah 7:20, 27:5, etc.

The reasons for reminding the reader of the entire history of prophecy from the beginning until the post-exilic days becomes clear in the final verses of the book. Does not God have greater pity and compassion on people, even pagans, than Jonah demands he have about a mere shrub? The book forcefully reminds Israel that prophecy had not simply been aimed at condemning all their enemies and making them feel important. Instead of claiming that their special place in God's covenant made them separate and better, they must recognize that God chose them to be witnesses to all peoples that God also loves them.

The message of course is more than just this one point. The story of Jonah has several lessons that work on many levels as we read it:

(1) it presents the universal love of God even for Gentiles
(2) it shows God's control over all of nature and all peoples
(3) it ridicules some of the narrow nationalism in Judah
(4) it is a satire on the actions of many prophets
(5) it affirms that God is not merely 'just' in his actions
(6) in fact, God acts in strange and sometimes humorous ways
(7) and we cannot figure God out according to our desires.

In short, Jonah is both entertainment and lesson, aimed at the community of Israel in the period after the exile. It reminds us that the spirit of Israel had not died or been frozen by Ezra's reforms and the growing sense of stability centred on the priesthood, the temple and the book of the law. Post-exilic Judaism kept alive its sense of covenant and election as a gift of Yahweh to be shared with the world.

## The Book of Daniel

In English translations of the Bible, Daniel is always found as the fourth of the major prophets, standing immediately after Ezekiel and before the twelve minor prophets. This follows the Greek traditions of the Septuagint and it is easy to tell why they thought it should be among the more important prophets. The book is filled with dreams and visions that reveal coming events. But, in contrast, the Hebrew Bible always places Daniel among the last of the writings, and does not consider it to be prophecy at all. Indeed, it can be readily understood as edifying examples of trust in God not much different from the stories of Esther, Judith and Tobit. Some scholars consider it to be prophecy, others to be wisdom, and others to be a whole new kind of literature called apocalyptic, because it speaks about the overthrow of the whole world order.

The entire book claims to take place in the sixth century BC and to report a series of visions that come to the boy Daniel, who is remarkable for his great wisdom and his ability to receive divine revelation about the future. Few scholars today, however, believe that this book originated in any way during the days of the Babylonian exile. And the ones who do usually have a very difficult time explaining the references to historical people and places which seem to be grossly wrong.

The first part of the book is a collection of tales that originated during the Persian era from 529 to 333. They reflect many Persian court customs and interests, such as astrology and dream interpretation. But they are written from a very Jewish point of view using a legendary hero who was taken captive in the exile as a young boy and brought up in the court of the Babylonian king. This Daniel carefully observes all the Jewish dietary laws and yet stays healthier than his comrades (chapter 1); he interprets dreams that no one else can understand (chapters 2 and 4); he predicts the fall of Babylon (chapter 5), and is thrown in to a lions' den for refusing to worship idols and yet is saved by God (chapter 6). These are all charming stories that make the point that God guards and blesses those who are faithful to him in following the law and in observing prayer. Because the stories are set in the moment of Israel's greatest persecution and disaster, they provide an example of how God delivers all who are faithful in their hour of greatest need.

The second part in chapters 7–12 with its four visions is also set during the Babylonian and early Persian years. Daniel is shown all the events of the centuries to come right down to the time of Antiochus IV Epiphanes and his persecution of the Jews.

The clear purpose of these visions is to predict in a veiled fashion the end of the kingdom of Antiochus Epiphanes and his persecution. This makes it highly probable that the author of chapters 7–12 was living through this terrible time and wrote these visions to give strength to Jews suffering for their faith with the promise that God would end both the persecutor and his persecution shortly.

Although the Book of Daniel is not intended to be primarily an historical record, it does reflect the general course of events in the post-exilic period from the time of Nebuchadnezzar down to the

Maccabees, a period of nearly four hundred years. Its whole purpose is to interpret that history without being wedded to the details. The authors were intensely interested in what was happening and what God would do about it. They were convinced that God really does act at every moment even when it may seem that he has abandoned his people. They also tried to answer why Israel suffered, and why God allowed people to be martyred for following his law. These were pressing problems at the time of the Maccabees, and the authors used all the skill at their command to create an answer, combining wisdom, prophecy and the new form of apocalyptic.

## The Book of Esther

The Book of Esther contains a thrilling tale of escape from mortal danger for the Jews. It is set in the Persian period under King Xerxes, who ruled from 486 to 465BC, and tells the story of a beautiful young Jewish maiden, Esther, who is chosen to be his queen when he becomes angry with his first queen and divorces her. Esther brings along her cousin and guardian, Mordecai, but soon he has enraged the Persian prime minister, Haman, by refusing him the proper signs of respect. In anger, Haman convinces the king that he should destroy all the Jews in a day of slaughter because they follow their own religion and do not worship as the Persians do. In this crisis, Mordecai convinces Esther to go before the king and change his mind. The king is won over when he realizes Haman's evil intentions, and he instead orders the prime minister to be slain while he gives the Jews permission to have their day of slaughter against their enemies. The book ends with the establishment of the feast of Purim, to be kept forever as a memorial of this great day of victory

Thus one purpose of the book is to give the reason for the feast of Purim. But another reason is to show that the Jewish people must always keep themselves separated from the dangers of pagan governments and be prepared to defend their own faith when it is in danger. Interestingly, although every other book of the Old Testament has been found at Qumran among the famous Dead Sea Scrolls, no copy of Esther is known. The reason for this may well be in the wild nature of the feast of Purim at the time. The Jewish rabbis who wrote the Talmud noted that the two-day festival (one day to celebrate the slaughter of enemies in Persia, the second to celebrate the slaughter of those in the provinces) became so carried away with wine and rejoicing that some could not distinguish between 'Blest be Mordecai' and 'Cursed be Haman'. For the sectarian Jews who lived a monastic life in the desert at Qumran, such levity was not tolerable.

But the Book of Esther was much appreciated in mainline Judaism. It became part of the Megilloth, the scroll of five short books that were to be read on feast days. Since the book was written to explain why a feast came to be, a real incident probably lies somewhere behind the present drama. Although the written story of Esther is played out on the level of the king and queen of Persia, it builds upon some local threat to the Jewish community that was averted by an unknown heroine. This small, original event became celebrated in prayer and story and from it the authors developed their final version. It is a difficult book to love since the spirit of vengeance seems to dominate the story. Moreover, it never mentions God or his direct help to his people. No one is sure why this is so, but it scandalized even the early Jewish translators of the Septuagint, who added to their translation prayers and petitions from Esther and Mordecai directly to God. The whole book must come from the latest Persian period or early Greek times. Its themes of divine help for persecuted Jews and the destruction of all their enemies are also found among other late books such as Judith and Daniel.

*Lawrence Boadt*

# STORIES FROM THE OLD TESTAMENT IN <u>LITERATURE</u>

## *Characters and Images*

# Characters and Images

## Abigail

The story in 1 Samuel 25:2–42 recounts how Abigail intervened to preserve her husband Nabal from sudden destruction at the hands of David and his men, only to become the handmaiden and bride of David after Nabal's death. Nabal and his flocks had been protected by David, but when David's messengers asked for hospitality from Nabal they were insulted and rebuffed; hence David's anger. Before David's avenging party could reach Nabal, Abigail met them on the road with gifts of food and a well-spoken apology for her churlish husband, who was on her account thus spared. Upon hearing of his narrow escape, Nabal became frightened, fell into a fit of despair (his 'heart turned to stone'), and died.

Abigail is noted in early Jewish commentary as the most important of David's wives, 'in whom beauty, wisdom and prophetical gifts were joined' (Ginzberg, *Legends of the Jews*, 4.117). She is reckoned with Sarah, Rahab, and Esther as one of the four most beautiful of all women (Megilla 15a; Seder Olam Rabba 21), and is also celebrated for her piety and quick-wittedness. Yet in some of the same sources it is observed that her appeal to David to 'remember thine handmaid' was really a form of coquetry and should not have been uttered to a man other than her husband (Megilla 14b; Sanhedrin 2.20b; 4.22b). In the 'Paradise of Women' she joins the wives of the patriarchs in supervising one of the seven divisions.

Prudence, in Chaucer's *Tale of Melibee*, intervening to temper her own husband's wrath, uses Abigail as perhaps a double-edged example to demonstrate the value of a virtuous wife's wit and prudent counsel (*Canterbury Tales*, 7.1099). In Dryden's *Absalom and Achitophel* (34) she becomes merely 'the Charming Annabel' whom 'Godlike' David could not deny himself. Mark Van Doren's 'Abigail' (*Collected and New Poems*, 1963) is a cunning and shrewd as well as beautiful envoy who, in a sense, condemns foolish Nabal even as she saves him from the retribution of another man with whom she has already fallen in love.

David L. Jeffrey
*University of Ottawa*

# Abishag

Abishag the Shunammite makes her appearance in 1 Kings 1:1–4 to 'cherish' old King David and minister to him, 'that my lord the king may get heat'. David is presented as weakened and nearing death (1:1), as indicated both by his inability to be warmed by the 'clothes' (better, 'blankets') put on his bed and by his inability to be sexually aroused by the maiden. The episode of old king and young virgin serves as transition to the drama of succession and the establishment of the Davidic dynasty.

Rabbinic interpretations follow the biblical account, assigning Abishag a limited yet significant and even heroic role. In Jewish tradition, Abishag is ancillary to David, and when Adonijah wants to marry her after David's death, the rabbis approve of Solomon's decision to eliminate his half-brother's oblique claim to the Davidic role by denying him her hand (1 Kings 2:13–25). Abishag does have a significant role in retellings of or references to the Davidic narrative until Dryden's 1681 *Absalom and Achitophel*, whose opening lines link David's political and sexual powers:

> Then *Israel's* Monarch, after Heaven's own heart,
> His vigorous warmth did, variously, impart
> To Wives and Slaves: and, wide as his Command,
> Scatter'd his Maker's Image through the Land.

Here Abishag's presence is only suggested as the terminus ad quem of David's procreative powers. An echo of these lines of Dryden's is added by Alexander Pope to his 1709 version of Chaucer's *Canterbury Tales*, '*David*, the Monarch after Heav'ns' own Mind, / Who lov'd our Sex, and honour'd all our Kind' (693–94). And there may be a similar hint of Abishag's role in Milton's *Paradise Lost* in the Archangel Michael's speech revealing the future to Adam (11:538–46).

In 'The Shunnamite' the self taught rural poet Stephen Duck produced what was acknowledged to be his best poem. In heroic couplets which echo Pope's diction and Dryden's choral structure, the woman of Shunem tells the story of how the prophet Elisha revived her son. After this Augustan compliment, more than seventy-five years elapsed before a poet was to refer to Abishag. She appears next in the first canto of Byron's *Don Juan* (1819), serving to fill out a stanza and cap a joke about the progress of young Don Juan's amorous education:

> Of his position I can give no notion:
> Physicians, leaving pill and notion,
> Prescribed, by way of blister, a young belle,
> When old King David's blood grew dull in motion,
> And that the medicine answer'd very well;
> Perhaps 'twas in a different way applied,
> For David lived, but Juan nearly died. (1.168)

While other Romantic writers and Victorians, for all their considerable interest in the Bible, do not refer to Abishag, some of the qualities of Byron's complex tone are present in Joseph Heller's 1984 novel *God Knows*, which begins with the demure and girlish Abishag ministering to David, who compares her to the worldly 'wide-hipped' Bathsheba, in a brilliant, wise-alecky monologue. Similarly, Julius Leibert's witty 1962 play *The Wives of King David* takes the form of a dramatic monologue recited by Abishag. Some modern works emphasize Abishag's place in the folk imagination. Thus, Aldous Huxley's aging Earl of Hauberk in *After Many a Summer* (1939) records in his diary that 'I have tried King David's remedy against old age and found it wanting,' as if Abishag were part of the lore of folk-medicine; Robert Frost's poem 'Provide Provide' makes her a Hollywood beauty queen and uses the biblical episode as a folk warning: 'The witch that came (the withered hag) / To wash the steps with pail and rag / Was once the beauty Abishag.' Neither invites reflection on the biblical account; the Abishag episode (and by extension the Bible) is considered hardly more than a warehouse of stock literary references. A more cynical view is offered by the debunking *David: The Biography of a King* (English version, 1965), written by the scholar and politician Juan Bosch. By contrast, in Shirley Kaufman's recent poem Abishag takes back her identity as a woman despite her status as object in the folk imagination ('Abishag', *Claims*, 1984), and like Karen Gershon's lyric ('David and Abishag', *Coming Back from Babylon*, 1979) makes a complex Zionist statement which brings her readers to a deeper reading of the original biblical tale.

In much 20th-century Yiddish poetry, Abishag becomes King David's equal. The meeting of the two – great king and little woman at his service – marks out the area Yiddish literature made its own, focusing in particular on the encounter of the world-historical Jewish king and the *pintele yid*, the anonymous Jew, who makes up the substratum of Jewish life so often unreflected in its national consciousness. In the 1926 poem by Jacob Glatstein ('Abishag', English version in *The Golden Peacock*, 1939), as well as in the cycle of four poems by Itsik Manger, their encounter is ironic and full of wit and feeling. Manger's Abishag knows – because she has read her story in the Bible – that for her deeds she will only receive 'A line in the bible, A line for her young flesh, the years of her youth. A line of ink on parchment for the whole long truth' ('Abishag Writes a Letter Home', English translated by Ruth Whitman, *An Anthology of Modern Yiddish Poetry*, 1966; cf. his 'Abishag', 'Abishag's Last Night in the Village', and 'King David and Abishag', *Lied un Balade*, 1952).

As country girl meets city king, Manger rescues Abishag from her subservient position in the David chronicle and transforms her into a symbolic figure powerfully expressing the predicament of the modern Jewish immigrant to the metropolis. Rooted in the biblical tale, in these poems the figure of Abishag takes on the Chagallian hues of the shtetl faced with its disintegration before the force of the modern world.

These Abishag poems make reference to a famous literary topos of Western culture, that of the *senex amans*. In their silence on the subject, the rabbis suggest the extent of their embarrassment at what the biblical story includes in a matter-of-fact way as part of the history of the Davidic era. Both Manger's and Glatstein's poems echo the biblical account. Unlike Boccaccio's senescent males or Chaucer's January lusting after May, the Yiddish writers depict a *senex amans* despite himself. Old King David's impotence takes on a personal rather than social value, which enables them to focus on Abishag's role, and transforms her into his equal by allowing her the right of speech.

By contrast Abishag plays a mythic role in Rainer Maria Rilke's poem 'Abisag' (English translated by J.B. Leishman, *Rainer Maria Rilke: New Poems*, 1964), developing his thematic concern with the relation of singing, poetry, and knowledge which draws on the rich history of biblical exegesis. She appears with the same lyric force in

Gladys Schmitt's magisterial 1946 historical novel *David the King*. Alexandre Arnoux's 1925 fantasy novel *Abishag* has her come to life like Pygmalion (along with David and Solomon) from a carving in a medieval Church. A year later a translation of the play *The Shunamite*, by the important Yiddish and Hebrew writer Yehoash – the pen name of Solomon Bloomgarden, who was also a brilliant translator of the Hebrew Bible – was performed by the Menorah Societies of Harvard and Radcliffe in Cambridge. Here the fiery poet-warrior is forever young in Abishag's songs and woos her for the old King David. Like Bloomgarden's work, David Pinski's play *Abishag* (*King David and his Wives*, 1923) introduces Abishag as a mythic erotic figure by presenting her through the eyes of King David:

> My whole life I have been fire and motion, and I thought I was like that bush that burned and was not consumed... You are my riddle. Desire for you will waken all my powers... The yearning for you will be the sharp goad that will neither let me sleep nor freeze. But if you were to be my wife, then you would become a riddle solved. What would then keep King David warm?

Two Hebrew poems of the 1940s expand the brevity of the biblical account by dramatizing Abishag's thoughts about her situation. For Yaakov Fichman, Abishag serves David the poet while ministering to the king; for Anda Finkerfeld-Amir, Abishag, who first rebels against her fate in warming a dying old man, is recalled to her king's service by his art. Both poems are monologues spoken by Abishag: Finkerfeld-Amir's free verse is stormy and dramatic, while Fichman's rhymed couplets are subtly restrained ('Abishag', translated by Robert Friend, *Voices from the Ark*, 1980; see also 'Abishag HaShunamit', *Lifnim Mishurat Hashir*, 1975).

In these Hebrew presentations of Abishag one encounters Abishag as contemporary. This is a strategy used by James Joyce in *Ulysses*, where in the middle of the Circe episode – Nightown, Joyce called it – Leopold Bloom remembers his father's dying moments and makes a bathetic comparison: 'Near the end, remembering King David and the Sunamite, he shared his bed with Athos, faithful after death...' Joyce's interest in Abishag depends upon the interpenetration of the contemporary and biblical worlds, thereby signalling the ways in which the strategies of midrashic retelling are once more available to the modern writer.

Murray Baumgarten
*Kresge College, University of California, Santa Cruz*

## Abner

Abner was commander of the Israelite army under Saul and Ishbosheth – perhaps Saul's cousin or uncle (1 Samuel 14:50; 1 Chronicles 8:33; 9:39) – who introduced young David fresh from his conquest of Goliath to the king's court (1 Samuel 17:57). He also accompanied Saul in pursuit of David, and was rebuked by the latter for not more carefully guarding his liege (chapter 15). Abner took up the claim of Ishbosheth to the throne. In a formal battle against Joab and David's supporters, he lost and fled, suffering the further loss of 360 men in flight. Despite the fact that he made peace with David, Joab eventually slew Abner to avenge the murder of his brother; he 'smote him there under the fifth rib' (2 Samuel 3:27). David sincerely mourned Abner's death, though in fact it sped his ascension to the throne. *Under the Fifth Rib* (1932) is the title of a novel by C.E.M. Joad; the phrase is used cryptically by John Galsworthy in 'Soames and the Flag' and Henry James in 'The Death of the Lion'.

In early Jewish commentary Abner is a figure of considerable interest. A giant of a man in size and strength, he is said to be not only the cousin of Saul but also a son of the Witch of Endor. Proud of his vast strength, he is said to have exclaimed, 'If only I could seize the earth at some point, I should be able to shake it!' (Ginzberg, *Legends of the Jews*, 4.73). He is elsewhere credited with being a saint (Sota 176) and a 'lion in the Torah' (Midrash Tehillim 7.67) whose name, signifying 'father of light', was granted to him as head of the Sanhedrin (Ginzberg, *Legends of the Jews*, 6.240). He is of less interest to medieval Christian commentators, except as a dim foil to David, and appears too early in the David narrative to attract interest from John Dryden (*Absalom and Achitophel*). In Vittorio Alfieri's *Saul* (1784, translated into English 1815, 1821) Abner turns the king's heart against David with envious insinuations, whereas in Browning's *Saul*

(1845; 1855) David favourably recalls Abner's calling upon him to solace the stricken Saul with music. Abner appears in Charles Heavysage's three-part drama *Saul* (1857) and in Mark Van Doren's 'Michal' (1946), where Abner forces a separation between Michal and her husband Palatiel, ordering her back to the harem of David.

David L. Jeffrey<br>
*University of Ottawa*

## Absalom

Absalom was the third son of King David. The account of his rebellion against his father (2 Samuel 13–18) is widely regarded as a masterpiece of Old Testament prose narrative. The events of Absalom's life form the sequel to the preceding narrative of David's sin with Bathsheba (2 Samuel 11–12), bringing to fulfilment Nathan's prophecy that, as a consequence of that sin, the sword would never be lifted from his house (2 Samuel 12:10–11). David's transgressions of lust, treachery, and murder are mirrored in the conduct of his sons, whose wilful repetition of their father's sins ironically becomes the instrument of divine retribution upon David's house.

The portrayal of Absalom's extraordinary beauty and luxurious hair (2 Samuel 14:25–26), which underscores his virility, power, and personal appeal, serves also to identify the nature of Absalom's hubris; the very qualities which favour his rebellion ultimately ensnare him and prove his undoing, a fact graphically dramatized in the ignominious manner of his death. According to the biblical text Absalom was caught by his head in the boughs of a tree, leaving him vulnerable to attack by Joab's men. Subsequent tradition (as early as Josephus) maintains that he was suspended by his hair, a significant alteration in the narrative which underscores the poetic justice of his humiliating end. 'As he rode along at full speed, he was lifted up by the unsteady motion, and his hair became entangled in a rugged tree… and in this strange fashion he remained suspended' (*Antiquities* 7.238–39). Andrew Willet, in his *Harmonie upon the Second Book of Samuel* (1614), points out that to be hanged aloft between heaven and earth is a death accursed by God (cf. Galatians 3:13), a curse Absalom shares with his co-conspirator Ahithophel who, Judas-like, takes his own life by hanging himself. Jewish tradition held that Absalom failed to cut himself down with his sword because he saw hell yawning beneath him, hence preferring to remain hanging (L. Ginzberg, *Legends of the Jews*, 4.106). But the circumstance that most frequently arouses commentary is David's grief over the death of his errant son. Augustine expresses the prevailing view in *De doctrina Christiana*, 3.21.30:

> He mourned over his son's death, not because of his own loss, but because he knew to what punishment so impious an adulterer and parricide had been hurried. For prior to this, in the case of another son who had been guilty of no crime [2 Samuel 12:15–23], though he was dreadfully afflicted for him while he was sick, yet he comforted himself after his death.

Literary response to the story of Absalom evidences three distinct, though by no means exclusive, phases. Poets of the Middle Ages were fascinated with Absalom as an ideal of physical beauty, though their treatment of this tradition was usually heavily didactic. This preoccupation gave way in Renaissance and Restoration literature to an almost exclusive emphasis on the political implications of the story. Finally, with the advent of the novel in the 18th century, writers increasingly drew attention to the pathetic, human elements of the narrative, especially David's heart-rending lament upon the death of his son.

In medieval literature, the most celebrated Absalom is Chaucer's 'joly Absolon' in *The Miller's Tale*. Chaucer's description of the hapless parish clerk emphasizes his effeminacy and fastidiousness: 'Crul was his heer, and as the gold it shoon, / And strouted as a fanne large and brode – / Ful streight and evene lay his joly shode' (1.3314–16). In portraying Absolon in this way Chaucer reflects a marked inclination among medieval poets to transmute the biblical Absalom into a type of feminine beauty. Peter Riga's use of the rhetorical device of the *effictio* in his description of Absalom in the *Aurora* or *Biblia Versificata* is the most prominent instance of this tendency, but Chaucer himself, with calculated irony, includes Absalom and his 'gilte tresses clere' in the catalogue of beautiful women which inaugurates his 'balade' in praise of Alceste (Prologue

37

to *The Legend of Good Women*). The didactic impulse which underlies this emphasis on Absalom's beauty is underscored by Adam Scotus, who warns in his *De Triplici Genere Contemplationis*, 'Woe unto you, O perfidious Absalom, weighed down by your hair – that is, by carnal excess, concupiscence of the eyes, and the pride of life!'

Writers of the Renaissance were more responsive than their medieval counterparts to the tragic dimensions of Absalom's history and frequently reflect these sympathies in the more than sixty 16th- and early 17th-century European plays deriving their inspiration from the David story. Though some of these dramas are now lost, two notable works have survived: Thomas Watson's Latin *Absalom* and George Peele's *The Love of King David and Fair Bethsabe: With the Tragedie of Absalon* (1594). The former work exploits elements in the narrative which readily adapt themselves to a Senecan formula: 'the blood-feud which works itself out within a noble family, the exile who nourishes resentment, the hypocritical reconciliation masking revengeful purpose, the suicide of a highly placed personage, and the political ramifications of an emotional situation' (Blackburn, 82). Peele's treatment of the story differs from those of his contemporaries in its awareness of the moral ambiguity of the situation; his Absalom, rather than embracing David's concubines, vehemently denounces them as symbols of the king's lust, and the play ends not with the rebel's eternal damnation but with a vision of his participation in heavenly bliss.

Peele's tragedy is striking in its divergence from the received interpretation of the Absalom story. Tudor Royalist political doctrine predictably demanded that rebels be portrayed as coming to a bad end. Thus the 1574 'Homily against Disobedience and Wilful Rebellion' points to the example of Absalom to illustrate the moral that 'neyther comelinesse of personage, neither nobilitie, nor fauour of the people, no nor the fauour of the king himselfe, can saue a rebell from due punishment.' Numerous homilists and biblical commentators in the period, including Archbishop Cranmer, enforce this doctrine, as do John Marbecke in *Holie Historie of King David* (1579) and Anthony Munday in *The Mirrour of Mutabilitie*.

Renaissance writers also display a keen interest in Absalom's reputation for false eloquence (2 Samuel 15:1–6), a proverbial attribute of the political schemer. In Shakespeare's *1 Henry IV*, the king, himself a usurper of the throne, describes to his son Hal the manner in which he swayed public opinion: 'And then I stole all courtesy from heaven, / And dress'd myself in such humility / That I did pluck allegiance from men's hearts' (3.2.50–52). His words echo the biblical report of Absalom's campaign for public support: 'So Absalom stole the hearts of the men of Israel' (2 Samuel 15:6). Similarly, in book 6 of *The Faerie Queene*, Spenser describes Sir Calidore as a man of 'comely guize', who through 'gracious speach, did steale mens hearts away' (6.1.2).

Protestant polemicists found in David's trials and suffering at the hands of Absalom a powerful analogue to their own precarious state, a parallel which St Thomas More detects in Tyndale's veiled reference to himself as Chusai in his *Answer unto More's Dialogue* (1531): 'As though the princes that would repress heresies were as Absalon with his army, and Achitophel therein, that persecute King David' (*The Confutation of Tyndale's Answer*, 1973, 138). In the course of rejecting Tyndale's self-characterization More expounds Tyndale's implicit allegorization of Absalom's rebellion in a manner which anticipates Dryden's subsequent adaptation in *Absalom and Achitophel* (1681): 'And then hath Tyndale a trust that some Chusy... shall by his high wisdom... beguile all the company, and so scatter them and make them to be taken and slain as Absolon was and his folk' (*Confutation*, 138). This allegorizing tendency grows more pronounced in the polemics arising out of the civil conflict of the 17th century, as the title of one anonymous pamphlet (1645) indicates: 'Absalom's Rebellion... with some Observations upon the Severall Passages Thereof. Too fit a Patterne for the present Times, whereinto we are Fallen'.

Dryden, in fashioning his parallel history, found several models ready to hand. Nathaniel Carpenter's *Achitophel, or, the Picture of a Wicked Politician* (1627) lays out the general lines of characterization which Dryden was to adopt. Another pamphlet, *David's Troubles Remembred* (1638), describes Absalom in verses which directly anticipate those of Dryden: 'In all the Kingdomes of the East not one / Was found, for Beauty like to Absolon' (cf. *Absalom and Achitophel*, 17–18). Other references likening Absalom's rebellion to contemporary political events occur in *Absalom's Conspiracy; or, The Tragedy of Treason* (1680), *Character of a Rebellion* (1681), and Francis Gifford's *The Wicked Petition* (1681).

With characteristic subtlety, Dryden adapts this long polemical tradition to his defense of Charles II against the attacks of his Whig opponents during the time of the Popish plot (1678–81). Unlike Carpenter, who introduces some of the more repugnant aspects of Absalom's conduct, such as his public rape of David's concubines, Dryden adopts a more conciliatory tone, portraying his hero as a fine young man misled by the consummate treachery of Ahithophel and dazzled, like Narcissus, by his own noble attributes. The portrayal required great tact because his original, Charles' illegitimate son, the Duke of Monmouth, still retained his father's affection. At the level of explicit statement Absalom emerges as an attractive person deceived by subtler men than he, but his own speeches reveal a mind only too willing to receive the blandishments of others. From a historical point of view, perhaps the most striking feature of Dryden's poem is its tone. The ironic and sardonic treatment of the scriptures anticipates a new and increasingly secular attitude towards biblical narrative which places it alongside classical mythology as a kind of miscellany of allusions.

In Byron's passing reference to David's lament over his son in the poem 'Oscar of Alva' ('Oscar! my son! – thou God of Heaven, / Restore the prop of sinking age!'), biblical allegory has dwindled into incidental metaphor; this is typical not only in Byron's canon (see also *Cain*, 3.1.381; *Two Foscari*, 3.1.340) but also in those of Melville, Longfellow, Whittier, and Crane. Byron's choice of this episode underscores the increasing admiration which writers, particularly novelists, expressed for the poignant scene in which David mourns Absalom's death: 'O my son Absalom, my son, my son Absalom! would God I had died for thee, O Absalom, my son, my son!' (2 Samuel 18:33). Thomas Hardy pronounced this chapter of the Bible the 'finest example of [prose narrative] that I know, showing beyond its power and pathos the highest artistic cunning' (*Fortnightly Review*, August 1887, 304–06). Sir Walter Scott, in *The Fair Maid of Perth* and in *Woodstock*, underscores moments of heightened emotion (such as the Duke of Rothesay's death) by alluding to David's lament. Hardy, by contrast, eschews such pathos; in *Desperate Remedies*, there is irony in his reference to Manston as an 'unmoved David' for displaying no emotion at the news of his wife's death.

Faulkner's profound reenactment of the narrative in his novel *Absalom, Absalom!* (1936) is centred around the triad of Thomas Sutpen, his son Henry, and Henry's half-brother Charles Bon, a triangle reflecting the David/Absalom/Amnon relationship in 2 Samuel 13. Like Absalom, who murders his half-brother Amnon in revenge for the latter's rape of Absalom's sister Tamar, Henry kills Charles to forestall his incestuous and miscegenational marriage to Henry's sister Judith. In killing Charles, Henry is more a victim than a murderer, and his act is motivated by love rather than anger or revenge. Nevertheless, Sutpen's house, like David's, is doomed to play out the consequences of the father's sin: 'Who should do the paying if not his sons, his get, because wasn't it done that way in the old days?' In both families the failure of love ends in fratricide and civil war.

Another modern novelist powerfully attracted to this biblical chronicle of a house divided is Alan Paton, who shares Faulkner's reluctant inheritance of a society built upon racial enmity and division. Paton weaves an extended allusion to Absalom into the very structure of his novel *Cry, the Beloved Country* (1948). Like his biblical namesake, Stephen Kumalo's wayward son, Absalom, rejects his family and his tribe, commits a murder, and hangs for his crime. In the course of his quest to find and reclaim his son, Stephen Kumalo encounters another bereaved father, James Jarvis, whose son is the victim of Absalom's violence; though their sorrow seems irreconcilable, the two fathers find comfort and redemption in their mutual grief. When Kumalo finds his son in prison, he utters the words 'My child, my child' in echo of David's lament, and during his mountain vigil on the morning of his son's execution he cries out, 'My son, my son, my son'. These anguished words at the end of the novel are a cry not only for his own son but also for Jarvis', and ultimately blend with countless other voices lamenting all the sons of South Africa: 'Cry, the beloved country, for the unborn child that is the inheritor of our fear.'

Perhaps the most revisionist reading of the Absalom story in modern literature is Christopher Fry's play, *A Sleep of Prisoners*. In it four British soldiers captured by the Germans are confined in a church, where they reenact in their dreams the lives of various Old Testament characters whose circumstances in some way mirror their own. Private Peter Able, a pacific young man, plays Abel to the belligerent David King's Cain in the opening dream sequence; King's own dream follows, in which he assumes the role of King David and Able becomes Absalom. But this Absalom is a Christ-like figure who responds to David's tyrannical efforts to 'make a soldier of him' with words which echo the language of the gospels: 'You and your enemies! Everlastingly / Thinking of your enemies. Open up. / Your enemies are friends of mine.'

Frans De Bruyn
*University of Ottawa*

# Ahab

Ahab, whose Hebrew name suggests 'God is a close relative', is notorious for behaving as though the opposite were true. Seventh king of Israel (c. 874–852BC), he entered into suspect alliances with neighbour states and even erstwhile enemies and, under the influence of his fanatical pagan queen Jezebel, came to worship Baal (1 Kings 16:31–33), to pursue political tyranny (1 Kings 21), and to engage in religious persecution (18:4) and human sacrifice (16:34). These actions put him in conflict with the prophets, notably Elijah and Micaiah; at Jezebel's request, he massacred Hebrew prophets and then installed prophets of Baal as counsellors in his court (18:4, 19).

Jewish commentators note both the great power of Ahab and his almost unprecedented wickedness. At his order the gates of Samaria are said to have borne the inscription 'Ahab denies the God of Israel' (Sanhedrin 102b, 103b; cf. Tan. Shemot 29). His miserable fate under divine judgment (1 Kings 22) is said to be occasioned above all by his murder of Naboth for his vineyard (Sanhedrin 48b; Tosefta 4.6). This occurred when Ahab, having decided to make war with the Arameans, asked his 400 prophets of Baal for advice and received unanimous encouragement – exactly what he wanted to hear (1 Kings 22:6, 11–13). Micaiah (a faithful prophet of God) then being sent for – someone whom Ahab hated, for, as he said, 'he doth not prophesy good concerning me, but evil' (v. 8) – the judgment of God was rendered as a vision of the court of heaven deciding how Ahab should be 'tricked' into his death. The device suggested by 'the Spirit' (which Sanhedrin 89a identifies as that of murdered Naboth) was simple concurrence with the raving 400 prophets of Baal – to reiterate the promise of victory, and so encourage Ahab to attack at Ramoth-gilead. In a powerfully ironic conclusion the narrator records that though Ahab apprehensively disguised himself, one of the enemy archers, drawing his bow at random (KJV 'at a venture', v. 34), struck the king in the tiny place between the joints of his armour. Despite his plea to be taken out of the battle, his officers strapped him into his chariot upright lest the troops (who knew his identity) be demoralized, and as the battle wore on, he bled to death. At the end of the day the army fled in disarray, Ahab's corpse was removed, 'and one washed the chariot in the pool of Samaria, and the dogs licked up his blood' (22:38). The archer, nameless in the text, is identified by Josephus (*Antiquities*, 18.15.5; cf. Midrash Tehillim, 78.50) with Naaman, the leprous Syrian commander who was healed by Elisha (2 Kings 5).

In patristic commentary Ahab is either an epitome of wickedness (e.g., St Jerome, *Epistle* 77.4) or else his actions are divorced, in a sense, from his character so as to allow for topical allegorization (e.g., *Glossa Ordinaria*, *Patrologia Latina*, 113.605–10). Pseudo-Fulgentius characterizes him as an exemplum of one who, though he had been witness by day to Elijah's miracles and other clear signs of God's divine authority, 'yet at night he drank in the poison of his wife Jezebel's vicious persuasion' (*Of the Ages of the World*, 8, translated by Whitbread) and so perished eternally.

In his fourth Latin elegy Milton compares his former tutor, then a chaplain to English merchants in Germany, to Elijah fleeing 'from the hands of King Ahab' (99–100). Satan in Milton's *Paradise Regained* boasts of being the spirit who proposed to all God's angels 'to draw the proud King Ahab into fraud / That he might fall at Ramoth' (1.372–77), a superposition of the Job contestation onto the Micaiah story, probably following Lavater's commentary *In Libros Paralipomenon sive Chronicorum* (which Milton annotated). On the random arrow, Merrick, in Montague's *Right off the Map*, alludes to biblical precedent sarcastically: "'Bow drawn at a venture", was it?

Lots of first-class scientific fighting in the Bible' (16.2). While there are numerous incidental allusions to Ahab in modern literature (e.g., Stephen Dedalus is compared to Ahab in *Ulysses*), the most important characterization is undoubtedly Melville's Captain Ahab in *Moby Dick*, who drinks in his own species of poison at night, rails against God, and goes to his death following a false rather than true prophecy. His fate is foreshadowed early in the narrative when one of the characters proclaims, 'Ahab's above the common... He's *Ahab*, boy; and Ahab of old, thou knowest, was a crowned King!' – only to receive the rejoinder, 'And a very vile one. When that wicked King was slain, the dogs, did they not lick his blood?'

David L. Jeffrey
*University of Ottawa*

## Ahithophel

Ahithophel (Achitophel in Vulgate) appears in the account of Absalom's rebellion against his father, King David (2 Samuel 15:12 – 17:13). For whatever motives – he may have been the grandfather of Bathsheba (see 2 Samuel 11:3; 23:34; and 1 Chronicles 3:5) – Ahithophel, a counsellor to David, betrayed the king and joined forces with the son. Sagacious, pragmatic, but unscrupulous, he advised Absalom to secure his position by taking David's concubines and by killing the king. As an exercise in realpolitik, Ahithophel's was good advice. But when Absalom accepted instead the counsel of Hushai, David's spy, because 'the Lord had appointed to defeat the good counsel of Ahithophel, to the intent that the Lord might bring evil upon Absalom' (2 Samuel 17:14), Ahithophel hanged himself.

Mentioned little in early Christian tradition, Ahithophel becomes in English literature a conventional tag for traitor, wicked politician, and suicide. In *The Canterbury Tales* Chaucer's Parson admonishes that 'wikked conseil yeveth is a traytour. For he deceyveth hym that trusteth in hym, *ut Achitofel ad Absolonem*' (*The Parson's Tale*, 10.635–40). If he were to betray his love, says a character in *The Book of the Duchess*, he would be 'wers than was Achitofel' (1118). In refuting Tyndale St Thomas More alludes to Absalom's revolt, implicitly comparing Henry VIII to Absalom and his chancellor to

Ahithophel. George Peale dramatizes Ahithophel's treachery in *The Love of King David and Fair Bethsabe. With the Tragedie of Absalom* (1599); Shakespeare's Falstaff calls a merchant who refuses him credit 'A whoreson Achitophel' (*2 Henry IV*, 1.2.35).

Later in 17th-century England, as numerous writers drew parallels between the life of David and contemporary political affairs, Ahithophel became a commonplace. In tracts, sermons, and poetry, from Nathanael Carpenter's *Achitophel, or the Picture of a Wicked Politician* (1627) to Dryden's satire *Absalom and Achitophel*, the most skilful literary rendering of the story in the language, Ahithophel is a synonym for political machination and rebellion. A verb was even coined out of his name, one poet writing of a group of plotters being 'out-Achitophel'd' by another.

After the 17th century, references to Ahithophel are few and scattered. Burns alludes to him as a suicide (*Letters*, ed. J. De Lancey Ferguson, 1931, 1.120); Blake ranks him with Caiaphas, Pilate, and Judas: 'Achitophel is also here with the cord in his hand' (*A Vision of the Last Judgment*, 608); Scott in *The Fair Maid of Perth* (chapter 13) writes of the 'wisdom of Achitophel, crafty at once and cruel'.

Larry Carver
*University of Texas, Austin*

## Bathsheba

2 Samuel 11 tells the story of King David and the beautiful Bathsheba, daughter of Eliam and wife of Uriah the Hittite. Her name may derive from Hebrew *bat-sheba* ('daughter of fullness'); but cf. 1 Chronicles 3:5: 'Bath-shua'). David's seduction of Bathsheba while her husband was away at war left her pregnant, news of which prompted the king to recall Uriah in an attempt to conceal the adultery. The valiant Uriah refused to return home to his wife while his comrades in arms were doing battle; David then surreptitiously arranged for his death at the siege of Rabbah at the foremost point of attack. Once her mourning was over, Bathsheba was brought to David and taken as his wife. The prophet Nathan publicly denounced the king's secret sins, prophesying truly the early death of the child born of their adulterous union. With the help of this same prophet in later years (1 Kings 1),

the politically astute Bathsheba was instrumental in the accession of Solomon, her second child by David, to the throne of Israel. According to 1 Chronicles 3:5, she also bore other sons – Shimea, Shobab, and Nathan. Matthew 1:6 lists her in the genealogy of Jesus Christ, though not by name: 'And David the king begat Solomon of her that had been the wife of Urias.'

Because of their commitment to see David as an ante-type of Christ, the typical strategy of early medieval commentators was either to evade the obvious import of the Bathsheba incident or to allegorize it elaborately. St Augustine, whose David was 'not lustfull, though he fell into adultery' (*De doctrina Christiana*, 3.21), was less engaging of Bathsheba's role than later commentary. The *Glossa Ordinaria* (*Patrologia Latina*, 113.571–72) gives the meaning of her name as 'well of fullness' or 'seven-fold well', contributing thereby to the iconography of the bathing/temptation scene in medieval and Renaissance iconography.

Bathsheba's place in subsequent English literature is small. George Peele's *The Love of King David and Fair Bethsabe*, which closely follows 2 Samuel, assigns her approximately one-twentieth of the play's lines (Uriah, who appears in but one scene, is given as many). Bathsheba is here a radiantly beautiful and chaste wife betrayed by her charms and obedience to her liege: 'The Kings poore handmaid will obey my lord' (117). She disappears from the stage at the end of scene 6, but returns in the final scene to help secure with Nathan's assistance the succession of Solomon to his father's throne, finishing the play a wise counsellor and supportive wife. It is in this role of *eminence grise* that Robert Cleaver remembers her in his *Bathshebaes instructions to her sonne Lemvel: containing a fruitful and plaine exposition of the last chapter of the Proverbs. Describing the duties of a great-man, and the vertues of a gracious woman* (1614). In accordance with the rabbinic tradition, which takes the name Lemuel ('belonging to God') to refer to Solomon (cf. Ginzberg, *Legends of the Jews*, 6.277), Cleaver identifies Bathsheba as the mother whose instructions concerning prudent kingship and the dangers of intemperance are recorded in Proverbs 31. She does not appear at all in Cowley's unfinished epic *Davideis, a Sacred Poem of the Troubles of David*. Similarly, Herbert omits any mention of Bathsheba in his reflections on the ethical aspects of

David's adultery (*Brief Notes on Valdesso's 'Considerations'*, 62). She is mentioned by name in Dryden's *Absalom and Achitophel*, but only in passing and as a stand-in for the Duchess of Portsmouth, a mistress to the promiscuous Charles II: the king 'Is grown in Bathsheba's embraces old' (710). Christopher Smart's *A Song to David* leaps directly from the Michal of David's youth to the Abishag of his old age without even a passing mention of Bathsheba.

Bathsheba does play a significant role, though again by association, in *Far from the Madding Crowd*. Hardy's heroine, the enticing Bathsheba Everdene (in a manner suggestive of her biblical namesake), grows through suffering and misfortune into a wise woman. In *Tess of the D'Urbervilles*, Angel Clare reflects belatedly on his desertion of Tess because of her past sexual relations with another man; remembering 'the wife of Uriah being made a queen', he regrets having failed to judge Tess 'by the will rather than by the deed'. In *The Scarlet Letter*, the story of David and Bathsheba serves Hawthorne well: a good widow gives her brooding pastor Dimmesdale the sunniest room, hung all around with tapestries 'representing the scriptural story of David and Bathsheba, and Nathan the Prophet, in colours still unfaded, but which made the fair woman of the scene almost as grimly picturesque as the woe-denouncing seer' (chapter 9).

A number of minor works of 20th-century literature – including Stephen Phillips' pseudo-Elizabethan verse drama *The Sin of David* – recall the wife of Uriah. Gladys Schmitt's *David the King*, a historical novel, develops Bathsheba's feelings of uncertainty as an obedient subject powerless before her king and as a woman made pregnant by someone other than her husband. David Robert Perry Marquis' *David and Bathsheba (As Interpreted by the Old Soak)* is democratic in the manner of Twain: 'Oh, what the hell, it's Spring! / And just for the sake of argyment, / I'll show 'em who is king.'

Camille R. La Bossière
*University of Ottawa*

# Daniel

The twelve chapters of the book of Daniel in the Hebrew canon represent two quite distinct literary genres. The first six chapters are narrative, presenting a series of popular edifying stories about Daniel, his three companions, and their trials and accomplishments at the courts of various foreign rulers. The last six contain four apocalypses or visions of this same Daniel. In addition there are several deuterocanonical sections lacking in the Hebrew but found in the Greek text: (a) two hymns, the Prayer of Azariah (Septuagint 3:24–45) and the Song of the Three Young Men (Septuagint 3:51–90), together with a short narrative passage connecting them (Septuagint 3:46–50); (b) the story of Susanna (chapter 13); (c) the stories of Bel and the Dragon (14:1–30), and (d) a second story of Daniel in the lions' den, perhaps a doublet of the narrative in chapter 6 (14:31–42).

Josephus devotes more attention to Daniel than to any other prophet, giving a detailed picture of his life (*Antiquities*, 10.10–11). The earliest patristic commentary on Daniel is that of St Hippolytus (died 235), which emphasizes apocalyptic themes (Sources chrétiennes, 14; Ante-Nicene Fathers, 5.177–94). By far the most important patristic commentary is that of St Jerome (*Patrologia Latina*, 25.491–584 = Corpus Christianorum 75A). It was composed in 407, partly in response to Porphyry, a Neoplatonist who had denied that the book of Daniel was written by the biblical figure Daniel during the Exile and had argued instead that it was composed by someone living in Judea at the time of Antiochus Epiphanes, so that the book did not so much foretell the future as relate the past. Since Porphyry's work has not survived, we are indebted to Jerome for Porphyry's position, which is essentially that of most modern critics. Jerome's commentary also cites earlier Christian writers whose works are now lost and, in addition, offers valuable testimony concerning early Jewish interpretations of specific passages in Daniel (cf. J. Braverman, *Jerome's Commentary on Daniel*, 1978). Important medieval commentaries are those of St Albert the Great and Nicholas of Lyra, and the section on Daniel in Peter Comestor's *Historia Scholastica*; Calvin later devoted important lectures to Daniel, and S. Münster exercised considerable influence on the early English versions of the text (cf. Montgomery, *A Critical and Exegetical Commentary on the Book of Daniel*, 1950, 108).

The Old English *Daniel* treats the episodes in the first five chapters as found in the Vulgate, presenting them as part of a struggle waged by Daniel and his friends against Nebuchadnezzar and his line.

This poem is much more than a mere paraphrase of the biblical narrative, making important changes in emphasis in order to further the thematic concerns of the Old English poet. The Middle English poem variously titled *Purity* or *Cleanness* has a long section (1143–1804) imaginatively retelling the story of Belshazzar's Feast (Daniel 5) and making several references to other episodes in Daniel as well.

Chaucer's *Monk's Tale* (7.2151–54) reiterates a rabbinic tradition (cf. Braverman, 53–71) based on Daniel 1:3–4 and mentioned by Jerome (*Patrologia Latina*, 25.496 = Corpus Christianorum 75A.779.51–59) that Daniel was a eunuch of royal descent. Christian tradition generally, however, has emphasized instead the theme of Daniel's chastity. For St Augustine, Daniel represents the celibate state in the Church (*Patrologia Latina*, 37.1731 = Corpus Christianorum 40.1929.1–1930.15), and in the Middle English *Vices and Virtues* this theme is related to Daniel's renunciation of fine food (Daniel 1:8–16), which is taken as representative of all fleshly pleasures (Early English Text Society, old series 89, 1888, 43). Daniel's diet of pulse is often mentioned in relation to fasting and moderation in eating, as, for example, by Milton (*Comus*, 720–23), Sir Thomas Browne (*Works*, 1964, 3.10–11), Cowper ('The Progress of Error', 215–16), and Longfellow (Samuel Longfellow, *The Life of Henry Wadsworth Longfellow*, 1886, 1.36).

According to rabbinic tradition, Daniel's wisdom outweighed that of all the wise men of the heathen world (Yoma 77a; cf. Ezekiel 14:14, 20; 28:3), and Daniel's wisdom is often alluded to in Christian literature. Commenting on the question 'Who is wiser than Daniel?' (Vulgate Ezekiel 28:3), St Ambrose writes glowingly of him as uniquely blending a prophet's calling with the offices of a teacher of wisdom (*De officio clericorum*, 2.11.57–58). In the Middle English *Purity* the queen recommends Daniel to Belshazzar because of 'his depe divinite and his dere sawes' ('his profound learning and his excellent advice'), and his knowledge of 'derne coninges' ('secret branches of knowledge') (1609–11). Shakespeare, in *The Merchant of Venice*, 4.1.333–34, makes ironic reference to 'a Daniel come to judgment' – a proverb based on Daniel's judicial acumen in the history of Susanna where he demonstrates Susanna's innocence and exposes the wickedness of her accusers. In Hawthorne's *Scarlet Letter* a townsman reflects upon the question of who may be the father of Hester Prynne's child: 'Of a truth, friend, that matter remaineth a riddle; and the Daniel who shall expound it is yet a-wanting' (chapter 3). Many allusions to Daniel's wisdom refer to the story in Daniel 5 of the handwriting on the wall or to the stories in the deuterocanonical additions (chapters 13 and 14) of Susanna and Bel and the Dragon.

Because of his wisdom in interpreting two dreams of Nebuchadnezzar (chapters 2 and 4), Daniel is often mentioned in literary discussions of dreams and their significance, as in Chaucer's *Nun's Priest's Tale* (7.3127–28), *Piers Plowman* (A.8.137–44; B.7.151–58; C.10.304–07), *Handlyng Synne* (Early English Text Society, old series 119, 1901, 443–60). There is even an alphabetical dream interpretation manual, the *Somniale Danielis*, which purported to give Daniel's authoritative interpretations of the dreams of the people of Babylon. This work probably originated in Greek; Latin versions are numerous throughout the Middle Ages and beyond. There are also versions in Old English and Middle English, including one in Middle English verse (cf. L. Martin, ed., *Somniale Danielis*, 1981). In later literature Daniel continues to be mentioned as a wise interpreter of dreams, as in Charlotte Brontë's novel *Shirley* (chapter 1) and Emerson's poem 'The Miracle' (25–30). In E.L. Doctorow's novel *The Book of Daniel*, however, Daniel Lewin reflects upon his biblical namesake: 'Daniel seems to be a modest man, brave, and more faithful to God than wise, for it is by means of prayer and piety that he learns from God the dream interpretations he must make to the King in order to survive' (1971, 11).

In Daniel 6 Daniel appears as a courtier whose success is envied by subordinates; they trap Daniel by exploiting his piety, and cause him to face the ordeal of the lions' den. Their intended victim miraculously escapes, and they must then suffer the fate they had planned for him. The intrigue, suspense, and irony of this story have naturally appealed to many writers. King Darius' capricious action is used as a humorous motif in Vachel Lindsay's poem 'Daniel Jazz', where the motivation for Daniel's being put into the lions' den is stated by the king to Daniel's mother and sweetheart: 'Your Daniel is a dead little pigeon. / He's a good hard worker, but he talks religion'

(32–33). More serious approaches to this story emphasize the qualities of Daniel's character for which he was persecuted, as, for example, in Jerome's commentary (*Patrologia Latina*, 25.526 = Corpus Christianorum 75A.836.394–402) and in Aelfric's sermon 'On the Memory of the Saints' (Early English Text Society, old series 82, 1885, 78–82). In both Jewish and Christian tradition, Daniel's actions in this episode make him the model of a man of prayer (Midrash Tehillim 66; Josippon 3.8b; Jerome, *Commentarii in Danielem, Patrologia Latina*, 25.524 = Corpus Christianorum 75A.832.296–303), while in a more secular context Thomas Hardy takes Daniel as representative of the refusal to conform as he 'persisted in kneeling eastward when reason and common sense said that he might just as well follow suit with the rest' (*Far from the Madding Crowd*, chapter 13). Other writers have focused on Daniel's miraculous escape as exemplifying the justification and survival of the just person. Mrs Mary Rowlandson, in her account of being carried off by Indians in 1675, reflects on her survival: 'God showed his Power over the Heathen in this, as he did over the hungry Lyons when Daniel was cast into the Den' (R. Pearce, ed., *Colonial American Writing*, 1950, 126). In two poems Whittier compares the escape of Quakers from Puritan persecution to Daniel's miraculous escape from the lions ('The King's Missive', 65–68; 'Cassandra Southwick', 4 and 148).

Several treatments of the lions' den episode amplify the biblical account. In one of the deuterocanonical sections of the book of Daniel (14:31–42), God transports the prophet Habakkuk from Judea to Babylon, having an angel carry him by the hair, so that he can bring food to Daniel in the lions' den. Allusion is made to this story in the Middle English *Life of St Katherine* (Early English Text Society, old series 80, 1884, 1845–48), and Longfellow introduces his collection of verse dramas *Christus: A Mystery* with a dialogue between Habakkuk and the angel who is carrying him through the air (*Works*, 1886, 5.21–24). In Jewish legend the lions receive Daniel like loyal dogs, wagging their tails and licking him or allowing him to ride upon their backs (Josippon 3.8b). Similar romantic touches are found in a homily of the Syrian church father Aphrahat (cf. Hartman and Di Lella, Anchor Bible 23, 1978, 22), and the behaviour of the lion towards Una in Spenser's *Faerie Queene* perhaps suggests the influence of this tradition (1.3.6.1–3), particularly in view of Una's 'wronged innocence' (cf. Daniel 6:22). In Saul Bellow's novel *Henderson the Rain King* King Dahfu frolics with a lion in its den, and numerous allusions to the book of Daniel throughout the novel suggest that this, too, may reflect a romantic tradition concerning Daniel's experience in the lions' den (chapter 16).

Lawrence T. Martin
*University of Akron*

## David

The basic source for David's life is found in the books of 1 and 2 Samuel and 1 Kings. The first part of this account (1 Samuel 16:1 to 2 Samuel 2:11) is a fairly continuous narrative covering David's first thirty years. The second part (2 Samuel 2:12 to 1 Kings 2:46), more thematically selected and arranged, relates certain highlights of his forty-year reign.

David first appears as the youngest son of Jesse the Bethlehemite, good-looking but scarcely noticed alongside his more accomplished brothers, yet chosen by God to be Saul's successor and already identified by God as 'a man after his own heart' (1 Samuel 13:14). Samuel anoints him, and the Spirit of the Lord, having 'departed from Saul', comes upon him (16:13–14). David is a shepherd, already tried in adventures against wild animals and possessing an air of confidence which combines self-assurance with trust in God (17:34–37). His reputation as a harpist, as well as for valour and prudence, reaches the court, and when the king is stricken with melancholy David is summoned to minister to him with music. Strongly drawn to the young man, Saul appoints him an armourbearer. When, later, David is moved by the shame of Israel's failure to respond to the Philistine champion's challenge, he persuades Saul to let him confront Goliath, unarmed save for his stones and sling and a firm trust in God. In an account emphasizing how hubris and blasphemy are punished, David fells the boaster with a single shot and carries off his head in triumph.

David is now firmly established as part of the king's retinue, captain and prospective son-in-law of the king and covenanted friend of the prince Jonathan, but a powerful ambivalence governs Saul's attitude towards him. He sees the popular young man as both a support and a threat; at some level he is aware that the divine favour has been transferred from himself to David. When oppressed again by 'the evil spirit from God' (18:10), he calls the harpist to soothe him but twice tries to pierce him with a javelin. He advances David to the captaincy of 1,000 troops but is only made the more afraid by the youth's mature handling of his responsibility and growing popularity. After reneging once on a marriage offer, he allows David to have his second daughter, Michal, only upon performance of a formidable task designed to cost David his life (18:25); yet David and his men killed not 100 Philistines as required, but 200. Despite Saul's oath to the contrary (19:6), there follow other attempts on David's life, all of them frustrated by David's own watchfulness (19:10) or with the aid of Michal (19:11–17), of Jonathan (19:1–7; 20:31–42), or directly of God (19:19–24). Finally David quits the court for good and assumes the life of an outlaw.

The years of exile are the proving ground for the qualities of leadership which will make David a great king. The narrative reveals in David exquisite honour and sensitivity towards his own people. He feels personally responsible for the tragic fate of the Nobites (22:22–23); he insists on equal shares in booty for camp guards who are prevented from the actual fighting (30:21–25); when his fury against Nabal is mollified by Abigail's conciliatory behaviour, he blesses her for averting bloodshed (25:32–33); when Saul falls into his power he will not let anyone harm him (chapters 24 and 26); he is loyal in friendship to the king's son (23:18); and, when Saul and Jonathan are killed in battle, he laments them eloquently and acts to avenge them (2 Samuel 1).

Prominence is also given to David's reverence for the sacred; for example, 'who can stretch forth his hand against the Lord's anointed, and be guiltless?' (1 Samuel 26:9; cf. v. 23; 24:6–12; 2 Samuel 1:14). David's close relationship to God and his enjoyment of divine favour (1 Samuel 25:26–31) are recognized by Abigail, among others. In warfare David has God's aid (23:14, 19–26; 24:4) and even a direct line of counsel from the Almighty (23:1–5, 9–13; 30:7–8).

In the succeeding chapters – part two of the narrative – are interwoven two main themes. The first involves the consolidation and expansion of David's power after Saul's death. The second concerns the establishment of the Davidic dynasty, with a strong admixture of domestic and personal tragedy which have proven an especially fruitful field for subsequent creative artists.

Prominent features of this narrative are the emphasis on David's devotion to cultic observances (2 Samuel 5:19, 21, 23–24; 8:11–12; 24:18–25) and the repeated attribution of his success to the Lord's being with him (5:10, 12, 19, 23–25; 7:1; 8:14; 23:1; cf. 6:12). In establishing Jerusalem as his capital David aims to make it the centre of religious as well as political life and to this end he erects a tabernacle for the Ark of the Covenant, which he brings up to Jerusalem from Kirjath-jearim (6:1–19) with music and dancing. David intends to house it in a permanent structure as elegant as his own palace instead of a tent (7:2). The prophet Nathan first endorses the plan but then is instructed by the Lord to veto it. The Israelites, their wanderings over, will 'dwell in a place of their own' (7:10), but God's house can wait. Instead, 'the Lord... will make [David] an house' – that is, a dynastic line: 'thy throne shall be established for ever' (7:11, 16). It will be left to David's son to build the Temple. If the ruler sins, he will be chastened, 'but my mercy shall not depart away from him, as I took it from Saul' (7:15).

Despite this divine promise, however, the question of succession becomes central in the later episodes, especially as David is no longer able to control affairs so firmly as he had done. His adultery with Bathsheba, followed by his arranging the death of her husband Uriah (chapter 11), brings Nathan's sharp rebuke. The prophet first asks the king to judge a legal case involving the theft of a lamb – thus alluding to both David's former and present occupations in what is actually a parable concerning the abuse of power. After David passes judgment, in effect, on himself, Nathan speaks directly: 'Thou art the man' (12:7). David's prompt repentance cancels his own death sentence, but the other consequences of his wrongdoing remain: David himself will be dishonoured by the open defilement of his wives, the child Bathsheba conceived adulterously will not live, and 'the sword shall never depart from thine house' (12:10–14). Thus the king's taking of Bathsheba is seen as the root of the troubles which follow. These begin with the death of the young boy (12:15–23) – after which, however, Bathsheba has other children, including Solomon, whose destined succession is indirectly confirmed at once by Nathan (12:24–25) and at some point directly promised by David (1 Kings 1:17, 30).

Solomon has many older brothers, however, of whom three in particular are obstacles to his succession: Amnon the firstborn (2 Samuel 3:2), Absalom, and Adonijah – none of them, as the narrative reveals, having the character proper to a king. Amnon rapes and then ruthlessly casts off his half-sister Tamar, and is murdered for his crime two years later by Absalom. Absalom himself, angry at his father for failing to intervene on Tamar's behalf, conceives an ambitious plot to overthrow him. His rebellion, which precipitates civil war, is eventually put down and Absalom killed, against David's express orders, by Joab, David's military commander. Upon hearing the news, David weeps for his son, 'Would God I had died for thee', and thus 'the victory that day was turned into mourning' (18:33; 19:2).

With David 'old and stricken in years' (1 Kings 1:1), even beyond arousal by the young, beautiful Abishag, who is brought to 'minister' to him, the struggle for succession breaks out openly. Adonijah, backed by Joab and Abiathar the priest, attempts a coup (1:5–10, 25), but Nathan and Bathsheba appeal directly to David to honour his promise to Solomon, who as a result is immediately anointed and proclaimed king. Adonijah, initially granted a probationary pardon, is later executed (2 Samuel 2:17, 22–25; cf. Deuteronomy 22:30) when he asks for Abishag as his wife.

These accounts contain a great wealth of narrative, but what the name of David signified for many centuries thereafter, so far as the records we have indicate, consisted of just a few key theological and ideological points. For instance, the remaining sections of the books of Kings emphasize continuity: of Jerusalem, regularly designated 'city of David'; of the Temple, which finally comes to fulfilment under Solomon (1 Kings 8:14–20); and of the dynasty. Subsequent events in the descent of kings are connected with God's promise to David, who is repeatedly cited as the model of the ideal ruler. Thus the summary of David's life (1 Kings 15:5) is that he did 'right in the eyes of the Lord, and turned not aside... all the days of his life, save only in the matter of Uriah the Hittite.' Similarly, the account in 1 Chronicles 10–29 omits everything up to Saul's death and all the stories of David's and Solomon's rivals, to concentrate on the greatness of David's reign, his victories, his enjoyment of divine favour, and – greatly expanded – his devotion to cultic activities and facilities. Several references in 2 Chronicles reflect a continuing association of David with the liturgical side of worship, particularly the singing.

The same theological and ideological points dominate the treatment of David elsewhere in the Old Testament, including the Apocrypha, and in rabbinical tradition. David as poet, musician, and liturgical reformer is mentioned by Amos (6:5), eulogized by Jesus ben Sirach (47:8–10), and of course most fully memorialized in the Psalms, nearly half of which have the ambiguous heading 'of David', which has frequently been taken as an ascription of authorship. Fourteen psalm headings associate their poems with specific occasions in David's life. Apocryphal writings include psalms attributed to David after his anointing (Pseudo-Philo 59:4), in exorcising Saul (60:2–3), and after his victory over Goliath (Psalms 151, LXX).

The celebration of God's special favour to David, his chosen 'servant' (Psalms 78:70; 89:3, 20), in establishing his throne dominates Psalms 132 and 89. In the latter, however, references to later events (89:38ff.; cf. 78:69) show that the Davidic covenant is being cited as an event in national history on which, in more dismal times, hope for a renewal of God's favour may be based. The age of David, when the nation was united, powerful, and prosperous, had come to represent a longed-for ideal. Such is the way the prophets use the name of David (Isaiah 9:7; Jeremiah 33:17; Amos 9:11; Hosea 3:5); he is a byword for the faithfulness of God (Isaiah 55:3, 'the sure mercies of David'; Jeremiah 33:20–21). When the prophetic vision came to focus on an individual expected deliverer, his connection with the line of David was stressed (Isaiah 11:1; Jeremiah 23:5; Micah 5:2; 4 Ezra 12:32), and he was even designated by the name 'David' (Jeremiah 30:9) and further identified as a king-shepherd after the Davidic tradition (Jeremiah 23:4–5; Ezekiel 34:23–24; 37:24–25; cf. 2 Samuel 7:8; Ps. 78:70–71). Psalms used in coronation ritual became interpreted as referring to the coming Anointed; in fact, many psalms were given messianic interpretations in rabbinic teaching. By c. 50BC the use of the term Messiah and description of the expected deliverance by reference to David's conquest were explicit (Psalms of Solomon 17). David had progressed from being a type of the ideal king (both in goodness and in greatness) to being a type of the Messiah.

David symbolized a conquest which was spiritual and moral as well as military and political. His victory over Saul's evil spirit was a forecast of the subduing of Satan (Pseudo-Philo 60.3). He was an exemplum not only of confidence in God's power (Zechariah 12:8; 1 Maccabees 4:30; Sirach 47:5; Scroll of the War of the Sons of Light against the Sons of Darkness 11.1–3) but also of mercy (1 Maccabees 2:57), care for his subjects, devotion to the study of Torah, ascetic discipline (4 Maccabees 3:6–18), thankfulness (Sirach 47:8), and prayer (4 Ezra 7:108). So much was made of his superior virtue (Sirach 47:2; cf. 1 Kings 15:5 and the eulogy by Josephus, Antiquities 7.15) that attempts were even made to excuse his adultery and homicide, and he was honoured alongside the three great patriarchs by the phrase 'the God of David' (Isaiah 38:5).

For the writers of the New Testament David is an example of the faithful life (Hebrews 11:32; cf. Acts 13:22), one whose behaviour could in itself provide a strong ethical argument (Matthew 12:3–4 and parallels), a divinely inspired poet (Romans 4:6; Hebrews 4:7), but above all, one who was intimately associated in various ways with the messianic hope. Essential marks identifying Jesus as the Anointed, the Christ, included his Davidic birthplace (Matthew 2:4–6; Luke 2:4; John 7:42) and ancestry (Matthew 1:1–16; Luke 1:27, 69; Romans 1:3; 2 Timothy 2:8; cf. Revelation 5:5; 22:16). It was in those terms, and thus as heir to the throne promised to David, that he was acclaimed upon entering Jerusalem (Matthew 20:30–31; 21:9–15 and parallels, especially Mark 11:10). 'The son of David' was in fact a popular designation for the Messiah (Matthew 12:23). So firmly established was the Davidic pattern of the messianic hope (Luke 1:32–33; Acts 1:6; 15:16) that Jesus found it necessary to assert unequivocally the superiority of the fulfilment over the type (Matthew 22:42–45 and parallels). By a similar argument in his Pentecost sermon Peter traced in Christ the fulfilment of Psalms 16:8–10 and 110 (Acts 2:24–35; cf. 13:35–37). David was considered not only a type but also a prophet (Luke 24:44; Acts 2:30; cf. 2 Samuel 23:2). Drawing in some cases on messianic interpretations already established in rabbinic teaching, Jesus and his followers applied at least fifteen of the Psalms to himself and the circumstances of his life and death (cf. John 2:17; 15:25; 19:36; Matthew 21:9, 16, 42; 27:35, 39, 46, 48; Luke 23:46; Acts 1:16–20; 4:11, 25–28; 13:33; Romans 15:3; Hebrews 1:5–13; 2:6–9; 5:5–6; 10:5–7; 1 Peter 2:7).

Such views were perpetuated (and elaborated) in subsequent Christian tradition. David's designation as prophet is regularly assumed by the Fathers and in medieval literature – as in the *Ordo Prophetarum* plays or in various versions of the 'harrowing of hell' narrative, where David identifies Christ as the light penetrating the darkness of Limbo. Chaucer, in *The Canterbury Tales,* refers to David both as 'the psalmist' and 'the prophet', as do a host of other medieval writers.

David is one of the most important Old Testament types of Christ for St Athanasius, Origen, St Augustine, and other early Fathers; the details of his life are frequently seen as prefiguring specific aspects of the earthly life of Jesus. But David's notorious sins of adultery with Bathsheba and the murder of her husband Uriah could hardly be accommodated to this straightforward prefigurative scheme and needed to be handled in a different way. A commentary on the books of Kings attributed to St Eucherius treats 'The Adultery of David' as a complex allegory of the Messiah (David), the Law (Bathsheba), and the Jewish people (Uriah). St Isidore of Seville chooses rather to follow St Augustine (*Contra Faustum*, 22.87) in interpreting Bathsheba as the Church, Uriah as Lucifer, and David as the beloved Redeemer 'who has liberated us from the Devil through his mercy' (*Patrologia Latina*, 83.411–12, translated by J. Wojcik, in *The David Myth*, 34).

On another level, David is also, despite these crimes (temporary, though flagrant, lapses, according to Augustine, and not indicative of a continuing disposition of heart), seen as a moral exemplum, a man of faith, or in Nicholas of Lyra's term, a viator who has set a standard for Christian conduct. He is perhaps most important in this regard as a model of penitence and a guide in spiritual reformation. His 'penitential psalms', identified by the 6th century – cf. Cassiodorus, *Patrologia Latina*, 70.371–72 – were prominent in medieval liturgy and private devotion. They were subsequently translated by Pietro Aretino, Sir Thomas Wyatt, and others and imitated by Petrarch.

David's sin, punishment, and repentance form the centre of dramatic interest for a host of early playwrights: it is this part of his story which governs his treatment in the Cornish *Ordinale de Origine Mundi*, John Bale's *Chief Promises of God unto Man*, a 'new interlude of the ij synnes of kynge DAVYD', Thomas Watson's *Absalom*, and George Peele's *Love of King David and Fair Bethsabe*. Interest in David's complex personality and varied experience effects his gradual translation from theology and devotional literature to imaginative literature, in which he is assigned four principal roles: king, epic hero, lover, and poet-musician.

With the institution of the Holy Roman empire David was studied as a model of the divinely appointed king, a ruler whose religious duties were concomitant with political ones. The ideals of Davidic kingship, as well as David's personal and domestic tragedy, have a formative influence on much of Britain's Arthurian literature. David's refusal to slay Saul, the Lord's anointed, and his character under persecution by Absalom became arguments for both sides in the 17th-century Puritan–Royalist debates. Marvell attempted to legitimize Cromwell politically by investing him with qualities of the Davidic king (see J. Mazzeo), while Dryden argued, in *Absalom and Achitophel*, for Stuart right to rule.

For those attempting to accommodate pagan heroic themes to Christian subjects, David proved an especially viable subject. John Marbecke offers *The Holie Historie of King David* (1579) as a substitute to 'lewd' works, while Thomas Fuller makes an epic of David's spiritual development in *David's Heinous Sin, Hearty Repentance, and Heavy Punishment* (1631). David's encounter with Goliath receives epic treatment in Drayton's *David and Goliah*, and provides a model for the Samson–Harapha episode in Milton's *Samson Agonistes* (see Steadman). Abraham Cowley's *Davideis* (1656), of which only four books of the projected twelve were completed, was to be a classical epic 'after the pattern of our master Virgil'; according to his Preface, one of its principal themes is the relationship between David and Jonathan, here seen in the light of classical ideals of friendship.

For some writers, the story of David's adultery provided a pretext for writing erotic poetry, such as Francis Sabie's epyllion 'David and Beersheba' (1596) or engaging in risqué dramaturgy: George Peele opens his play *David and Fair Bethsabe* (1599) with Bathsheba naked in her bath. So great were David's sensual excesses considered to be that Dryden could achieve sly comic effect in opening *Absalom and Achitophel* with a comparison of libertine Charles II to him. Throughout the early 18th century a controversy raged as to the propriety of including David in Sacred Writ at all.

Modern writers have sometimes characterized David's relationship with Jonathan and/or Saul as having an explicit or implicit homosexual character. Herman Melville defines the nature of Claggart's feeling for Billy Budd by referring to Saul's obsession with the comely shepherd boy (cf. André Gide's *Saul*). D.H. Lawrence used David and Jonathan as a model for homosexual relations in several of his novels.

David's skill as a musician and poet were celebrated early by St Jerome, who explained that 'David, who is our Simonides, Pindar, and Alcaeus, our Horace, our Catullus, and our Sirenus all in one, sings of Christ to his lyre.' David was indeed, throughout the Middle Ages, the quintessential Christian poet. In Renaissance debates on the morality and usefulness of poetry, David is cited by Sidney and Lodge; and in the movement to create a body of religious poetry, David's name is consistently invoked (see B. Lewalski, *Protestant Poetics*, 1979, 231–50). Ralph Knevet alludes to the psalmist / musician in expressing his praise for 'Pious Herbert': 'For it was Hee who rightly knew to touch Davids Harpe.' For many poets, David is a conscious model as well as subject; thus, Thomas Traherne delights in celebrating David's own delight in creation, and Christopher Smart praises the 'Blessed light' which David brought into the world.

The power of David's harp-playing to cure Saul's melancholy and madness was often emphasized. Lydgate follows an old tradition when he couples David with Orpheus in their power to produce a melody 'so heuenly and celestiall' (*Reason and Sensuality*,

5599–5612). Cowley makes a long digression on 'The mystick pow'rs that in blest *Numbers* dwell' when he narrates David's playing to Saul in *Davideis*. While Byron treats David's libertinism humorously in *Don Juan* (1.168), he also poignantly praises 'The Harp the Monarch Minstrel Swept' in his *Hebrew Melodies*. Following Byron's depiction of melancholic Saul as a spiritually troubled man, Browning, in *Saul*, uses David to speak of the poet's ability to express 'the new law'.

The human experience of David has attracted, finally, a number of inferior dramatists in addition to J.M. Barrie (*The Boy David*), D.H. Lawrence (*David*), and Christopher Fry (*A Sleep of Prisoners*), as well as such diverse novelists as Charles Dickens (*David Copperfield*), Thomas Hardy (*Far from the Madding Crowd; The Mayor of Casterbridge*), William Faulkner (*Absalom, Absalom!*), and Joseph Heller (*God Knows*). Such emphasis on his complex humanity, however, has never obscured his religious dimension: for Smart and his contemporaries David represents the 'intense and personal overflowing of religious emotion' praised by Bishop Lowth in *The Sacred Poetry of the Hebrews* (1753); for Byron and Browning he is still the man of faith capable of rousing others from the black slough of despair.

Charles A. Huttar
*Hope College*
Raymond-Jean Frontain
*University of Central Arkansas*

## Elijah

The varied and colourful career of Elijah the Tishbite may be divided into seven distinctive episodes: his sudden appearance on the national scene of Israel, as he announces to King Ahab the forthcoming drought and immediately flees (on God's command) to the brook Cherith, where he is fed by ravens (1 Kings 17:1–7); his reviving of the son of the widow of Zarephath (1 Kings 17:8–24); his successful contest with the prophets of Baal at Mount Carmel (1 Kings 18:20–40); his flight from the wrath of Ahab's wife Jezebel, in the course of which he despairs, falls asleep under a broom (KJV 'juniper') tree, is awakened and fed by an angel, and then fasts for forty days and forty nights at Mount Horeb (1 Kings 19:1–18); his judgment upon Ahab and Jezebel in the matter of Naboth's vineyard (1 Kings 21:1–29); his intervention in Ahaziah's attempted embassy to Baal-zebub (2 Kings 1:1–18); and his translation into heaven in a fiery chariot (2 Kings 2:1–12).

In Christian tradition, the gospels' association of Elijah with John the Baptist (Matthew 11:14; Luke 1:17; 9:8; 9:19; John 1:21) complicates the understanding of his role. In Christian pictorial iconography his appearance usually follows New Testament descriptions of John – a tendency justified in part by Elijah's habit of living (by choice or necessity) in the wilderness. The Desert Fathers and other ascetics trace their lineage not only to Christ's sojourn in the wilderness, but back through John to Elijah. (A 3rd-century Apocalypse of Elijah strongly resembles the book of Revelation.)

In general, however, the attention the Fathers give to Elijah is slight. He is typically seen as exemplifying absolute devotion to God in the face of enmity and persecution – a position modified by Luther, who in a polemical vein compares the Reformers to Elijah and the Roman church to the prophets of Baal (Works, edited by T. Bachmann, 1960, 35.200–201) – or, through his dealings with the prophets of Baal, as providing justification for the slaying of God's enemies. For St Clement of Rome, Elijah is a type of the simplicity and poverty to which Christians are called (1 Clement 17:1). Many Christian commentators have identified Elijah and Enoch, the other biblical character who did not experience a natural death, as the two witnesses of Revelation 11 who will appear in the last days.

Many of the theological uses of the Elijah narrative are repeated in literature. In Chaucer's Summoner's Tale, the prophet is cited as an example of the virtue of fasting (3.1890–93). The same tale's friar asserts that both Elijah and Elisha were friars (3.2116–18), an allusion to the traditional identification of Elijah as the founder of the Carmelites. Milton, in his Apology for Smectymnuus, sees Elijah's mockery of the prophets of Baal as an example of humour used properly for instruction – in response to Bacon, who had called such tactics into question. Swinburne, however, turns Elijah's mockery of the prophets of Baal against Christians in his 'Hymn of Man':

Is he drunk or asleep, that the rod of his wrath is unfelt and
unseen?... Cry aloud till his godhead awaken; what doth he
to sleep and to dream? Cry, cut yourselves, gash you with
knives and scourges, heap on to you dust; Is his life but as
other gods' lives? Is not this the Lord God of your trust?...
O fools, he was God, and is dead.

Hardy, in *Tess of the D'Urbervilles*, is similarly sceptical, implicitly
comparing the silence of the Christian God with that of Baal: after Tess
is raped, his narrator asks, 'Where was Tess' guardian angel? where
was the Providence of her simple faith? Perhaps, like that other god of
whom the ironical Tishbite spoke, he was talking, or he was pursuing,
or he was on a journey, or he was sleeping and not to be awaked.'
Howard Nemerov recalls the contest on Carmel to make a different
kind of point:

> ... when Elijah on Mount Carmel brought the rain
> Where the prophets of Baal could not bring rain,
> Some of the people said that the rituals of the prophets of Baal
> Were aesthetically significant, while Elijah's were very plain.
> ('On Certain Wits')

Milton makes significant use of Elijah in *Paradise Regained*, where he
cites Elijah's sojourns in the wilderness as types and patterns for
Christ's own desert fast. Christ himself, addressing Satan disguised as
an inquiring stranger, calls attention to Elijah's example (1.351–55).
Andrew and Simon, unable to find Jesus, fear that he has been 'caught
up to God... like the great Tishbite', and seek him 'as those young
Prophets then with care / Sought lost Elijah' (1.1–20). This
connection is further explored when Christ dreams that he sees Elijah
fed by the ravens, then fed by the angel under the juniper (2.260–78).
This incident comes in for ironic treatment in Butler's *The Way of All
Flesh*, where it becomes a concern of Ernest Pontifex, thanks to a
painting of 'Elijah or Elisha (whichever it was) being fed by ravens in
the desert' which hung in the dining room.

> When Ernest was a very small boy it had been a constant
> matter of regret to him that the food which the ravens carried
> never actually reached the prophet... One day... he had

clambered up to the picture and with a piece of bread and butter traced a greasy line right across it from the ravens to Elisha's mouth, after which he had felt more comfortable.

Later Ernest, as a young priest, angered his Bishop by preaching a sermon on 'what kind of little cake it was that the widow of Zarephath had intended making when Elijah found her gathering a few sticks. He demonstrated that it was a seed cake.'

Although the notion of inheriting another's mantle (from 2 Kings 2:1–12) has become common enough to lose the force of allusion, some English writers have recalled the source. Robert Burns, in his prefatory 'Dedication' of his *Poems* ('to the Noblemen and Gentlemen of the Caledonian Hunt'), writes that 'The poetic genius of my country found me, as the prophetic bard Elijah did Elisha – at the plow; and threw her inspiring mantle over me.' In *Billy Budd*, Melville describes the dawn of the day on which Billy was hanged: 'Like the prophet in the chariot disappearing in heaven and dropping his mantle to Elisha, the withdrawing night transferred its pale robe to the peeping day.' Dryden produces an ironic reversal of the story. As his Elijah (Flecknoe, the dullest of poets) sinks, the mantle rises up to Mac Flecknoe:

> Sinking he left his drugget robe behind,
> Borne upwards by a subterranean wind.
> The mantle fell to the young prophet's part,
> With double portion of his father's art.
> (*Mac Flecknoe*, 214–17)

Another common phrase deriving from the Elijah narrative is the 'still small voice' of 1 Kings 19:9–12 – modified in Wordsworth's 'Tintern Abbey' to 'the still, sad music of humanity', and in Tennyson's 'Break, Break, Break' to 'the sound of a voice that is still'.

William Blake refers to Elijah more generally as a great exemplar of uncompromising prophetic power. In *Milton* (plate 24, 68–71)

> Los is by mortals nam'd Time...
> But they depict him bald & aged who is in eternal youth
> All powerful and his locks flourish like the brows of morning
> He is the Spirit of Prophecy the ever apparent Elias.

In *The Marriage of Heaven and Hell* (plates 22–24), Blake creates 'A Memorable Fancy' in which an angel – convinced by a devil that 'no virtue can exist without breaking [the] ten commandments', and that 'Jesus was all virtue, and acted from impulse, not from rules' – embraces the 'flame of fire' out of which the devil speaks, and thus '[is] consumed and [arises] as Elijah'.

Melville's *Moby Dick*, in which Ahab is so prominent, is not without an Elijah, although his appearance is brief (chapter 19, 'The Prophet'). Just before he boards the *Pequod*, Ishmael is confronted by an apparently crazy old man, an ambiguous prophet – 'wants to be, will be, and then again, perhaps it won't be, after all' – who warns vaguely of disaster to come. On finding that the man's name is Elijah, Ishmael is worried, but soon shrugs off his concern. This Ahab will be spared nothing – perhaps because his Elijah is so peripheral to his story.

Alan Jacobs
*Wheaton College*

## Elisha

The career of Elisha, although intimately connected with that of the prophet Elijah, has a distinctive history to which both commentators and writers have attended. His independent prophetic vocation begins at 2 Kings 2:13, as he picks up the mantle of the departed Elijah; his story continues (with occasional interruptions) through 2 Kings 13:21, which describes how a dead man, tossed into Elisha's tomb, was restored to life upon coming into contact with the prophet's bones. This final miracle is alluded to in Ecclesiasticus 48:12–14, where it is said of Elisha, 'No word could overcome him, and after his death his body prophesied. He did wonders in his life, and at his death were his works marvellous.'

Theological commentators, both Jewish and Christian, tend to focus on two special problems arising from the biblical account. The first revolves around the proper interpretation of Elisha's claim to 'a double portion of [Elijah's] spirit' (2 Kings 2:9). The events related in the text hardly seem to support the conclusion that Elisha was twice as great a prophet as Elijah (the Hebrew phrase itself, meaning literally 'a mouth of two' or a double mouthful, is ambiguous); yet St Jerome,

Martin Luther, and many other translators and interpreters have tried to save the 'plain sense'. Rabbinical commentators argue that Elisha performed twice as many miracles as Elijah, sixteen to eight (Baraita of 32 Middot, 1); the medieval Christian theologian Peter Damian uses the same argument, but attributes twenty-four miracles to Elisha, twelve to Elijah (*Acta sanctorum*, July 20). The second issue which has prompted extensive commentary is the incident in which Elisha called bears down upon a group of boys who taunted him (2 Kings 2:23–25): was the prophet following the will of God? Here the rabbis are particularly inventive: the Haggadah argues that those who mocked Elisha were not boys, but men behaving like boys; other commentators say that Elisha saw, with his prophetic gifts, that the boys were the sons of evil parents and would grow up to be evil themselves, and furthermore argue that God punished him for yielding to his anger by visiting him with a serious illness (Sota 46b–47a).

The morbid humour associated with this incident is not lost on Charles Lamb, who writes of one Thomas Coventry that he 'made a solitude of children wherever he came, for they fled his insufferable presence, as they would have shunned an Elisha bear' ('The Old Benchers of the Inner Temple'). Joyce provides a modification of the Vulgate rendering of the taunt of the boys in *Ulysses* ('Proteus' episode): '*Descende, calve, ut ne nimium decalveris*' ('Come down, bald one, lest you become even balder'). In his poem 'Baldhead Elisha', A.M. Klein comments on 'the horrible / Vengeance that bears / Wreaked for the honour / Of forty-two hairs!'

Elisha's miracle of making 'iron swim' (2 Kings 6:5–7) is alluded to by Milton in his 'Animadversions', when he says that his opponent needs a better foundation for argument than the trivial one he has provided, 'which you may now deplore as the axehead that fell into the water and say, "Alas, master, for it was borrowed," unless you have as good a faculty to make iron swim, as you had to make light froth sink.' Of all Elisha's miracles, however, his revival of the dead son of the Shunammite woman (2 Kings 4:8–37) is the most thoroughly detailed, and has produced some of the most intriguing echoes. A sermon of John Donne (edited by Potter and Simpson, 1953–62, 2.300) is particularly striking:

And as *Elisha* in raysing the *Shunamits* dead child, put his mouth upon the childs mouth, his eyes, and his hands, upon the hands, and the eyes of the child; so when my crosses have carried me up to my Saviours Crosse, I put my hands into his hands, and hang upon his nailes, I put mine eyes upon his, and wash off all my former unchast looks, and receive a soveraigne tincture, and a lively verdure, and a new life into my dead teares, from his teares. I put my mouth upon his mouth, and it is I that say, *My God, My God, why hast thou forsaken me?* and it is I that recover againe, and say, *Into thy hands, O Lord, I commend my spirit.*

Alan Jacobs
*Wheaton College*

## Esther

The heroine of the book of Esther recalls, even in her name, the plight of Jews in exile. First named Hadassah (Hebrew for 'myrtle'), she later took the Persian name Esther (from 'star' or possibly from the goddess Ishtar). An orphan or foundling Jewess raised by her cousin Mordecai, she was chosen to succeed Vashti as consort to King Ahasuerus. As queen she prevailed on Ahasuerus to save her people from the treacherous designs of Haman, a prominent court official.

The historicity of the book of Esther is problematic. Its composition followed Persian hegemony and is probably to be placed during the 2nd century BC. Numerous additions to the core narrative are found in the LXX, Targum, Talmud, Midrash, and Josephus. While Queen Esther does not match any known Persian consort, King Ahasuerus has been tentatively identified with Xerxes I (486–485BC), partly on account of there being a notable courtier, Marduka (Mordecai?), in Xerxes' court. Esther is a late addition to the canon, unnoted in Sirach, the New Testament, and the Qumran scrolls or the Pirqe ' Abot (c. 180BC). In the Midrash, however, it is called Megillah, 'the Scroll', chief among the Megilloth of five scrolls appropriated to chief festivals (Ruth, Song of Songs, Ecclesiastes, Lamentations, and Esther), Esther being read at Purim. Maimonides valued the book next after the Pentateuch, signalling its growing importance in medieval Jewish community life.

The story is mainly didactic and aetiological, accounting for the Festival of Purim (Esther 9:20–32), which celebrates the ultimate failure and demise of Haman the Agagite, Ahasuerus' favourite, who conspired to eliminate the Jewish exiles. When Haman sent instructions throughout the kingdom 'to destroy, to kill, and to cause to perish, all Jews, both young and old, little children and women, in one day... and to take the spoil of them for a prey,' Esther courageously broached court decorum to appeal for her people before the king. Haman was hanged on the gallows he had erected for Mordecai, and Mordecai was elevated to prominence in the court, whereby the Jews gained continuing advocacy for their cause.

Esther's fabled loyalty and courage are not depicted as being especially religious; there is no mention of God in the account, and the concluding theme of vengeance is handled in a way which has raised doubts among canonists from the rabbis at Jamnia (c. AD80) to Martin Luther. Greek apocryphal additions to Esther spiritualize the narrative by introducing divine agency and prophecy through dream interpretation. Copious midrashic commentary subsequently synthesizes the secular and religious aspects of Esther's history: her concern for her endangered people exemplified the Jews' relationship with God, while Haman's perfidy not only tested divine providence but foreshadowed Seleucid and Roman oppression (Pesahim 117a; Yoma 29a; Megilla 6b–7a, 10b–11a, 12a n.1, 13a–b, 15a–b, 16a–b, 19a; Yebamot 24b; Sanhedrin 74b, 93a). Esther entered Jewish legend as a figure of female virtue, piety, resolve, and national resistance, akin to Deborah, Judith, and Hannah; occasionally she is also regarded as a prophetess. Talmudists and midrashic commentators also stress her extraordinary beauty, making her one of the four most beautiful women in the world (along with Rahab, Sarah, and Abigail).

The Fathers of the Christian Church and later commentators built upon this Jewish legendary foundation. St Ambrose regards Esther as an exemplar of virtuous and courageous action in the face of danger (*De officis ministrorum*, 3.21.123). St Jerome (*Epistle* 53.8) regards her as a type of the Church defending the faithful against iniquity and persecution (typified by Haman). She is seen also to prefigure the Virgin Mary, similar to her in chaste beauty and in intercessional efficacy.

Franciscan lyricists typically were indebted in such typology to St Anthony's famous treatise *In Annuntiatione Sanctae Mariae* (3.836b); in another medieval lyric Esther becomes *mater misericordi* (R. Greene, ed., *The Early English Carols*, 1977, no. 210; cf. no. 194).

Geoffrey Chaucer refers to Esther *ad sensus literalis* four times: predictably, in *The Book of the Duchess* and *Legend of Good Women* she is a model of womanly and saintly virtue. Prudence advances her as an example of woman's good counsel in *The Tale of Melibee*. And in *The Merchant's Tale* the beautiful, loyal Esther of medieval legend is contrasted with January's treacherous bride. In a rare application of the Esther story as political parody, the anonymous *New Enterlude of Godly Queene Hester* (1560–61) coyly invites the audience to identify Ahasuerus with King Henry VIII, Haman with Cardinal Wolsey, and Esther with Catherine Parr, emphasizing the conspiratorial features of the narrative (cf. the contemporary 16th-century play *Queen Esther and Proud Haman*). Racine, in 1689, composed a dramatic versification of Esther for the Sisters of St Cyr to read or chant, finding Esther an ideal subject for such a community, because the heroine exemplifies *'de détachement du monde au milieu du monde même'* (preface).

Post-Reformation references to Esther, such as Milton's in *Reason of Church Government* (3.1.188) or Gray's in his 'Extempore on Dr Keene, Bishop of Chester', conventionally allude either to Esther's extraordinary beauty or to her virtue, themes which persist in the few Joycean references to her (e.g., *Finnegans Wake*). An exception to the pattern of casual allusion is Browning's reversion in *The Ring and the Book* to the climactic moment of the biblical narrative. Browning cites the Queen's defiance of royal courtly protocol, at risk of her own life, in order to treat it ironically in terms of masculine dreams of power over women. The relationship between the orphaned Esther Summerson of Dickens' *Bleak House* and her guardian-wooer John Jarndyce, is suggestive of the somewhat mysterious connection between the biblical Esther and Mordecai. Esther's memory is romanticized by a variety of 19th-century authors (e.g., Tennyson's 'The Princess'; cf. also Melville's 'The Bell Tower') as well as in a modern and more cynical vein by the poet A.M. Klein in 'Five Characters'. Klein's Esther, like a 'new star's sudden naissance', walks moonlit in the palace garden, her pardon the sequestered token of her gratifying the 'Persian-hot passion' of Ahasuerus.

Mark S. Madoff (deceased)
Royal Road Military Academy, Victoria, British Columbia

## Feet of Clay

One of the dreams of Nebuchadnezzar recorded in the book of Daniel is of a great composite giant, gold, silver, and bronze from head through torso but with legs of iron and 'his feet part of iron and part of clay' (Daniel 2:33). The insubstantial support is shattered by a stone and the giant falls with a crash, reduced to powder. This description has given rise to the English expression 'feet of clay' – meaning to be vulnerable out of proportion to superficial appearances. In Tennyson's 'Merlin and Vivien' the magician condemns Vivien for, 'harlot'-like, slandering Arthur's knights, judging 'all nature from her feet of clay'. Oscar Wilde's *An Ideal Husband* makes a generic complaint: 'Why do you place us on monstrous pedestals? We have all feet of clay, women as well as men' (chapter 2). In the same vein, Dolly, in Somerset Maugham's *Theatre*, is determined not to grant her admirer 'a peep at her feet of clay' (chapter 22). In his *Studies in Classic American Literature* D.H. Lawrence laments Melville's homecoming from South Sea island adventures to 'a wife: a thing with clay feet'. The association in modern literature is thus typically with sexual frailty, something not implicit in the biblical source.

David L. Jeffrey
University of Ottawa

## Goliath

Goliath was the giant of Gath and champion of the Philistines who was eventually defeated and killed by the boy David (1 Samuel 17:4–23; 21:9; 22:10; 2 Samuel 21:19; 1 Chronicles 20:5ff.). Scholars speculate that he was not, strictly speaking, a Canaanite but was perhaps of aboriginal stock such as the Anakim, some of whom were still to be found near Gath in the reign of Saul (2 Samuel 21:22; 1 Chronicles 20:8). According to the usual reckoning of a cubit as

45 centimetres, Goliath would have been almost 3 metres (9 ft) tall ('six cubits and a span').

Haggadic commentary suggests that Goliath was descended from Samson, the enemy of giants (Targum 1 Samuel 17:4); he wore into his battle with David the insignia of the Canaanite deity Dagon, whose temple was in Gaza (Tehillim 18.160; 144.533; Shemuel 21.109). Patristic and later Christian commentary typically allegorizes him as a type of Satan, contesting against Christ: *'Goliath vero superbiam diaboli significat: quam David, id est Christus...'* (*Glossa Ordinaria, Patrologia Latina,* 113.556).

Because of the popularity of the David–Goliath narrative, Goliath's name has become in modern literature a byword for prodigious strength and size. The lance of Ivanhoe is compared by Isaac in Scott's *Ivanhoe* to 'that of Goliath the Philistine, which might vie with a weaver's beam' (chapter 10). Huck Finn compares the burly Hines to 'Goliar' (*Huckleberry Finn,* chapter 29). American poet Anthony Hecht pictures Goliath lying 'on his back in Hell', a Miltonic conflation (cf. *Patrologia Latina,* 1.196–98), in *'La Masseur de ma Soeur'*. A.M. Klein's 'Sling for Goliath' in 'Five Weapons against Death' uses the giant as an image for the reversal of fortune, the victory of death over life; and in Margaret Avison's *Winter Sun* poems Goliath acquires mythic attributes from yet another source, notably a 'purple beard' (92).

David L. Jeffrey
*University of Ottawa*

## Haman

The wicked Haman was a vizier of the Persian empire under Xerxes (Ahasuerus) and mortal enemy to Mordecai, cousin of Esther. His history is recorded in the book of Esther. Enraged that Mordecai, a devout Jew, would not bow down and reverence him, Haman plotted to achieve the destruction of the whole Jewish nation. Esther interceded with Ahasuerus, and Haman was himself hanged on the gallows he had prepared for Mordecai.

In Jewish legend Haman is an Iago-like figure, whose hostility towards the king's first consort Vashti precipitated her downfall (Abba Gorion 17; Esther Rabba 1.16), even as he intended to eradicate

Esther and her people. In Haman's lengthy iteration of charges against the Jews he gives a précis of their observance of the Torah, including its principal ritual laws and festal observances, at the conclusion of which God is said to remark: 'You did well to enumerate the holidays of the Jews, yet you forgot two – Purim and Shushan-Purim – which Jews will henceforth celebrate to commence your downfall' (2 Targum 3:8; cf. Megilla 13b; 'Aggadat Esther 30.34; Targum Esther 3.8–9).

Patristic commentary makes the first of Haman's sins his desire to be worshipped (Esther 3:1–2; *Glossa Ordinaria*, *Patrologia Latina*, 113.743). The reversal of the plot and Haman's ultimate condemnation (7:8–10) is cited by the *Glossa Ordinaria* as an example of 'the oppressor oppressed' or 'tormentor tormented' (113.745), a reading accorded prominence in many literary treatments of the narrative.

In Middle English lyrics, where the Virgin Mary is often compared to Esther, Haman is a type of Satan, the serpent whose head is struck off by the 'Second Eve' (e.g., R. Greene, *The Early English Carols*, no. 194). As one who was rightfully executed on a 'tree' (gallows), he is occasionally contrasted with Christ, in a typological juxtaposition of two victories over evil:

> Aman alsoo, the fende, oure foo,
> Thou hast hangyd vppon a tre;
> Thus thou hast brought mankynd fro woo,
> *Mater misericordie*. (Greene, no. 210)

Several Renaissance plays (*Queen Esther and Proud Haman*, *Godly Queen Hester*) as well as the 19th-century *The Death of Haman* consider Haman's fate.

David L. Jeffrey
*University of Ottawa*

## Handwriting on the Wall

The handwriting (or hand writing) on the wall (Daniel 5:5) is one of five incidents in the narrative section (chapters 1–6) of Daniel in which the power of God is proved to an unbelieving king. Of these incidents – Nebuchadnezzar's dream, the men in the furnace, Nebuchadnezzar's metamorphosis, Belshazzar's feast, Daniel in the lions' den – this is the only one in which the unbeliever is destroyed rather than reproved, because Belshazzar practises idolatry and desecrates the temple vessels (Daniel 5:3–4).

The inscription in Daniel 5:25, *mene', mene', teqel, upharsin* (KJV, Masoretic Text; cf. Septuagint, Vulgate, Josephus, *Antiquities* 10.11.3 *mane, thekel/tekel, phares*), describes the diminishing worthiness of the Babylonian kings from Nebuchadnezzar by means of a monetary metaphor. Debates too involved to be recounted here have arisen over the meaning of the inscription and the question of why in the Masoretic Text (and hence in the KJV) it differs from the interpretation given by Daniel (*mene, tekel, peres*) in Daniel 5:26–28. The inscription has been deciphered to read, 'a mina, a mina, a shekel, and half-minas (or half-shekels)'. The saying may be proverbial, and answer the riddling question, 'What is the worth of the kings of Babylon?' *Mene* may be repeated rhetorically, as in 'Babylon is fallen, is fallen' (Isaiah 21:9); or perhaps the first Aramaic *mn'* here means *menah*, 'he was weighed'. The Masoretic Text for Daniel 5:26–28 may represent the inscription differently from Daniel 5:25 because Daniel, in interpreting the inscription, altered it after the practice of eisegesis, a midrashic adaptive interpretation of texts, according to O. Eissfeldt ('Die Mene-Tekel Inschrift und ihre Deutung', *Zeitschrift für die alttestatementliche Wissenschaft* 63, 1951, 105–14).

Daniel's interpretation of the inscription is built on a paronomastic reworking of the Aramaic *mene', teqel*, and *upharsin*: 'MENE: God hath numbered [*menah*] thy kingdom and finished it. TEKEL: Thou art weighed [*teqiltah*] in the balances, and art found wanting. PERES: Thy kingdom is divided [*perisat*], and given to the Medes and Persians [*paras*].' (See *Interpreter's Dictionary of the Bible*, 3.348–49; *New Catholic Encyclopaedia*, 9.650.)

St Jerome's influential *Commentarius in Danielem* (*Patrologia Latina*, 25.519–21) sees Belshazzar's idolatry and sacrilege as instances of pride; Daniel 5 foreshadows typologically the downfall of Antichrist and the subsequent reign of the saints. This view was adjusted only slightly in the later Middle Ages; for example, Rupert of Deutz held that Belshazzar's punishment was a type of the destruction of Babylon the Great in Revelation 18:2–3 (*De Trinitate; In Danielem*, 9, *Patrologia Latina*, 167.1510). To Rupert, the hand which did the writing was that of Christ, the right hand of God (col. 1509). To Protestant commentators, however, the hand itself was incidental – perhaps only the 'appearance' of a hand (Calvin, *Commentaries on... Daniel*, trans. T. Myers, 1852, 322), or possibly that of the angel Gabriel (Matthew Poole, *Synopsis Criticorum Aliorumque Sacrae Scripturae Interpretum*, 1673, 3.1454).

If the story of Belshazzar's feast is excellent literary material, its earliest literary adapters were just as interested in its theological value as in its narrative strengths. The incomplete Old English Daniel stops before Daniel interprets the handwriting, but it provides enough of Daniel 5 directly and through foreshadowing (675–94) to bring out a clear parallel between Belshazzar's feast and the sins of the Jews before the Captivity. This parallel suggests that the theme of *translatio imperii*, God's handing over imperial rule from a just to an unjust people (see W. Goez, *Translatio Imperii*, 1958), may lie behind the poet's reworking of his source. Two 12th-century Latin Daniel plays (see K. Young in *Drama of the Medieval Church*, 1933, 2.276–301) are noteworthy examples of the literary tradition already well established by the Middle Ages. Middle English *Cleanness* includes a full and vivid retelling of Daniel 5 as the last of three Old Testament examples of sin which brought about God's angry retribution (1529–1804). Belshazzar's feast is one of Chaucer's Monk's illustrations of tragedy, but the moral the Monk draws from it reveals only his own spiritual blindness, since he sees the story simply as a warning that misfortune may strike anyone at any time (7.2239–46).

Interest in the narrative and dramatic aspects of Daniel 5 prompted the creation of verse dramas by Hannah More ('Belshazzar', in *Sacred Dramas*, 1782) and the Oxford historian Henry Hart Milman, whose *Belshazzar* recounts Babylon's last day before the Persian conquest. Perhaps seeking to outdo Milman, Robert Eyres Landor, in *The Impious Feast* (1828), set the beginning of his exotic poetic epic two days earlier.

Belshazzar appealed to the Byronic imagination: Byron retells Daniel 5 in 'The Vision of Belshazzar', and in 'To Belshazzar' he places himself at the feast, where he urges Belshazzar to reform even as he recognizes that Belshazzar is 'unfit to govern, live, or die' (24). The fall of Napoleon prompted him to observe, in 'Ode to Napoleon

Buonaparte', that 'weigh'd in the balance, hero dust / Is vile as vulgar clay' (109–10). Describing the destruction of the Suez city Ismael by Russian troops, Byron ironically compared the victory message of Catherine the Great's general Suvarov to the handwriting on the wall (*Don Juan*, 8.133–34).

Colloquially, 'the handwriting on the wall' can refer simply to a warning of approaching (but not necessarily inevitable or divinely sent) disaster, and so it is often used in literature. Among the more original uses of the phrase are Milton's (*Paradise Lost*, 4.977–1015), where the Homeric golden scales in the heavens which Satan beholds after being chased from Eden by angels suggest not only that he is like Achilles, Hector, and Turnus, but that he is like Belshazzar. Swift's broadside, 'The Run upon the Bankers', resurrects the economic metaphor in Daniel 5:26–28 and applies it to bankers who lend their banks into bankruptcy; at Judgment

> Other Hands the Scales shall hold,
> And They in Men and Angels Sight
> Produc'd with all their Bills and Gold.
> Weigh'd in the Balance, and found Light. (61–64)

The Romantic period brought further adaptation of the handwriting motif. Keats' castle builder entertains guests lavishly in his apartment, in which he keeps a mirror inscribed with the handwriting; thus, he is both Belshazzar and Daniel to himself ('The Castle Builder', 54). Shelley inverted the balance image so that vice, not virtue, was found wanting, in *Defence of Poetry:* '[the great poets' moral] errors have been weighed and found to have been dust in the balance' (*Shelley's Poetry and Prose*, eds. D. Reiman and S. Powers, 1977, 506). The handwriting is the image of a past injury of crime in Dickens' *David Copperfield* and Hawthorne's *The Scarlet Letter.* In Dickens, the scar from the hammer wound on Rosa Dartle's lips becomes as pronounced as the handwriting during an argument between Rosa and Steerforth, a harsh judge (chapter 20; see J. Vogel, *Allegory in Dickens*, 1977, 179). In Hawthorne, Hester Prynne's offense is as mysterious to her neighbours as the handwriting (chapter 3). In *Moby Dick* (chapter 119), Ishmael prophetically calls the fire in the *Pequod*'s masts God's handwriting, whereas Ahab sees it only as a guiding light to the white whale. The narrator in Browning's 'Too Late', 92–94, attributes a supernatural power to the dead woman who rejected him in life, and imagines his heart inscribed with 'her mark, / *Tekel*, found wanting, set aside / Scorned!' (see L. Perrine, 'Browning's "Too Late"; A Reinterpretation', *Victorian Poetry*, 7, 1969, 339–45).

The handwriting is a symbol of guilt in Emily Dickinson's 'Belshazzar Had a Letter' (no. 1459). In Hardy's *Return of the Native* (1.6), the 'small human hand, in the act of lifting pieces of fuel into the fire' with which Eustacia Vye signals Wildeve appears dismembered, 'like that which troubled Belshazzar'. The allusion adds to the larger symbolism which makes Egdon Heath an agent of fate.

Robert Louis Stevenson makes a poignant allusion to the handwriting in *The Strange Case of Dr Jekyll and Mr Hyde*; in Jekyll's letter to his friend Utterson, he recalls the discovery that he had, asleep, transformed unwillingly into Hyde. 'This inexplicable incident, this reversal of my previous experience, seemed, like the Babylonian finger on the wall, to be spelling out the letters of my judgment.' Lawrence's short story 'Things' transmutes Emma Lazarus' poem at the base of the Statue of Liberty into both the handwriting and the first commandment in the American work ethic for a young American couple returning from years wasted gathering possessions abroad: 'Erasmus, of course, ought to get a job. This was what was written on the wall... the strange, vague threat that the Statue of Liberty had always held over them: "Thou shalt get a job!"' (*Complete Short Stories*, 1961, 850).

M.W. Twomey
*Ithaca College*

## Hezekiah

Hezekiah, son of Ahaz, was king of Judah in the time of the prophet Isaiah. His notable deeds are recorded in 2 Kings 18:1 – 20:21; 2 Chronicles 29:1 – 32:33; Isaiah 36–39; Sirach 48:17–25. He reigned from c. 716 to 687BC, during a time of fairly constant military threat from the Assyrians, of whose empire Judah under Hezekiah had become a vassal state. A pious king, he is celebrated for opposing idolatry and destroying the 'high places' of pagan worship as well as cleansing and opening the Temple. After a 'sickness unto death', he was instructed by the prophet Isaiah to 'set [his] house in order' in preparation for his death. Hezekiah 'turned his face to the wall' and appealed to God to extend his life. He received a promise that the Lord would indeed grant him fifteen more years and, as a sign of assurance, a reversing of the sun's shadow on 'the sun dial of Ahaz' by 10 degrees. When, after his recovery, Hezekiah foolishly showed the Babylonians the royal treasury and armour, Isaiah predicted disaster – plunder and destruction at the hands of his enemies and his own sons made eunuchs in the palace of the Babylonian king. Instead of anguish Hezekiah expressed relief, saying, 'For there shall be peace and truth in my [own] days' (Isaiah 39:1–8).

Rabbinic legends esteem Hezekiah as steeping the nation in the Law (Sanhedrin 94b) as well as fulfilling the whole Law himself (Lamentations Rabba 25). He was seen by some as the Messiah (Genesis Rabba 97; Leviticus Rabba 36.6; Ruth Rabba 7.2; cf. St Cyril, *Lectures*, 12.22), and one tradition credits him and his disciples with the composition of Isaiah, Proverbs, Canticles, and Ecclesiastes (Baba Batra 15a).

Hezekiah is chiefly remembered in Christian tradition for his piety and for the extraordinary answer to his prayer for a stay of death (e.g., Cyril, *Lectures*, 2.15; 12.22). In New England Puritanism he was sometimes adduced as a type of Christ (e.g., Thomas Frink, *A King Reigning in Righteousness*, 1758) and as a moral example for temporal magistrates.

Christopher Smart's poem of gratitude on recovering from spiritual depression in 1756 is drawn from the story of Hezekiah's recovery, expressing for Smart his 'second birth... a birth of joy' ('Hymn to the Supreme Being'). However, with the exception of biblical dramas, such as William Allen's *Hezekiah, King of Judah: or, Invasion Repulsed* (1798) and W.H.T. Gairdner's *King Hezekiah: A Tragical Drama* (1923), Hezekiah has a minimal place in English literature.

Several phrases drawn from the story have become commonplace. In Henry James' *The Wings of the Dove*, it is twice said of Milly that 'she turned her face to the wall' (cf. 2 Kings 20:2) in a Hezekiah-like gesture of resignation and acceptance of death (the same expression is used in James' 'The Abasement of the Northmores' and 'The Beldonald Holbein'). While A.W. Pinero's *His House in Order* (1906) makes conscious reference to the Hezekiah narrative (as does Kierkegaard's *Sickness Unto Death*), such phrases are most often used in a merely proverbial way, with no recollection of their biblical source.

David W. Baker
*Asland Theological Seminary*

## Isaiah

The greatest among Israel's prophets, and the one most quoted in connection with messianic prophecies, Isaiah lived in 8th-century-BC Judah. The book which bears his name was composed under the reigns of Uzziah, Jotham, Ahaz, and Hezekiah. The prophet is thought to have met his death at the hands of King Manasseh for making unflattering speeches (Ta'anit 26b; Yerushalmi 4.68d; Tosepta Targum Isaiah 66:1); according to the Mishnah, he was sawn in half (cf. Ascension of Isaiah; Sanhedrin 10.28c; Pesiqta Rabbati 4.14; Midrash 'Aggadah Numbers 30:15). This tradition entered into Christian literature via Justin Martyr's *Dialogue with Trypho* and the 2nd-century AD Jewish apocalypse the Ascension of Isaiah, and is reflected in St Isidore of Seville and the anonymous *De ortu et obitu patrum*.

Isaiah is celebrated for the brilliance of his style and metaphorical language – a brilliance not entirely lost in translation. His vocabulary is one of the richest among Hebrew writers. In the greatest of early Christian commentaries (*Patrologia Latina*, 24.17–678), St Jerome compares him to Demosthenes as an orator and poet, an opinion which has stood the test of time. Because of the strong note of messianic expectation and an attendant sense of hope and consolation – particularly in the latter half of Isaiah's prophecy – Christian commentators have often followed Jerome's lead in referring to his book as an Old Testament 'gospel'.

Although Isaiah is frequently cited in English literature, he seldom appears as a character. When he does, as in the various

'Prophets' plays of the medieval Corpus Christi cycle, his role is typically limited to a recitation of his messianic prophecies.

Isaiah's irradiations of phrasing commend themselves to Herbert's preacher (A Priest to the Temple, 7, 34). Milton recollects the prophet's calling and the lips seared with a coal in 'On the Morning of Christ's Nativity', and makes extensive use of the messianic prophecies in Paradise Lost and Paradise Regained.

David L. Jeffrey
University of Ottawa

## Jonah

Jonah, the son of Amittai, was the fifth of the twelve minor prophets of the Old Testament. Rejecting God's command to preach to the Gentiles of Nineveh, capital of Assyria, he fled in a ship bound for Tarshish, but the sailors, harassed by a storm, reluctantly cast him into the waves. Immediately 'a great fish' (often assumed to be a whale) swallowed him; after three days in its belly, he prayed and was regurgitated. Proceeding at last to Nineveh, he prophesied its destruction within forty days, and the terrified Ninevites repented. When God granted them a reprieve, however, Jonah callously resented that his prophecy of destruction was not fulfilled. To teach him the virtue of compassion for living creatures, God raised a gourd to shelter him from the sun and a day later sent a worm to kill it.

The brief (forty-eight verses) Old Testament book of Jonah proves an exception to the prophetic rule by not reporting the substance of Jonah's prophecy but rather the tale of his mission: his initial flight (chapter 1:1–16), his three-day sojourn in the belly of the fish (1:17 – 2:10), his successful ministry in Nineveh (chapter 3), and his petulant response to God's mercy extended to the repentant Ninevites (chapter 4). The disobedient prophet himself becomes the object of satiric attack in the book because he embodies the type of nationalism and religious ethnocentrism which regards God as the exclusive property of the Israelites. Jonah's bigotry is contrasted to the character of God, whose mercy extends beyond national bounds; this emphasis accounts for the reading of the book of Jonah on the Day of Atonement in the Jewish liturgical calendar.

Jewish sources provide extensive commentary, both serious and fanciful, on the book of Jonah. Early interpretations from the Targums link Jonah with Moses in that Moses ascended to the heights of Mount Sinai and Jonah descended to the depths of the sea. Midrash Rabbah equates the fleeing Jonah with the fallen Adam, who shunned God's presence (Genesis 21:5). Other Jewish sources include fantastic descriptions of the whale's belly and its contents, together with the legend that Jonah used the whale's eyes as windows into the depths.

In Matthew 12:41 and Luke 11:29–32 Jesus uses the repentance of the Ninevites as a standard by which to condemn the unbelief of his listeners. In Matthew 12:38–41 he foretells that, like Jonah in the whale's belly, he will remain for three days 'in the heart of the earth' (cf. Matthew 16:1–4; Luke 11:29–32). These prophetic words establish Jonah as a type of Christ, especially the resurrected Christ, and he figures as an emblem of the resurrection in nearly sixty early Christian paintings in the catacombs. Here he appears in company with other Old Testament figures who escaped certain death: Daniel in the lions' den (Daniel 6:16–24) and the three children in the fiery furnace (Daniel 3).

Jonah's history is frequently cited by the Church Fathers, who see it as a lesson on the efficacy of repentance and the greatness of God's mercy (e.g., St Clement of Rome, *Epistle to the Corinthians*, 7; Tertullian, *Adversus Marcionem* 2.17; 5.4; St John Chrysostom, *Epistle* 1.15). Following Matthew 12:38–41, many refer to Jonah as a type of Christ (St Justin Martyr, *Dialogue with Trypho*, 107–08; St Augustine, *De civitate Dei* 18.44). St Cyril of Jerusalem draws a detailed parallel between the lives of Jonah and Jesus and regards the whale's belly as an analogue of hell, which Christ harrowed (*Catechetical Lectures*, 14.17–20). Noting that the literal meaning of *Jonah* is 'dove', St Jerome associates the prophet with the Holy Spirit (*In Jonam*, 391). He further emphasizes that the conversion of the Ninevites, a non-Jewish people, typifies the transfer of faith from the Jews to the Gentiles. In line with midrashic exegesis, some of the Fathers regard Jonah's flight as emblematic of Adam's fall (e.g., St Irenaeus, *Adversus haereses* 3.20.1; St Methodius, *On the History of Jonah*). Augustine (*Epistle* 102), Jerome (*In Jonam*, 422), and St Gregory of Nazianzus (*Orationes*, 2.107–08) interpret Jonah's sorrow as grief for the passing of God's favour from Jews to Gentiles, while Origen (*Contra Celsum*, 7.53, 57), Augustine (*Epistle* 102), and Jerome (*In Jonam*, 406) counter the arguments of pagan scoffers at the miracle of the fish.

Although interest in Jonah is less marked in the Middle Ages, commentators follow the Fathers in observing his role as a type of Christ and the etymology of his name (e.g., *Glossa Ordinaria*, *Patrologia Latina*, 114.128, and Haymo of Halberstadt, *Patrologia Latina*, 117.128). Rupert of Deutz recalls St Cyril of Alexandria in his search for minute parallels between Jesus' life and that of Jonah (*Patrologia Latina*, 168.399–440). The Jewish Zohar (Exodus Rabba 199a–b) expounds Jonah's story as an allegory of the soul's experience in the mortal body (the ship), its descent into a grave (the whale), and its resurrection (regurgitation).

One persistent early tradition has it that Jonah was swallowed fully clothed by the whale and was vomited forth both naked and bald. A naked Jonah occurs on an early Christian sarcophagus from Arles. A bald Jonah appears in the 9th century, when he is mentioned in both the Midrash and the *De Cena Cypriani* by John the Deacon; the 12th-century goliardic Archpoet, in his poem '*Fama Tuba Dante Sonum*', mentions, likewise, that Jonah emerged bald from the whale.

Disdaining such fanciful speculation and distrusting allegorical hermeneutics, the Reformers emphasize the inner struggles of Jonah, whom they see as a fallible human being saved by grace, a man whose example should dispel spiritual despair. Calvin lays especial stress on Jonah's sin of disobedience (*Commentary on the Prophet Jonah*, 1559; cf. Luther, *Lectures on Jonah*, 1525, 1526; Tyndale, *Prologue to the Prophet Jonah*, 1531). In the Enlightenment, skeptics revive the pagan incredulity over the miracle of the great fish (e.g., Voltaire, 'Jonas', *La Bible enfin expliquée*, 1776; Paine, 'The Best Way to Serve God', *The Age of Reason*, pt. 1, 1794). Today the book of Jonah is widely regarded as didactic fiction.

In English literature Jonah serves as both a type and an exemplum. In a number of Old English sermons for Rogationtide he illustrates the power of prayer and the efficacy of fasting and good deeds. His emergence from the whale's belly in the fifth of the Chester mystery plays illustrates God's mercy and prefigures the Resurrection. A variation on the traditional moral interpretation appears in *Patience*, a 14th-century alliterative poem, which rebukes the prophet for repining at the lot God had decreed for him and uses the story as the occasion to teach by the negative example of Jonah's impatience the virtue announced in the title. In Jonah's fear of being 'on rode rwly to-rent with rybaudes mony' ('on a cross pitifully torn to pieces by many ruffians', 96) and his ordeal 'in saym and in sorwe [grease and filth] that savoured as helle' (275), the poet also glances at the prophet's role as a type of Christ.

Dramatizing Jonah's story in *A Looking Glasse for London and England* (c. 1590), Thomas Lodge and Robert Greene soften it by letting him announce to the Ninevites God's change of heart, but the main purpose of their play is to accuse England of the sins of Nineveh. In Francis Quarles' *A Feast for Wormes* (1620), a verse paraphrase of the biblical book, the emphasis is on God's mercy, the efficacy of repentance, and the saving power of faith, although the poem mentions that Jonah is 'the blessed Type of him, that di'de for us' (1.7). Blake, in *The Four Zoas*, turns Jonah into a type of fallen man oppressed by a Satanic spirit who boasts, echoing Jonah 2:3, 'I roll my floods over his body, my billows & waves pass over him, / The sea encompasses him' (ed. Keynes, 4.133–34; cf. 9.95–96 with Jonah 2:5). In chapter 9 of Melville's *Moby Dick* the devout Father Mapple sees in Jonah's story a lesson on the wickedness of disobeying God and on the importance of true faith to the penitent. In Mapple's sermon the motivation for Jonah's flight is not, as in the Bible, dismay over God's universal mercy, but fear of being an alien in the hostile pagan city of Nineveh, and the final application of the sermon is a warning against becoming what Jonah became, the archetypal outcast.

James Bridie's satirical comedy *Jonah and the Whale* (1932) presents Jonah as the killjoy tyrant of his village and undermines his claim to divine inspiration. Laurence Housman's short play *The Burden of Nineveh* (1942) explains away the miracles (replacing the fish, for example, with timber) to throw the whole emphasis on obedience to God's promptings and the fullness of his mercy. Free of marvels, likewise, is Robert Frost's *A Masque of Mercy* (1947), in which a modern American Jonah, a contemporary Paul, and an egalitarian discuss whether God can be both just and merciful. In a lighter vein, Aldous Huxley's and A.M. Klein's fanciful lyrics, both entitled 'Jonah'

(1917 and 1933 respectively), follow Jewish midrashic lore in romanticizing the wondrous innards of the fish: for Klein's prophet, indeed, the return to land ironically becomes an expulsion from a paradise. Wolf Mankowitz's *It Should Happen to a Dog* (1956) casts Jonah as a kind of travelling salesman who is timid to announce the prophecy and resentful of his lot (constantly complaining that what happens to him 'should happen to a dog'). Other modern versions of the story appear in David Compton's *Jonah*, a modern psychological drama with a priggish and unpleasant hero, and Gordon Bennett's *So Why Does That Weirdo Prophet Keep Watching the Water?*

There are numerous passing references to Jonah in English literature. His name is given to one who brings trouble on his companions (e.g., Milton, *Eikonoklastes*, bk. 5; Defoe, *Robinson Crusoe;* Emily Brontë, *Wuthering Heights*, chapter 9; Byron, *The Two Foscari*, act 4; Kipling, *Captains Courageous*, chapter 4). A transient good is referred to as a Jonah's gourd (Tennyson, *The Princess*, 4.292; Hardy, *Far from the Madding Crowd*, chapter 33). And the great fish is recognized as a stumbling block to faith (Browning, 'Easter-day', 1850, 180; Shaw, 'The All or Nothing Complex', Preface to *Farfetched Fables*, 1948).

Henry Summerfield
*University of Victoria*
Leland Ryken
*Wheaton College*
Laurence Eldredge
*University of Ottawa*

# Jonathan

Jonathan was King Saul's oldest son and David's closest friend. He is portrayed as gentle, brave, pure-hearted, kind, swift as an eagle and strong as a lion, devoted to his father despite disagreements, true to his friend even at the cost of his own claim to the throne, resourceful in snatching victory out of the jaws of defeat, and courageous in facing death at the side of his father.

Jonathan first appears in 1 Samuel 14, when he wins an important victory over the Philistines but finds himself condemned to

die for disobedience to a parental order. But because the people plead
for him he is spared. He reappears in chapter 18, when he makes a
covenant of friendship with David, and in chapters 19 and 20, when
he keeps this covenant, even risking his life to defend his friend
against his father's wrath. David's lament for Jonathan in 2 Samuel 1
ranks among the world's great dirges.

St John Chrysostom cites Jonathan as a preeminent example of
charity in his *Homilies on First Corinthians* (*Homily* 33, on 1
Corinthians 13:4), a view reflected by the Fathers and medieval
exegetes. Aelred of Rievaulx in his *De Spirituali Amicitia* observes that
'the sacred bond of friendship between David and Jonathan... was
consecrated not through hope of future advantage, but from
contemplation of virtue' (2.63). 'Jonathan was found a victor over
nature, a despiser of glory and of power, one who preferred the
honour of his friend to his own' (3.95) (*On Spiritual Friendship*,
translated by M.E. Laker, 1974).

In English literature, it is Jonathan's friendship for David which
receives most attention. Edmund Spenser includes, among the great
friendships which inspired brave thoughts and deeds, the friendship
of 'true Jonathan and David who were trusty and tried' (*Faerie Queene*,
4.10.27). George Herbert compares the relationship of David and
Jonathan to that of Christ and the beloved disciple John (*The Church
Porch*, st. 46).

In Lord Byron's 'Song of Saul Before His Last Battle' (included
in his *Hebrew Melodies* of 1816), the doomed monarch, foreseeing his
end, bids farewell to his warriors and chiefs but not to Jonathan. In the
last stanza, he expresses his affection for his son from whom he has
become estranged and with whom he will now share death in battle:

> Farewell to others, but never we part,
> Heir to my royalty, son of my heart!
> Bright is the diadem, boundless the sway,
> Or kingly the death, which awaits us today!

Jonathan plays an important role in Abraham Cowley's *Davideis*
(1656), a sacred epic in four books. In book 1, Lucifer's emissary
characterizes him as an unnatural fool cheated by friendship. Book 2
deals with Jonathan's relationship to David, depicting Jonathan as

gentle and innocent. He endures patiently his father's invective when accused of being a spy and agent of David. In book 4, Jonathan is idealized as a person of fine judgment, and a praiseworthy husband, master, father, son, friend.

Charles Jennens, who wrote the libretto for Handel's oratorio *Saul*, acknowledged his indebtedness to Cowley's epic. In Jennen's text Jonathan frustrates Saul's designs against David and risks his life by refusing to carry out the orders of his envious father to execute vengeance upon David.

In D.H. Lawrence's *David* (1926), Jonathan is torn between his father, the king, and his friend, the king-to-be. He concludes that his life belongs to his father but that his soul is David's. The last scene depicts the final parting of the two friends. Jonathan acknowledges that the hope of Israel is with David, but he himself will remain with his father. 'I would not see thy new day, David. For thy wisdom is the wisdom of the subtle and behind thy passion lies prudence. Thy virtue is in thy wit and thy shrewdness. But in Saul have I known the magnanimity of a man.'

J.M. Barrie's play *The Boy David* (1936) presents Jonathan as a boy of about twelve, cultured, handsome, honest, intelligent, but unimaginative. His dejection is contrasted with David's light-heartedness. The play ends with a covenant between the two boys ever to remain friends.

Sol Liptzin
*Hebrew University of Jerusalem*

## Michal

Michal, the beautiful younger daughter of King Saul (cf. Megilla 15a), was given in marriage to David as his first wife (1 Samuel 14:49; 18:20ff.). Saul attempted to use his daughter's love for David as a means to rid himself of a popular rival: he therefore set the *mohar* (bridal price) for Michal at 100 Philistine foreskins (1 Samuel 18:20–30). When David presented double that number, 'Saul saw and knew that the Lord was with David... and was yet more afraid... and became David's enemy continually' (vv. 27–29). When the jealous king subsequently tried to ambush David in his house, Michal helped him escape, and then lied about her assistance, saying that David had threatened her. Saul therefore gave her to Phalti (or Phaltiel) in marriage (1 Samuel 25:44; cf. Sanhedrin 19b–20a). Because there was no divorce, David demanded her back for his harem fourteen years later (2 Samuel 3:14ff.) in order to legitimate his succession to the throne. An embarrassed Michal rebuked David for dancing before the ark when it was brought to Jerusalem (2 Samuel 6), and was apparently bitter about his succeeding her father in God's favour – a rejection of God's ordinance to which her barrenness was attributed (2 Samuel 6:22ff.).

In D.H. Lawrence's play *David* Michal is presented as a passionate lover resentful of the religious motivation in David that seems to interfere with her total possession of him. Morris Raphael Cohen sees Michal as a tragic heroine in his *King Saul's Daughter* (1938), a five-act closet drama. Mark Van Doren's 'Michal', a poem from his 'The People of the Word' cycle, concentrates on the tragic moment of her separation from the weeping husband Palatiel, who follows her on her enforced route back to David's harem as far as he dare.

Gladys Schmitt's novel *David the King* (1946) conjectures that Michal was originally intended to be the wife of Agag, hacked to pieces by Samuel, and presents her as a perpetual victim of unrequited love. Stefan Heym's *The King David Report* (1972) allows an aged Michal to tell her side of the story, a narration which characterizes David in extremely negative terms and undercuts the official 'state history' being composed for posterity by the historian Ethan. Like Dryden's *Absalom and Achitophel*, the novel is a political allegory about the writer's own contemporary Europe.

David L. Jeffrey
*University of Ottawa*

## Naaman

Naaman was a Syrian military commander during the reign of Ben-hadad. When afflicted with leprosy he was urged by a Hebrew slave girl in his Damascus household to seek help of God's prophet, Elisha (2 Kings 5). When he arrived at the house of Elisha Naaman was instructed by the prophet to go to the river Jordan and there dip in its waters seven times (v. 10). Naaman was offended at what seemed summary treatment and at the notion that the tepid Jordan had cleansing powers: 'Are not Abana and Pharpar, rivers of Damascus, better than all the waters of Israel? May I not wash in them and be clean? So he turned and went away in a rage' (v. 12). His servants, however, prevailed upon him to do the prophet's bidding. When he did, 'his flesh came again like unto the flesh of a little child, and he was clean' (v. 14).

St Ambrose comments that 'being forthwith cleansed, he understood that it is not of the waters but of grace that a man is cleansed' (De mysteriis, 3.17). Both St Irenaeus (Fragments, 34) and Tertullian (Adversus Marcionem 9, 10) see the narrative as typifying the efficacy of baptism. A brief commentary in the Glossa Ordinaria characterizes Naaman as a figure for the conversion of the Gentiles, whose strength has been eroded by 'the leprosy of an idolatrous faith' but who when cleansed by the gospel have their strength recovered to a higher purpose (Patrologia Latina, 113.613–14).

The story attracts little attention in literature until the 19th century, when the narrative became popular in evangelical preaching such as that of Charles Spurgeon. Though Lamb's allusion, 'The Cam and the Isis are to him better than all the waters of Damascus' is learned ('Oxford in the Vacation'), most later references tend to echo the homiletic tradition. Trollope writes in Barchester Towers:

> Then his faith was against him: he required to believe so much; panted so eagerly to give signs of his belief; deemed it so insufficient to wash himself simply in the waters of Jordan; that some great deed, such as that of forsaking everything for a true church, had for him allurements almost past withstanding. (chapter 20)

In Butler's The Way of All Flesh the narrator, attending Theobald's old church, 'felt as Naaman must have felt on certain occasions when he had to accompany his master on his return after having been cured of his leprosy', and Christina 'was sure that she had grown in grace since she had left off eating things strangled and blood – this was as the washing in Jordan as against Abana and Pharpar, rivers of Damascus' (chapter 21).

David W. Baker
*Ashland Theological Seminary*

## Nathan

Nathan was the prophet who, after David's adultery with Bathsheba and murder of her husband Uriah the Hittite, told David a parable to confront him with his unconfessed sin. The parable concerned a rich man with many sheep who stole from a poor neighbour the 'one little ewe lamb' in his possession. David, outraged at the thought of such radical injustice, exclaimed, 'As the Lord liveth, the man that has done this thing shall surely die,' to which the prophet responded, 'Thou art the man' (2 Samuel 12:1–12).

Nathan's role in conveying God's judgment on the sin of David is largely bypassed in early commentary and literature in favour of allegorization or extenuation of the adultery, murder, and repentance. By the 19th century, however, attention had shifted to the prophetic task of Nathan himself and to the crafty way in which he unmasked David by luring him into interpretation and self-condemnation. Ruskin notes, in *Modern Painters*, the particular aptness of such a narrative for a genteel reader: when David's own story 'is told him under a disguise, though only a lamb is concerned, his passion about it leaves him no time for thought. "The man shall die" – note the reason – "because he had no pity." A vulgar man would assuredly have been cautious and asked, "Who was it?".'

The 'one little ewe-lamb' became a figure for one's most cherished possession or pleasure, so that the unfortunate Diggery Venn in Hardy's *The Return of the Native*, after having lost his love Thomasin to Wildeve, nevertheless worked nearby 'though he never intruded upon her who had attracted him thither. To be in Thomasin's heath, and near her, yet unseen, was the one ewe-lamb of pleasure left to him' (cf. *Far from the Madding Crowd*, chapter 26). In *The Mayor of Casterbridge* Hardy has Elizabeth-Jane, upon discovering that the wealthy Lucetta had stolen her lover, stutter 'in Nathan tones, "You-have-married Mr Farfrae!"' In Brontë's *Wuthering Heights*, Lockwood dreams of challenging the Rev. Jabes Branderham for preaching a self-indulgent sermon on sin, only to have Jabes upstage him by 'leaning over his cushion' and declaring, 'Thou art the man!' This latter phrase, as well as the larger narrative, was used by Whitefield, Wesley, and other revivalists for just such sermons as gave rise to Brontë's parody.

David L. Jeffrey
*University of Ottawa*

## Nebuchadnezzar

Nebuchadnezzar (or Nebuchadrezzar; KJV Apocalypse of Nabuchodonosar), king of Babylon 605–562BC, is mentioned in 2 Kings 24–25 as responsible for the destruction of Jerusalem and the Babylonian exile of Judah (587–537BC). Jeremiah regards Nebuchadnezzar as God's instrument for the punishment of Judah (e.g., Jeremiah 25), a theme also mentioned in Ezra 5:12. In the apocryphal book of Judith, Nebuchadnezzar appears unhistorically as king of Assyria. In Daniel 1–4 Nebuchadnezzar appears as Daniel's overlord and as the king responsible for the trial in the fiery furnace of Shadrach, Meshach, and Abednego.

The Old English *Daniel* begins with an account of Nebuchadnezzar's sacking of the Jerusalem temple and deportation of the Israelites (1–79), while the remainder of the poem treats the events of Daniel 1–5, presenting them as a struggle of Daniel and his friends against Nebuchadnezzar and his line. Although the Middle English *Purity* or *Cleanness* deals mainly with Belshazzar's Feast, there is a long section devoted to Nebuchadnezzar's conquest of Jerusalem (1157–1332), and the poet praises Nebuchadnezzar for his reverent treatment of the sacred vessels of the Temple (1309–20). Nebuchadnezzar's dream of the composite statue made of four metals, symbolizing four world empires, and Daniel's interpretation of that dream (Daniel 2) became part of the literary tradition which dealt with Daniel as an apocalyptic prophet. Nebuchadnezzar's condemnation of Shadrach, Meshach, and Abednego to the fiery furnace for their refusal to worship the golden statue which he had set up (Daniel 3) is referred to in Milton's 'Eikonoklastes' (chapter 15, *Works*, 1932, 5.215).

Nebuchadnezzar's importance in literary tradition, however, derives primarily from Daniel 4, which concerns Nebuchadnezzar's dream of a great tree reaching to heaven and a voice ordering it to be cut down (Daniel 4:10–17). Daniel interprets the dream as portending Nebuchadnezzar's fall from greatness and temporary exile to a beastlike existence (4:19–27), and the story concludes with the fulfilment of this prophecy.

In the biblical account the offence which apparently causes Nebuchadnezzar's fall is a boast about the great city which he has built (Daniel 4:30–31). In later tradition, however, his offence was often magnified into blasphemous emulation of God; in Jewish tradition, references are made to Nebuchadnezzar as a 'hater and adversary of God' (Lamentations Rabba, proem 23); he was also seen as proud (Exodus Rabba 30.1; Numbers Rabba 9.24) and insolent (Leviticus Rabba 7.6). Like the Roman emperors, he is accused of self-deification (Genesis Rabba 9.5; Exodus Rabba 8.2 on Isaiah 14:14). Commentators came to associate other biblical texts with the Nebuchadnezzar of Daniel 4 – including Judith 6; Ezekiel 28 and 31, and Isaiah 14:12, the latter of which forms the basis of the identification of Nebuchadnezzar with the devil in several medieval commentators (cf. Doob, 58–64). Chaucer's Monk emphasizes Nebuchadnezzar's pride and presumptuous emulation of God (*Monk's Tale*, 7.2159–69; 2562–63), as does Gower (*Confessio Amantis*, 1.2785–809) and the Middle English *Miroure of Man's Salvacionne* (ed. H. Huth, 1888, 128). Spenser likewise refers to Nebuchadnezzar's absurd pride: 'There was that great proud king of Babylon, / That would compell all nations to adore, / And him as onely God to call vpon' (*Faerie Queene*, 1.5.47.1–3). Matthew Arnold cites Nebuchadnezzar's pride and fall as a political warning against excessive confidence in the British empire (*Complete Prose Works*, 1973, 9.38), and Byron makes a similar application in his 'Ode to Napoleon Buonaparte' (127–35).

On the other hand, Christian tradition has also emphasized Nebuchadnezzar's final redemption from his colossal pride through his humiliation and exile. The dew which fell on Nebuchadnezzar (Daniel 4:33) was often interpreted as divine grace, and Albert the Great links the 'seven times' period of Nebuchadnezzar's exile (Daniel 4:23) to the seven parts of the Sacrament of Penance, thereby emphasizing the restorative aspect of the king's madness and exile (*Commentaria in Librum Danielis*, in *Opera Omnia*, 1893, 18.515; cf. Doob, 71–72). In a similar way Chaucer's Parson compares penitence with a tree, its roots being contrition, its leaves confession, and its fruit satisfaction, and he then refers to Nebuchadnezzar's dream of the great tree (*Parson's Tale*, 10.112–25). Chaucer's Monk also stresses Nebuchadnezzar's penance and acknowledgment of God's power (*Monk's Tale*, 7.2177–82), as does a Middle English lyric 'The Bird with Four Feathers' (C. Brown, *Religious Lyrics of the XIVth Century*, 1924, nos. 121, 145–64). In the Middle English *Purity* Daniel tells Belshazzar about Nebuchadnezzar's degradation and suffering, which ultimately led to his self-understanding in relation to God (1669–1704). In the Middle English romance *Robert of Sicily*, the proud king Robert is punished by being made a king's fool dressed as an ape. The English version of this romance is unique in having Robert remember Nebuchadnezzar's similar plight and follow his example of prayer and humility (eds. French and Hale, *Middle English Metrical Romances*, 1930, 325–76; cf. Lillian Hornstein in *PMLA* 79, 1964, 16). Anne Bradstreet's long historical poem *The Foure Monarchies* emphasizes the divine origin of Nebuchadnezzar's madness and his subsequent restoration to sanity and repentance (*Complete Works*, 1981, 66).

Medieval descriptions of madness, whether actual or literary, often reflect the symptoms of Nebuchadnezzar's condition (cf. Doob, 31–33), and Nebuchadnezzar remains the archetypal madman in later literature as well. A character in Mark Twain's *Huckleberry Finn* remarks: 'The nigger's crazy – crazy's Nebokoodnezzer' (chapter 41). In *Nature* Emerson bemoans the irrational separation of humanity from the natural world: 'We are, like Nebuchadnezzar, dethroned, bereft of reason, and eating grass like an ox' (*Collected Works*, 1971, 1.42). In an antislavery poem 'The Panorama', Whittier compares the madness of slavery to Nebuchadnezzar's madness (253–57).

References to Nebuchadnezzar's eating grass like an ox (Daniel 4:32–33) are frequent in literature. A clown in Shakespeare's *All's Well That Ends Well* says: 'I am no great Nebuchadnezzar, sir, I have not much skill in grass' (Riverside ed., 4.5.20–21), and the grotesque image of the great king grazing like a beast appealed to Donne ('The

Liar', 3–4), Byron (*Don Juan*, 5.6.472–75), Hazlitt (*Complete Works*, 1933, 17.270), and Ruskin (*Works*, 1905, 19.62). Melville characterizes Omoo's diet as 'the Nebuchadnezzar fare of the valley' (*Omoo*, 1968, 7), and Keats' sonnet 'Nebuchadnezzar's Dream' begins: 'Before he went to feed with owls and bats / Nebuchadnezzar had an ugly dream' (1–2).

In the biblical narrative the mad Nebuchadnezzar resembles a beast in his diet and in letting his hair and nails grow, but he is apparently not actually transformed into a beast. Commentators such as St Jerome and Peter Comestor emphasize that Nebuchadnezzar was not literally transformed (*Patrologia Latina*, 25.517; 198.1452), and the author of *Purity*, although describing the fallen Nebuchadnezzar in vivid bestial terms, reminds the reader that the king did not literally become a beast but only thought himself so in his delusion (1681–85). Sir Thomas Browne also states that Nebuchadnezzar, unlike Lot's wife (cf. Gen. 19:26), was not literally metamorphosed (*Works*, 1964, 1.48). In John Gower's romance-style retelling of the story, however, Nebuchadnezzar is actually transformed (*Confessio Amantis*, 1.2992–3039), and Gower emphasizes the pathos of the situation in his description of the king's restoration, for Nebuchadnezzar weeps as he becomes aware of his hairy coat,

> And thogh him lacke vois and speche,
> He gan up with his feet areche,
> And wailende in his bestly stevene
> He made his pleignte unto the heven.
> He kneleth in his wise and braieth (3023–27)

before his human form is restored. Spenser, too, seems to regard Nebuchadnezzar's transformation into a beast as actual (*Faerie Queene*, 1.5.47.5), as do Charlotte Brontë (*Jane Eyre*, chapter 37) and Edwin Arlington Robinson ('The Man against the Sky', 45–46).

In Saul Bellow's novel *Henderson the Rain King*, Nebuchadnezzar's transformation into a beast functions as a major theme in the story of Henderson's search for identity. Henderson is obsessed with Daniel's prophecy that Nebuchadnezzar will be driven from the realm of mankind and will dwell with the beasts of the field (chapter 16), and under the instruction of an African chieftain the troubled Henderson achieves a healing psychological transformation into a beast (chapter 18).

Lawrence T. Martin
*University of Akron*

## Nehemiah

Nehemiah was a post-exilic governor of Judah (c. 445BC) whose chief importance lies in his role in organizing the rebuilding of the walls of Jerusalem with the permission of Artaxerxes, king of Persia, to whom he was cupbearer. As narrator of the biblical book which bears his name, he records how he obtained the respect and cooperation of those who might have opposed his building project and instituted a number of social and religious reforms, including observance of the Feast of Booths, renewal of instruction in the Torah, and strictures against intermarriage. His assistant in all these activities was Ezra, a priest. Nehemiah's Babylonian name, according to talmudic sources, was Zerubbabel, and he is so identified regularly in Jewish commentary on the book (e.g., Sanhedrin 38a; Alphabet R. Aleiba 27–28; cf. Nehemiah 7:7). As Zerubbabel he is a figure of signal eminence, one of those said to be born circumcised and destined to be a 'messianic herald', at whose cry Michael and Gabriel will undertake a war of annihilation against the pagan world (cf. Kalir, in Lamentations; Pirqe Mashiah 75). He is chiefly identified in Christian commentary of the patristic period as one who 'cleanses' the Temple and reconsecrates the sacrifice (e.g., St Ambrose, *De officiis ministrorum*, 3.17.100–101).

As a builder of the walls of Jerusalem he is celebrated in post-Reformation Protestant exegesis as a type of the 'restorer of the Church' (e.g., Matthew Poole, *Annotations*). It is this tradition which informs the vision of American Puritan Jonathan Mitchell's *Nehemiah on the Wall* (1671); a century later Thomas Frink can still say that Nehemiah's Jerusalem 'does most graphically set forth in Figure this Wonderful Reformation of the World in these latter days' (*A Sermon Delivered at Stafford,* 1757). Thomas Tilston's *The Return from Captivity* (1793), a verse drama interspersed with songs and choruses, is based on Nehemiah, anticipating Eleanor Wood Whitman's *Nehemiah the Builder* (1926), a four-act American biblical drama with music (based on chapters 1–7; 12:27–47; 13:4–31). One of the best-known American adaptations of Nehemiah as a type of the spiritual builder is Cotton Mather's 'Nehemias Americanus', the appellation by which in *Magnalia Christi Americana* he salutes John Winthrop as one of the great builders of Christian civilization in the New World.

A.M. Klein's poem 'Nehemiah' considers the Persian king: he has been so swayed by his cupbearer Nehemiah's appeal that 'He dreams he sees dead streets and yawning jackals roam / Through the lone city' and, in a hint of his decree permitting Nehemiah to undertake the work, 'The king will drink a tear-drop in his wine.' For T.S. Eliot Nehemiah is a central figure in his choruses from *The Rock* (4–5), one who builds with 'The trowel in the hand, and the gun rather loose in the holster' (5). In Margaret Avison's 'The Earth That Falls Away', Roman soldiers in occupied Judea are restless on a watch:

> But in that night in the courtyard
> they hear the silence
> (the ancient voices:
> 'Hide not thy face from me')
> (the voice of Nehemiah:
> 'Let thine eyes now be open'). (*Winter Sun*, 131)

David L. Jeffrey
*University of Ottawa*

## Shadrach, Meshach, and Abednego

Shadrach, Meshach, and Abednego are the Babylonian names given to Hananiah, Mishael, and Azariah, the three companions of Daniel. They appear in Daniel 1, where they participate in Daniel's rejection of the king's food in favour of a simple diet of pulse and water, and they are the heroes in the story of the fiery furnace in chapter 3, in which Daniel himself does not appear. The story of the three young men in the fiery furnace belongs to the genre 'romance of the successful courtier' (Hartman and Di Lella, Anchor Bible 23, 55). The three youths' prestige at court is envied by their fellow courtiers, who turn the king against the heroes by taking advantage of their fidelity to the God of Israel. In the end, however, the youths are miraculously rescued from the furnace, and their faith is embraced by the king. The Septuagint version of the story, reflected also in the Latin Vulgate, contains several elements not found in the Hebrew text: (a) the song of Azariah (Septuagint 3:24–45), (b) a prose narrative which adds some details concerning happenings within the furnace (Septuagint 3:46–50), and (c) the song of the three young men, or 'three holy children' (Septuagint 3:51–90).

In the Old English *Daniel*, which deals with the episodes of Daniel 1–5, the section devoted to the story of the fiery furnace (168–451) is probably the most imaginative portion of the entire poem, emphasizing in particular the ironic reversal which has the Babylonian soldiers themselves perishing from the heat of the furnace (243–55, 265–68, 343–45). The poem includes compressed paraphrases of the songs of Azariah (279–332) and the song of the three young men (358–408). In the Exeter Book another Old English poem, *Azarias*, provides a fuller treatment of these two songs, with considerable expansion upon the nature imagery found in the biblical version.

The Rouen version of the Latin *Procession of Prophets* includes a dramatization of the fiery furnace story (Karl Young, *Drama of the Medieval Church*, 2.164, 168). This episode does not appear in any of the Middle English cycle plays, but there is a late 16th- or early 17th-century play attributed to Joshua Sylvester, *Nebuchadnezzars Fiere Furnace* (ed. Rösler, *Materials for the Study of Old English Drama*, ser. 2, 12). Christopher Fry's *A Sleep of Prisoners*, in which British prisoners of war relive the experiences of various Old Testament characters, concludes with the story of the three young men in the furnace (39–46).

The three young men are put forth as examples of courageous faith in 1 Maccabees 2:59, a theme used also in Sulpicius Severus' letter on the death of St Martin (*Patrologia Latina*, 20.179 = Corpus scriptorum ecclesiasticorum latinorum 1.143–44), in Aelfric's sermon 'On the Memory of the Saints' (Early English Text Society, old series 82, 1885, 71–77), in one of Anne Bradstreet's *Meditations* (no. 75, *Complete Works*, 1981, 208), and in one of Hazlitt's *Political Essays* (*Complete Works*, 1932, 7.241). Similarly, a sermon of John Donne refers to the three youths as examples of confidence in God (ed. Carrithers, *Donne at Sermons*, 246). The youths' deliverance from the furnace functions as an illustration of God's power to save the persecuted in the Middle English *St Juliana* (Early English Text Society, old series 51, 1872, 32) and in *The Life of St Katherine* (Early English Text Society, old series 80, 1884, 1426–38), while the *Ayenbite of Inwit* connects their escape with their rejection of the king's fancy food in Daniel 1:11–15, for such food is said to nourish lechery as oil does fire (Early English Text Society, old series 23, 1866, 205). The rescue of Quakers from Puritan persecution in Salem in 1658 is compared to the rescue of the three young men in Whittier's poem 'Cassandra Southwick' (3–4, 147–48). In Tennyson's play *Queen Mary*, ironic reference to the escape of the youths from the fiery furnace is addressed to Cranmer as he is about to be burned (4.3.59–61).

Wordsworth describes a boy uncontaminated by the world as 'Like one of those who walked with hair unsinged / Amid the fiery furnace' (*Prelude*, 7.369–70). A more jarring comparison to the rescue of the three youths is made in Melville's description of the processing of a captured whale in *Moby Dick*: after the whale is cut into pieces, he is 'condemned to the pots, and, like Shadrach, Meshach, and Abednego, his spermaceti, oil, and bone pass unscathed through the fire' (chapter 98). E.L. Doctorow's novel *The Book of Daniel* is introduced by a quotation from Daniel 3, and the protagonist, Daniel Lewin, reflects on the effect that the fiery furnace trial must have had on his biblical namesake, Daniel, whom he regards as the brother of the three young men in the furnace.

Nebuchadnezzar's setting up of the golden image to be adored (Daniel 3:1–6) represents the human tendency to make idols of material things and of wealth in Ben Jonson's *Bartholomew Fair* (3.6.49–53) and in Ruskin's *The Crown of Wild Olives* (*Works*, 1905, 18.457–58). In Robert Frost's *Masque of Mercy*, a rather startling application of this story occurs:

> We have all the belief that is good for us.
> Too much all-fired belief and we'd be back
> Down burning skeptics in the cellar furnace
> Like Shadrach, Meshach, and Abednego.
> (*Complete Poems*, 1964, 636)

A somewhat similar idea may lie behind a reference in Joyce's *Finnegans Wake* to 'the fierifornax being thrust on him motophosically'

– that is, thrust on him metaphysically (cf. Roland McHugh, *Annotations to Finnegans Wake*, 319).

In *Paradise Lost* Milton alludes to Nebuchadnezzar's command that the fire be heated 'seven times more than it was wont to be heated' (Daniel 3:19) in relation to God's creation of the fire of hell (2.170–72). Browning refers to this passage in the context of misused authority in *The Ring and the Book* (1961, 989–93), and Longfellow uses it in *Giles Corey of the Salem Farms* in a ranting speech of Cotton Mather against witchcraft (1.2, *Works*, 1886, 5.380). Hawthorne compares the heat of midsummer to Nebuchadnezzar's seven-times heated furnace (*American Notebooks*, 1932, 185), and Edwin Arlington Robinson makes a similar comparison in 'The Man against the Sky' (41–46). In Tennyson's *The Holy Grail*, Lancelot is prevented from seeing the grail by a heat 'as from a seven-times-heated furnace' (838–43). Shaw has Joan of Arc say that being 'shut up from the sight of sky, fields, and flowers' is 'worse than the furnace in the Bible that was heated seven times' (*St Joan*, *Collected Works*, 1930, 17.145).

The litany of musical instruments used to call the worshippers to Nebuchadnezzar's idol (Daniel 3:5) is used by Shakespeare in *Coriolanus*, 5.4, when the hero's mother, who has betrayed her son, is hailed by Rome as the city's patroness. The same passage is referred to in an attack on clergy who make music on the Sabbath in William Cowper's 'The Progress of Error' (128–33). Ruskin mentions it in relation to the morality of dancing (*Works*, 1907, 29.269), and Poe makes use of a very similar list of musical instruments in a call to prayer in 'A Tale of Jerusalem' (*Complete Works*, 1902, 2.219).

In the biblical narrative Nebuchadnezzar sees four men walking unhurt in the midst of the fiery furnace, and 'the form of the fourth is like the Son of God' (Daniel 3:25). St Jerome observes that most Christian commentators considered this fourth figure to be Christ, but he himself cannot see how 'an ungodly king could have merited a vision of the Son of God', and he therefore considers the fourth figure an angel, although the typological significance is Christ (*Patrologia Latina*, 25.511–12 = Corpus Christianorum 75A.807, 716–808). In the Old English *Daniel*, similarly, it is an angel that Nebuchadnezzar sees (273). This detail of the narrative is the basis for Nebuchadnezzar's appearance in the Latin *Ordo Prophetarum* as one of the Gentile prophets of Christ. Here he is characterized as a proud king who has learned humility at the sight of Christ (Young, 2.136, 142, 149, 165). William Blake makes use of the same incident in a complex allegorical framework (cf. John Beer, *Blake's Visionary Universe*, 36, 50). Christina Rossetti's 'Martyr's Song' offers the encouraging thought that in adversity, 'Be it furnace-fire voluminous, / One like God's Son will walk with us' (5–6). In Whittier's narrative poem 'Saint Gregory's Guest', which tells a legend of St Gregory the Great's kindness to a poor man who turns out to be Christ himself, the experience is compared to the vision of the fourth man in the fiery furnace (27–28). Whittier refers to this passage again in his poem 'Astrea at the Capital', which celebrates the abolition of slavery in the District of Columbia in 1862 (57–60). In the same vein, Newman's poem 'Temptation' addresses God: 'O Holy Lord, who with the Children Three / Didst walk the piercing flame' (1–2).

Lawrence T. Martin
*University of Akron*

## Sheba, Queen of

Sheba (Hebrew *Sheba'*; LXX *Saba*) is a name which appears in both Semitic and Hamitic genealogies. In Genesis 10:7 Sheba is a descendant of Ham, while another Sheba is listed in Genesis 10:28 as descended from Shem. But the Queen of Sheba (1 Kings 10:1–10, 13; 2 Chronicles 9:1–9, 12) is said to be a queen of the South (possibly modern Ethiopia and Yemen), who traveled to Jerusalem to visit King Solomon (cf. Matthew 12:42; Luke 11:31). She apparently came 'to test him with hard questions' and to see if the reports of his wisdom and the splendour of his palaces were justified. The chronicler reports that 'when the queen of Sheba had seen all of Solomon's wisdom, and the house that he had built... there was no more spirit in her' (1 Kings 10:4–5).

The first rabbinic account of a sexual liaison between Solomon and Sheba – the Alphabet of Ben Sira 21b – which suggests that Nebuchadnezzar was the offspring, is late. Some Islamic accounts follow Targum Job 1:15, in which Sheba is discovered by Solomon to have hairy feet and to be the night demon Lilith. Ethiopian accounts make Menelik I the child of Solomon and Sheba, and so trace their religious and national claim to succeed the Jews as God's chosen people to the liaison. Medieval Christian exegesis simply allegorizes the event: Solomon is Christ, the report of whose miracles prompts the Church to come and sit at his feet in pursuit of his wisdom and glory, which are recorded in the 'testimonies of Sacred Scripture' (*Glossa Ordinaria, Patrologia Latina,* 113.601–02). This interpretation tends to glorify representations of Sheba.

In Shakespeare's *Henry VIII,* Archbishop Cranmer is made to prophesy of the child Elizabeth that she will be

> a pattern to all princes living with her,
> And of all that shall succeed. Saba was never
> More covetous of wisdom and fair virtue
> Than this pure soul shall be. (5.5.22–25)

Milton makes a similar epic comparison in praising Queen Christine of Sweden as a 'queen of the north... worthy to appear in the court of the wise king of the Jews, or any king of equal wisdom' (*Second Defense*). Descending towards cliché, in Scott's *Kenilworth* Dame Amy is seen by Anthony to appear 'as proud and as gay as if she were the Queen of Sheba' (chapter 5). The sagging spirit of the Queen of Sheba emerges as a counter-motif in modern literature, with Hardy offering a pertinent example. When Angel Clare asks Tess why she appears dejected, Tess answers that she feels her life is a litany of lost opportunities. 'When I see what you know, what you have read, and seen, and thought, I feel what a nothing I am! I'm like the poor Queen of Sheba who lives in the Bible. There is no more spirit in me' (chapter 19). This last phrase has also become a tag (cf. Dorothy Sayers, *The Unpleasantness at the Bellona Club,* chapter 13; Rose Macaulay, *Told by an Idiot,* 2.15).

David L. Jeffrey
*University of Ottawa*

## Solomon

Solomon was the third king of Israel (c. 961–922BC) and the second son of David (2 Samuel 12:18, 24). His kingdom, excluding Philistia and Phoenicia, stretched from Kadesh in the north to Ezion-geber in the south (1 Kings 4:21). Largely free from external threat, Solomon built extensively in Jerusalem, his best-known structure being the Temple. He strategically established fortified cities throughout the empire and negotiated trade agreements with other nations. On the Gulf of Aqabah and from Phoenicia, he developed maritime trade (9:26–28; 10:11, 22–29). But his legendary, wealthy reign (v. 23) bled the nation's resources, requiring heavy taxation and forced corvées (4:7; 5:13–14; 9:21).

Unlike Chronicles, which omits a negative assessment, 1 Kings traces Solomon's decline largely to religious syncretism provoked by marriage to 'many foreign women' (11:1–3, RSV). For these he built cultic sites and permitted worship of alien deities (vv. 7–8). The nation's strong unity faded under this influence (cf. Sirach 47:13–21).

Solomon's celebrated wisdom reportedly 'excelled the wisdom' of 'the east country, and all the wisdom of Egypt' (4:20–34). Notably illustrated in the episode with the two harlots (3:16–28) and the visit of the Queen of Sheba (10:1–29), this wisdom expressed itself in riddles and proverbs, as well as in extraordinary judicial acumen. Solomon's sagacity was sufficiently renowned that he was frequently credited with later canonical, apocryphal, and pseudepigraphal literature (e.g., the biblical 'wisdom' books as well as Wisdom of Solomon, Psalms of Solomon, Odes of Solomon, and Testament of Solomon). In the New Testament, Jesus mentions both Solomon's splendour (Matthew 6:29; Luke 12:27) and his wisdom (Matthew 12:42; Luke 11:31).

Jewish tradition assigns Solomon extensive knowledge of many subjects (Wisdom of Solomon 7:17–22; Gittin 59a). He is said to have authored works on medicine, mineralogy, and magic. Legends of Solomon's liaison with the Queen of Sheba (Balkis), also known in Arabic and Ethiopian versions, tell how Solomon married Balkis and gained control of Sheba. Arabic lore makes Solomon a devout follower of Allah and prototype of Mohammed. With the winds and demons at his disposal (Koran, *Sura* 21:82), he visits the Valley of the Ants (*Sura* 27:16–17) and the Queen of Sheba (vv. 20–45). One legend, resembling the *Arabian Nights*, has the jinn weave an enormous carpet on which Solomon goes on a hajj to Mecca, where he prophesies the birth of Mohammed.

In both Judaism and Christianity, the association of Solomon with demonology and magic flourished during late antiquity. According to the Testament of Solomon, Solomon received a magic ring seal from the archangel Michael with which to subjugate the demons and set them to building (1.5–7); Josephus connects magical seal rings with Solomon in an account of exorcism (*Antiquities*, 8.42–49). Scores of Jewish and Christian amulets and talismans invoke his power over demons. One amulet declares, 'Seal of Solomon, drive away all evil from him who wears [this]' (E.R. Goodenough, *Jewish Symbols*, 1953–68, 2.238). This notion of Solomon's power gives rise to the legend of his conquest of Asmodeus, the prince of demons, and his acquisition of the stonecutting *shamir* (Gittin 68a–69b).

Patristic theology, on the other hand, focuses on Solomon's sagacity as a king and judge (cf. St Ambrose, *De fide*, book 1, prologue) and often portrays him as a type of Christ (cf. Ambrose, *De interpellatione Iob et David*, 4.4.15). Debate among the Fathers concerning whether Solomon repented his fall into luxury constitutes a tacit criticism of his wisdom, as does the medieval tale of Solomon's besting by Marcolphus the dullard and Morolf the dwarf.

While interest in Solomon as magician is strong in the Middle Ages – many books of magic, including the *Clavicula Salomonis*, are ascribed to him – he is, above all else, seen as a great moral teacher and leader. *The Ancrene Riwle* invokes him as an author of wise sayings (Camden Society, 1883, 64) who judges rightly (90). In Dante's *Paradiso*, the voice of St Thomas Aquinas introduces Solomon as the brightest of the twelve lights of philosophy (10.109–14), then argues for him as the model of kingly prudence (13.94–108). The fate of Solomon is the subject of speculation in *Piers Plowman*. In the 'C' text, Conscience uses the case of Solomon to argue that God's blessings can be withdrawn if the recipient proves unworthy (C.4.326–34) and concludes that Solomon is now in hell (see also B.12.266–74). The presence of Solomon the magician can be detected in Chaucer's *Squire's Tale* (*The Canterbury Tales*, 5.248–51). The successor of David appears elsewhere in *The Canterbury Tales* as 'he that so wel teche kan' (*Summoner's Tale*, 3.2085) and as 'the wise man' (*Parson's Tale*, 10.664). He is cited extensively as an authority and fount of trustworthy counsel in *The Tale of Melibee*. For Luther, Solomon is the 'Wise Man' (*Works*, 1955–57, 45.306), a type of Christ (14.327), and a magus, having 'secret knowledge of nature' (52.161).

Solomon appears principally as the great castigator of human folly and ignorance in Renaissance literature. As Rosalie L. Colie points out, satirists such as Brant and Erasmus unleash the wisdom of Ecclesiastes on all fools, themselves included (*Paradoxia Epidemica*, 1966, 6–23, 458). If Tottel's *Miscellany* of 1557 takes Solomon for a 'sober wit' (Arber ed., 1870, 168), Sir Thomas Browne is less restrained: his *Religio Medici* counsels its reader to follow Solomon's advice (Proverbs 6:6) and go to insects for genuine wisdom (1.16). In Butler's *Hudibras*, a lady contrasts contemporary fools with the ancient Solomon (3.195). More directly constructive, Bacon's *New Atlantis* envisions a programme of empirical sciences in the 'House of Solomon'. Bunyan works out a typology in *Solomon's Temple Spiritualized*. For the major neoclassical satirists from Dryden to Johnson, Horace or Juvenal rather than Solomon provides the exemplary analogue of the combatant against vanity, unreason, and the realm of dunces.

The Solomon of the 19th century comes in many guises. Walter Scott's *Anne of Geierstein* recalls the man of wit so unlike the fool (chapter 30); and Dickens refers to 'sentiment... Solomonic' in *Little Dorrit* (1.13) and in *Dombey and Son* has his Captain Cuttle make a warmhearted philanthropist of Solomon, quick to share a good bottle with the less fortunate (chapter 15). By contrast, the last paragraph of Thackeray's *Vanity Fair* calls up the sombre wisdom of Solomon's Ecclesiastes: 'Ah! *Vanitas Vanitatum!*' In Browning's 'Mr Sludge, "The Medium"', the charlatan caught in a deception turns the moral indignation of his superficial Boston patron back on the accuser, pronouncing as the most hateful form of foolery that of 'the social sage, Solomon of saloons / And philosophic diner-out' (773–74). A story of 'Wisdom in the abstract facing Folly in the concrete' (chapter 13), Hardy's *Far from the Madding Crowd* alludes to Solomon as misogynist (chapter 22) and womanizer (chapter 7). In *King Solomon's Mines*, a popular romance of fabulous hidden wealth and exotic adventure, H. Rider Haggard exploits another memory of that monarch.

Melville centres his entire work after *Typee* and *Omoo* on Solomon's view of earthly wisdom as folly. 'I read Solomon more &

more, and every time see deeper & deeper and unspeakable meanings in him', he writes to Hawthorne (Leyda, *The Melville Log*, 1951, 1.413). In *Moby Dick*, the sceptical Ishmael invokes the 'unchristian Solomon's wisdom' in confirmation of the nullity he perceives at the centre of the entire creation: 'the truest of all books is Solomon's, and Ecclesiastes is the fine hammered steel of woe. "All is vanity." ALL' (chapter 96). The blank, perfectly balanced stone signed 'Solomon the Wise', which encapsulates Melville's theme in *Pierre, or The Ambiguities*, is a text devoid of all light: the reflexive logic of the sceptic's foolish wisdom is self-cancelling. Such annihilating doubt is alien to Solomon Swap, Lot Sap Sago, and Jonathan Ploughboy, the shrewd, homely Yankee characters of the early 19th-century popular American stage who were derived from Solomon Gundy, the French Cockney of George Colman the Younger's *Who Wants a Guinea?* The stories of 'ole King Sollermun' in Twain's *Huckleberry Finn* serve to poke fun at more than just the languor and unprofitableness of royalty. The 'learned' Huck recalls that Solomon 'had about a million wives', and the wise Jim, who understandably reckons Solomon a fool for having a 'harem' of that size, foolishly misconstrues that king's most celebrated act of judicial wisdom (chapter 14).

In Conrad's *Typhoon*, a tale of wise ignorance or ignorant wisdom, the avuncular and enlightened chief engineer, Mr Solomon Rout, 'Old Sol', who rarely sees the light of day, writes entertaining letters filled with sagacious observations comically mistaken for his biblical namesake's. By tale's end, he finds that his obtuse captain, MacWhirr, who writes uninspired letters, is a rather wise and clever man. More recently, the Solomon of Langston Hughes' poem 'Brass Spittoons' delights in wine cups, like the reveller of James Ball Naylor's *Ancient Authors*:

> King David and King Solomon
>   Led merry, merry lives,
> With many, many lady friends
>   And many, many wives.

Camille R. La Bossière
*University of Ottawa*
Jerry A. Gladson
*Psychological Studies Institute, Atlanta, Georgia*

## Witch of Endor

The witch of Endor is a figure in the history of King Saul who received this designation in the chapter heading of early printings of the KJV; in the KJV text itself (1 Samuel 28) she is referred to as 'a woman [at Endor] that hath a familiar spirit'. On the eve of his final battle against the Philistines at Mt Gilboa, Saul was anxious and fearful. Since the Lord had refused to resolve his doubts by dreams, by lot, or by prophets, and in spite of his earlier banishment of mediums and wizards, he came in disguise to consult the woman of Endor and asked her to call up Samuel. Afraid of being denounced by Saul, she at first refused, but after being reassured, she agreed. Samuel's ghost offered Saul no more comfort than the living Samuel had done; he repeated his earlier declaration (15:27–28) that the Lord had stripped the kingdom from Saul and predicted that Saul and his sons would die in battle the next day. At these words Saul collapsed.

1 Chronicles 10:13 stresses Saul's sinfulness in consulting a medium; in 1 Samuel the emphasis is rather on the horrifying effect of Samuel's message. With its nocturnal setting, its elements of disguise and recognition, 'gods ascending out of the earth', Samuel in his mantle, and Saul's abrupt collapse, the episode forms a vivid and arresting narrative. Lord Byron called it 'the finest and most finished witch-scene that ever was written or conceived... It beats all the ghost scenes I ever read' (quoted in Ashton, 174).

From a theological point of view the text has been a focus of considerable controversy. Early Christian exegetes were, like their Jewish counterparts, much concerned with the nature of the apparition. Was it really Samuel's spirit which appeared? If so, how could it have been raised by a witch? If it was a devil in disguise, how could it have delivered a true prophecy? (St Augustine, *De octo Dulcitii quaestionibus*, *Patrologia Latina*, 40.162–65; Fathers of the Church 16.452–58; Tertullian, *De anima*, chapter 57). Smelik provides a thorough survey of these arguments, as well as of their rabbinic counterparts, up to AD800, when they are reflected in Aelfric's treatment of the Witch of Endor passage in *De Auguriis*, and they continue to appear in Simon Patrick's *Commentary upon the Historical Books of the Old Testament* (4th ed., 1732), in Coleridge's *Notebooks* (ed. Kathleen Coburn, vol. 3, no. 3753), and in 19th-century commentaries. Literary echoes of the same questions occur in Chaucer's *Friar's Tale*, 1506–12, and in Abraham Cowley's 'Reason: The Use of It in Divine Matters' (stanza 3). The episode continued to have an important role in 17th-century controversies about the reality of witchcraft (see Stock). Thomas Henry Huxley saw it as a kind of theological fossil, revealing a primitive stage of Hebrew religion ('The Evolution of Theology', 1886; *Science and Hebrew Tradition*, vol. 4 of *Collected Essays*, 1900, 290–307).

Byron's 'Saul', in *Hebrew Melodies*, retells the story, and it is alluded to briefly in *Manfred* (2.2.180–82). Twice Byron invokes the ghost of Samuel with the wish that modern monarchs could be as terrified as Saul was (*Don Juan*, 'Dedication', st. 11, and *The Age of Bronze*, 380–82). An illustration of the witch and the ghost obsessed the young Charles Lamb ('Witches, and Other Night-Fears', *Essays of Elia*). Browning's 'Mr Sludge, "the Medium"', cites the story in defence of his own trade (843–47). Kipling's powerful 'En-Dor, 1914–19– ?' depicts hordes of war widows and orphans seeking the perilous consolation of communion with their dead. Like Byron, Hardy alludes repeatedly to the witch. Perhaps most notably, in chapter 26 of *The Mayor of Casterbridge* a weather prophet plays her role as part of the parallel with Saul and David which permeates the novel (see Moynahan, 126–27). In Robert Frost's *Masque of Reason*, Job's wife claims the witch as a friend.

Saul's visit to the woman of Endor forms the climax of many of the plays devoted to him. In the prologue to Arthur Russel Thorndike's *Saul: A Historical Tragedy in Five Acts* (1906), she is shown writing mysterious words in the dust (an allusion to Jesus' act in John 8:6–8). She has an expanded role as a prophet of truth in opposition to the conniving Samuel in Laurence Housman's play *Samuel the Kingmaker* (1944), but in Howard Nemerov's powerful one-act play *Endor* she is central, the unwilling agent of a divine predestination she can no more control than Samuel can when she calls up to say as much. She then echoes his words: 'I do nothing. And yet there is nothing which is not done.'

William Kinsley
*Université de Montréal*

# STORIES FROM THE
# OLD TESTAMENT

## Volume II

### Part One: David and Saul

### Part Two: David the King

## Part Three: The Golden Age of Solomon

## Part Five: The Kings of Judah

## *Part Six: The Return from Exile*

## Part Seven: The Story of Jonah

## Part Eight: The Story of Daniel

## Part Nine: The Story of Esther

# David and Saul

## GOD CHOOSES A NEW KING
### 1 Samuel 16:1–13

The Lord said to Samuel, 'How long will you grieve because I have rejected Saul as king of Israel? Fill your horn with oil and take it with you; I am sending you to Jesse of Bethlehem; for I have chosen myself a king from among his sons.' Samuel answered, 'How can I go? If Saul hears of it, he will kill me.' 'Take a heifer with you,' said the Lord; 'say you have come to offer a sacrifice to the Lord, and invite Jesse to the sacrifice; then I shall show you what you must do. You are to anoint for me the man whom I indicate to you.' Samuel did as the Lord had told him, and went to Bethlehem, where the elders came in haste to meet him, saying, 'Why have you come? Is all well?' 'All is well,' said Samuel; 'I have come to sacrifice to the Lord. Purify yourselves and come with me to the sacrifice.' He himself purified Jesse and his sons and invited them to the sacrifice.

When they came, and Samuel saw Eliab, he thought, 'Surely here, before the Lord, is his anointed king.' But the Lord said to him, 'Pay no attention to his outward appearance and stature, for I have rejected him. The Lord does not see as a mortal sees; mortals see only appearances but the Lord sees into the heart.' Then Jesse called Abinadab and had him pass before Samuel, but he said, 'No, the Lord has not chosen this one.' Next he presented Shammah, of whom Samuel said, 'Nor has the Lord chosen him.' Seven of his sons were presented to Samuel by Jesse, but he said, 'The Lord has not chosen any of these.'

Samuel asked, 'Are these all the sons you have?' 'There is still the youngest,' replied Jesse, 'but he is looking after the sheep.' Samuel said to Jesse, 'Send and fetch him; we will not sit down until he comes.' So he sent and fetched him. He was handsome, with ruddy cheeks and bright eyes. The Lord said, 'Rise and anoint him: this is the man.' Samuel took the horn of oil and anointed him in the presence of his brothers, and the spirit of the Lord came upon David and was with him from that day onwards. Then Samuel set out on his way to Ramah.

## DAVID ENTERS SAUL'S SERVICE
### 1 Samuel 16:14–23

The spirit of the Lord had forsaken Saul, and at times an evil spirit from the Lord would seize him suddenly. His servants said to him, 'You see how an evil spirit from God seizes you; sir, why do you not command your servants here to go and find someone who can play on the lyre? Then, when an evil spirit from God comes on you, he can play and you will recover.' Saul said to his servants, 'Find me someone who can play well and bring him to me.' One of his attendants said, 'I have seen a son of Jesse of Bethlehem who can play; he is a brave man and a good fighter, wise in speech and handsome, and the Lord is with him.'

Saul therefore dispatched messengers to ask Jesse to send him his son David, who was with the sheep. Jesse took a batch of bread, a skin of wine, and a kid, and sent them to Saul by his son David. David came to Saul and entered his service; Saul loved him dearly, and David became his armour-bearer. Saul sent word to Jesse: 'Allow David to stay in my service, for I am pleased with him.' And whenever an evil spirit from God came upon Saul, David would take his lyre and play it, so that relief would come to Saul; he would recover and the evil spirit would leave him alone.

## DAVID AND GOLIATH
### 1 Samuel 17

The Philistines mustered their forces for war; they massed at Socoh in Judah and encamped between Socoh and Azekah at Ephes-dammim. Saul and the Israelites also mustered, and they encamped in the valley

114

of Elah. They drew up their lines of battle facing the Philistines, the Philistines occupying a position on one hill and the Israelites on another, with a valley between them.

A champion came out from the Philistine camp, a man named Goliath, from Gath; he was over nine feet in height. He had a bronze helmet on his head, and he wore plate armour of bronze, weighing five thousand shekels. On his legs were bronze greaves, and one of his weapons was a bronze dagger. The shaft of his spear was like a weaver's beam, and its head, which was of iron, weighed six hundred shekels. His shield-bearer marched ahead of him.

The champion stood and shouted to the ranks of Israel, 'Why do you come out to do battle? I am the Philistine champion and you are Saul's men. Choose your man to meet me. If he defeats and kills me in fair fight, we shall become your slaves; but if I vanquish and kill him, you will be our slaves and serve us. Here and now I challenge the ranks of Israel. Get me a man, and we will fight it out.' When Saul and the Israelites heard what the Philistine said, they were all shaken and deeply afraid.

David was the son of an Ephrathite called Jesse, who had eight sons, and who by Saul's time had become old, well advanced in years. His three eldest sons had followed Saul to the war; the eldest was called Eliab, the next Abinadab, and the third Shammah; David was the youngest. When the three eldest followed Saul, David used to go from attending Saul to minding his father's flocks at Bethlehem.

Morning and evening for forty days the Philistine came forward and took up his stance. Then one day Jesse said to his son David, 'Take your brothers an ephah of this roasted grain and these ten loaves of bread, and go with them as quickly as you can to the camp. These ten cream-cheeses are for you to take to their commanding officer. See if your brothers are well and bring back some token from them.' Saul and the brothers and all the Israelites were in the valley of Elah, fighting the Philistines.

Early next morning David, having left someone in charge of the sheep, set out on his errand and went as Jesse had told him. He reached the lines just as the army was going out to take up position and was raising the war cry. The Israelites and the Philistines drew up their ranks opposite each other. David left his things in the charge of the quartermaster, ran to the line, and went up to his brothers to greet them. While he was talking with them the Philistine champion, Goliath from Gath, came out from the Philistine ranks and issued his challenge in the same words as before; and David heard him. When the Israelites saw the man they fell back before him in fear.

'Look at this man who comes out day after day to defy Israel,' they said. 'The king is to give a rich reward to the man who kills him; he will also give him his daughter in marriage and will exempt his family from service due in Israel.' David asked the men near him, 'What is to be done for the man who kills this Philistine and wipes out this disgrace? And who is he, an uncircumcised Philistine, to defy the armies of the living God?' The soldiers, repeating what had been said, told him what was to be done for the man who killed him.

David's elder brother Eliab overheard him talking with the men and angrily demanded, 'What are you doing here? And whom have you left to look after those few sheep in the wilderness? I know you, you impudent young rascal; you have only come to see the fighting.' David answered, 'Now what have I done? I only asked a question.' He turned away from him to someone else and repeated his question, but everybody gave him the same answer.

David's words were overheard and reported to Saul, who sent for him. David said to him, 'Let no one lose heart! I shall go and fight this Philistine.' Saul answered, 'You are not able to fight this Philistine; you are only a lad, and he has been a fighting man all his life.' David said to Saul, 'Sir, I am my father's shepherd; whenever a lion or bear comes and carries off a sheep from the flock, I go out after it and attack it and rescue the victim from its jaws. Then if it turns on me, I seize it by the beard and batter it to death. I have killed lions and bears, and this uncircumcised Philistine will fare no better than they; he has defied the ranks of the living God. The Lord who saved me from the lion and the bear will save me from this Philistine.' 'Go then,' said Saul; 'and the Lord be with you.'

He put his own tunic on David, placed a bronze helmet on his head, and gave him a coat of mail to wear; he then fastened his sword on David over his tunic. But David held back, because he had not tried them, and said to Saul, 'I cannot go with these, because I am not used to them.' David took them off, then picked up his stick, chose five smooth stones from the wadi, and put them in a shepherd's bag which served as his pouch, and, sling in hand, went to meet the Philistine.

The Philistine, preceded by his shield-bearer, came on towards David. He looked David up and down and had nothing but disdain for this lad with his ruddy cheeks and bright eyes. He said to David, 'Am I a dog that you come out against me with sticks?' He cursed him in the name of his god, and said, 'Come, I shall give your flesh to the birds and the beasts.' David answered, 'You have come against me with sword and spear and dagger, but I come against you in the name of the Lord of Hosts, the God of the ranks of Israel which you have defied. The Lord will put you into my power this day; I shall strike you down and cut your head off and leave your carcass and the carcasses of the Philistines to the birds and the wild beasts; the whole world will know that there is a God in Israel. All those who are gathered here will see that the Lord saves without sword or spear; the battle is the Lord's, and he will put you all into our power.'

When the Philistine began moving closer to attack, David ran quickly to engage him. Reaching into his bag, he took out a stone, which he slung and struck the Philistine on the forehead. The stone sank into his head, and he fell prone on the ground. So with sling and stone David proved the victor; though he had no sword, he struck down the Philistine and gave him a mortal wound. He ran up to the Philistine and stood over him; then, grasping his sword, he drew it out of the scabbard, dispatched him, and cut off his head.

When the Philistines saw the fate of their champion, they turned and fled. The men of Israel and Judah at once raised the war cry and closely pursued them all the way to Gath and up to the gates of Ekron. The road that runs to Shaaraim, Gath, and Ekron was strewn with their dead. On their return from the pursuit of the Philistines, the Israelites plundered their camp. David took Goliath's head and carried it to Jerusalem, but he put Goliath's weapons in his own tent.

As Saul watched David go out to meet the Philistine, he said to Abner his commander-in-chief, 'That youth there, Abner, whose son is he?' 'By your life, your majesty,' replied Abner, 'I do not know.' The king said, 'Go and find out whose son the stripling is.' When David came back after killing the Philistine, Abner took him and presented him to Saul with the Philistine's head still in his hand. Saul asked him, 'Whose son are you, young man?' and David answered, 'I am the son of your servant Jesse of Bethlehem.'

## JONATHAN'S LOVE AND SAUL'S JEALOUSY
### 1 Samuel 18:1–27, 19:10 – 21:15

That same day, when Saul had finished talking with David, he kept him and would not let him return any more to his father's house, for he saw that Jonathan had given his heart to David and had grown to love him as himself. Jonathan and David made a solemn compact because each loved the other as dearly as himself. Jonathan stripped off the cloak and tunic he was wearing, and gave them to David, together with his sword, his bow, and his belt.

David succeeded so well in every venture on which Saul sent him that he was given command of the fighting forces, and his promotion pleased all ranks, even the officials round Saul.

At the homecoming of the army and the return of David from slaying the Philistine, the women from all the cities and towns of Israel came out singing and dancing to meet King Saul, rejoicing with tambourines and three-stringed instruments. The women as they made merry sang to one another:

'Saul struck down thousands,
but David tens of thousands.'

Saul was furious, and the words rankled. He said, 'They have ascribed to David tens of thousands and to me only thousands. What more can they do but make him king?' From that time forward Saul kept a jealous eye on David.

Next day an evil spirit from God seized on Saul. He fell into a frenzy in the house, and David played the lyre to him as he had done before. Saul had a spear in his hand, and he hurled it at David, meaning to pin him to the wall; but twice David dodged aside. After this Saul was afraid of David, because he saw that the Lord had forsaken him and was with David. He therefore removed David from his household and appointed him to the command of a thousand men. David led his men into action, and succeeded in everything that he undertook, because the Lord was with him. When Saul saw how successful he was, he was more afraid of him than ever. But all Israel and Judah loved David because he took the field at their head.

Saul said to David, 'Here is my elder daughter Merab; I shall give her to you in marriage, but in return you must serve me valiantly and fight the Lord's battles.' For Saul meant David to meet his end not at his hands but at the hands of the Philistines. David answered Saul, 'Who am I and what are my father's people, my kinsfolk, in Israel, that I should become the king's son-in-law?' However, when the time came for Saul's daughter Merab to be married to David, she had already been given to Adriel of Meholah.

But Michal, Saul's other daughter, fell in love with David, and when Saul was told of this, he saw that it suited his plans. He said to himself, 'I will give her to him; let her be the bait that lures him to his death at the hands of the Philistines.' So Saul proposed a second time to make David his son-in-law, and ordered his courtiers to say to David privately, 'The king is well disposed to you and you are dear to us all; now is the time for you to marry into the king's family.' When they spoke in this way to David, he said to them, 'Do you think that marrying the king's daughter is a matter of so little consequence that a poor man of no account, like myself, can do it?'

The courtiers reported what David had said, and Saul replied, 'Tell David this: all the king wants as the bride-price is the foreskins of a hundred Philistines, by way of vengeance on his enemies.' Saul was counting on David's death at the hands of the Philistines. The courtiers told David what Saul had said, and marriage with the king's daughter on these terms pleased him well. Before the appointed time, David went out with his men and slew two hundred Philistines; he brought their foreskins and counted them out to the king in order to be accepted as his son-in-law. Saul then married his daughter Michal to David...

That night Saul sent servants to keep watch on David's house, intending to kill him in the morning. But David's wife Michal warned him to get away that night, 'or tomorrow', she said, 'you will be a dead man'. She let David down through a window and he slipped

119

away and escaped. Michal then took their household god and put it on the bed; at its head she laid a goat's-hair rug and covered it all with a cloak. When the men arrived to arrest David she told them he was ill. Saul, however, sent them back to see David for themselves. 'Bring him to me, bed and all,' he ordered, 'so that I may kill him.' When they came, there was the household god on the bed and the goat's-hair rug at its head. Saul said to Michal, 'Why have you played this trick on me and let my enemy get away?' Michal answered, 'He said to me, "Help me to escape or I shall kill you."'

Meanwhile David made good his escape, and coming to Samuel at Ramah, he described how Saul had treated him. He and Samuel went to Naioth and stayed there. When Saul was told that David was at Naioth, he sent a party of men to seize him. But at the sight of the company of prophets in a frenzy, with Samuel standing at their head, the spirit of God came upon them and they fell into prophetic frenzy. When this was reported to Saul he sent another party; these also fell into a frenzy, and when he sent men a third time, they did the same. Saul himself then set out for Ramah and came to the great cistern in Secu. He asked where Samuel and David were and was told that they were at Naioth in Ramah. On his way there the spirit of God came upon him too and he went on, in a prophetic frenzy as he went, till he came to Naioth in Ramah. There he too stripped off his clothes and like the rest fell into a frenzy before Samuel and lay down naked all that day and throughout that night. That is the reason for the saying, 'Is Saul also among the prophets?'

David made his escape from Naioth in Ramah and came to Jonathan. 'What have I done?' he asked. 'What is my offence? What wrong does your father think I have done, that he seeks my life?' Jonathan answered, 'God forbid! There is no thought of putting you to death. I am sure my father will not do anything whatever without telling me. Why should my father hide such a thing from me? I cannot believe it!' David said, 'I am ready to swear to it: your father has said to himself, "Jonathan must not know this or he will resent it," because he knows that you have a high regard for me. As the Lord lives, your life upon it, I am only a step away from death.' Jonathan said to David, 'What do you want me to do for you?' David answered, 'It is new moon tomorrow, and I am to dine with the king. But let me go and lie hidden in the fields until the third evening, and if your father misses me, say, "David asked me for leave to hurry off on a visit to his home in Bethlehem, for it is the annual sacrifice there for the whole family." If he says, "Good", it will be well for me; but if he flies into a rage, you will know that he is set on doing me harm. My lord, keep faith with me; for you and I have entered into a solemn compact before the Lord. Kill me yourself if I am guilty, but do not let me fall into your father's hands.' 'God forbid!' cried Jonathan. 'If I find my father set on doing you harm, I shall tell you.' David answered Jonathan, 'How will you let me know if he answers harshly?' Jonathan said, 'Let us go into the fields,' and so they went there together.

Jonathan said, 'I promise you, David, in the sight of the Lord the God of Israel, this time tomorrow I shall sound my father for the third time and, if he is well disposed to you, I shall send and let you know. If my father means mischief, may the Lord do the same to me and more, if I do not let you know and get you safely away. The Lord be with you as he has been with my father! I know that as long as I live you will show me faithful friendship, as the Lord requires; and if I should die, you will continue loyal to my family for ever. When the Lord rids the earth of all David's enemies, may the Lord call him to account if he and his house are no longer my friends.' Jonathan pledged himself afresh to David because of his love for him, for he loved him as himself.

Jonathan said, 'Tomorrow is the new moon, and you will be missed when your place is empty. So the day after tomorrow go down at nightfall to the place where you hid on the day when the affair started; stay by the mound there. I shall shoot three arrows towards it as though aiming at a target. Then I shall send my boy to find the arrows. If I say to him, "Look, the arrows are on this side of you; pick them up," then you can come out of hiding. You will be quite safe, I swear it, for there will be nothing amiss. But if I say to him, "Look, the arrows are on the other side of you, farther on," then the Lord has said that you must go; the Lord stands witness between us for ever to the pledges we have exchanged.'

David hid in the fields, and when the new moon came the king sat down to eat at mealtime. Saul took his customary seat by the wall, and Abner sat beside him; Jonathan too was present, but David's place was empty. That day Saul said nothing, for he thought that David was absent by some chance, perhaps because he was ritually unclean. But on the second day, the day after the new moon, David's place was still empty, and Saul said to his son Jonathan, 'Why has the son of Jesse not come to the feast, either yesterday or today?' Jonathan answered, 'David asked permission to go to Bethlehem. He asked my leave and said, "Our family is holding a sacrifice in the town and my brother himself has told me to be there. Now, if you have any regard for me, let me slip away to see my brothers." That is why he has not come to the king's table.' Saul's anger blazed up against Jonathan and he said, 'You son of a crooked and rebellious mother! I know perfectly well you have made a friend of the son of Jesse only to bring shame on yourself and dishonour on your mother. But as long as Jesse's son remains alive on the earth, neither you nor your kingdom will be established. Send at once and fetch him; he deserves to die.' Jonathan answered his father, 'Deserves to die? Why? What has he done?' At that, Saul picked up his spear and threatened to kill him; and Jonathan knew that his father was bent on David's death. He left the table in a rage and ate nothing on the second day of the festival; for he was indignant on David's behalf and because his father had humiliated him.

Next morning Jonathan, accompanied by a young boy, went out into the fields to keep the appointment with David. He said to the boy, 'Run ahead and find the arrows I shoot.' As the boy ran on, he shot the arrows over his head. When the boy reached the place where the arrows had fallen, Jonathan called out after him, 'Look, the arrows are beyond you. Hurry! Go quickly! Do not delay.' The boy gathered up the arrows and brought them to his master; but only Jonathan and David knew what this meant; the boy knew nothing. Jonathan handed his weapons to the boy and told him to take them back to the town.

When the boy had gone, David got up from behind the mound and bowed humbly three times. Then they kissed one another and shed tears together, until David's grief was even greater than Jonathan's. Jonathan said to David, 'Go in safety; we have pledged each other in the name of the Lord who is witness for ever between you and me and between your descendants and mine.'

David went off at once, while Jonathan returned to the town. David made his way to Nob to the priest Ahimelech, who hurried out to meet him and asked, 'Why are you alone and unattended?' David answered Ahimelech, 'I am under orders from the king: I was to let no one know about the mission on which he was sending me or what these orders were. When I took leave of my men I told them to meet me in such and such a place. Now, what have you got by you? Let me have five loaves, or as many as you can find.' The priest answered David, 'I have no ordinary bread available. There is only the sacred bread; but have the young men kept themselves from women?' David answered the priest, 'Women have been denied us as hitherto when I have been on campaign, even an ordinary campaign, and the young men's bodies have remained holy; and how much more will they be holy today!' So, as there was no other bread there, the priest gave him the sacred bread, the Bread of the Presence, which had just been taken from the presence of the Lord to be replaced by freshly baked bread on the day that the old was removed. One of Saul's servants happened to be there that day, detained before the Lord; his name was Doeg the Edomite, and he was the chief of Saul's herdsmen. David said to Ahimelech, 'Have you a spear or sword here at hand? I have no sword or other weapon with me, because the king's business was urgent.' The priest answered, 'There is the sword of Goliath the Philistine whom you slew in the valley of Elah; it is wrapped up in a cloak behind the ephod. If you want to take that, take it; there is no other weapon here.' David said, 'There is no sword like it; give it to me.'

That day David went on his way, fleeing from Saul, and came to King Achish of Gath. The servants of Achish said to him, 'Surely this is David, the king of his country, the man of whom they sang as they danced:

"Saul struck down thousands,
but David tens of thousands."'

These comments were not lost on David, and he became very much afraid of King Achish of Gath. So he altered his behaviour in public and acted like a madman in front of them all, scrabbling on the double doors of the city gate and dribbling down his beard. Achish said to his servants, 'The man is insane! Why bring him to me? Am I short of madmen that you bring this one to plague me? Must I have this fellow in my house?'

## DAVID THE OUTLAW
1 Samuel 22:1 – 23:29

David stole away from there and went to the cave of Adullam, and, when his brothers and all the members of his family heard where he was, they went down and joined him there. Everyone in any kind of distress or in debt or with a grievance gathered round him, about four hundred in number, and he became their chief. From there David went to Mizpeh in Moab and said to the king of Moab, 'Let my father and mother come and take shelter with you until I know what God will do for me.' He left them at the court of the king of Moab, and they stayed there as long as David remained in his stronghold.

The prophet Gad said to David, 'You must not stay in your stronghold; go at once into Judah.' David went as far as the forest of Hareth. News that the whereabouts of David and his men was known reached Saul while he was in Gibeah, sitting under the tamarisk tree on the hilltop with his spear in his hand and all his retainers standing about him. He said to them, 'Listen to me, you Benjamites: do you expect the son of Jesse to give you all fields and vineyards, or make you all officers over units of a thousand and a hundred? Is that why you have all conspired against me? Not one of you told me when my son made a compact with the son of Jesse; none of you spared a thought for me or told me that my son had set against me my own servant, who is lying in wait for me now.'

Doeg the Edomite, who was standing with Saul's servants, spoke up: 'I saw the son of Jesse coming to Nob, to Ahimelech son of Ahitub. Ahimelech consulted the Lord on his behalf, then gave him food and handed over to him the sword of Goliath the Philistine.' The king sent for Ahimelech the priest and his whole family, who were priests at Nob, and they all came to him. Saul said, 'Now listen, you son of Ahitub,' and the man answered, 'Yes, my lord?' Saul said to him, 'Why have you and the son of Jesse plotted against me? You gave him food and a sword, and consulted God on his behalf; and now he has risen against me and is at this moment lying in wait for me.' 'And who among all your servants', answered Ahimelech, 'is like David, a man to be trusted, the king's son-in-law, appointed to your staff and holding an honourable place in your household? Have I on this occasion done something profane in consulting God on his behalf? God forbid! I trust that my lord the king will not accuse me or my family; for I know nothing whatever about it.' But the king said, 'Ahimelech, you shall die, you and all your family.' He then said to the bodyguard attending him, 'Turn on the priests of the Lord and kill them; for they are in league with David, and, though they knew that he was a fugitive, they did not inform me.' The king's men, however, were unwilling to raise a hand against the priests of the Lord. The king therefore said to Doeg the Edomite, 'You, Doeg, go and fall on the priests'; so Doeg went and fell upon the priests, killing that day with his own hand eighty-five men who wore the linen ephod. He put to the sword every living thing in Nob, the town of the priests: men and women, children and babes in arms, oxen, donkeys, and sheep.

One of Ahimelech's sons named Abiathar made his escape and joined David. He told David how Saul had killed the priests of the Lord, and David said to him, 'When Doeg the Edomite was there that day, I knew that he would certainly tell Saul. I have brought this on all the members of your father's house. Stay here with me, have no fear; he who seeks your life seeks mine, and you will be safe with me.'

The Philistines had launched an assault on Keilah and were plundering the threshing-floors. When this was reported to David, he consulted the Lord and asked whether he should go and attack these Philistines. The Lord answered, 'Go, attack them, and relieve Keilah.' But David's men said to him, 'Here in Judah we are afraid. How much worse if we challenge the Philistine forces at Keilah!' David consulted the Lord once again and got the answer, 'Go down at once to Keilah; I shall give the Philistines into your hands.' David and his men marched to Keilah, fought the Philistines, and carried off their livestock; they inflicted a heavy defeat on them and relieved the inhabitants of Keilah.

When Abiathar son of Ahimelech fled and joined David at Keilah, he brought an ephod with him. It was reported to Saul that

David had entered Keilah, and he said, 'God has put him into my hands; for he has walked into a trap by entering a walled town with its barred gates.' He called out all the army to march on Keilah and besiege David and his men.

When David learnt how Saul planned his overthrow, he told Abiathar the priest to bring the ephod, and then he prayed, 'Lord God of Israel, I your servant have heard that Saul intends to come to Keilah and destroy the town because of me. Will the townspeople of Keilah surrender me to him? Will Saul come down as I have heard? Lord God of Israel, I pray you, tell your servant.' The Lord answered, 'He will come.' David asked, 'Will the citizens of Keilah surrender me and my men to Saul?' and the Lord answered, 'They will.' At once David left Keilah with his men, who numbered about six hundred, and moved about from place to place. When it was reported to Saul that David had escaped from Keilah, he called off the operation.

David was living in the fastnesses of the wilderness of Ziph, in the hill-country, and though Saul went daily in search of him, God did not put him into his power. David was at Horesh in the wilderness of Ziph, when he learnt that Saul had come out to seek his life. Saul's son Jonathan came to David at Horesh and gave him fresh courage in God's name: 'Do not be afraid,' he said; 'my father's hand will not touch you. You will become king of Israel and I shall rank after you. This my father knows.' After the two of them had made a solemn compact before the Lord, David remained in Horesh and Jonathan went home.

The Ziphites brought to Saul at Gibeah the news that David was in hiding among them in the fastnesses of Horesh on the hill of Hachilah, south of Jeshimon. 'Let your majesty come down whenever you will,' they said, 'and it will be our business to surrender him to you.' Saul replied, 'The Lord's blessing on you; you have rendered me a service. Go now and make further enquiry, and find out exactly where he is and who saw him there. They tell me that he is crafty enough to outwit me. Find out which of his hiding-places he is using; then come back to me at such and such a place, and I shall go with you. So long as he stays in this country, I shall hunt him down, if I have to go through all the clans of Judah one by one.' They left for Ziph without delay, ahead of Saul.

David and his men were in the wilderness of Maon in the Arabah to the south of Jeshimon. Saul set off with his men to look for him; but David got word of it and went down to a refuge in the rocks, and there he stayed in the wilderness of Maon. On hearing this, Saul went into the wilderness after him; he was on one side of the hill, David and his men on the other. While David and his men were trying desperately to get away, and Saul and his followers were closing in for the capture, a runner brought a message to Saul: 'Come at once! The Philistines are invading the land.' Saul called off the pursuit of David and turned back to face the Philistines. This is why that place is called the Dividing Rock. David went up from there and lived in the fastnesses of En-gedi.

## DAVID AND ABIGAIL
### 1 Samuel 25:2–44

There was a man in Maon who had property at Carmel and owned three thousand sheep and a thousand goats; and he was shearing his flocks in Carmel. His name was Nabal and his wife's name Abigail; she was a beautiful and intelligent woman, but her husband, a Calebite, was surly and mean. David heard in the wilderness that Nabal was shearing his flocks, and sent ten of his young men, saying to them, 'Go up to Carmel, find Nabal, and give him my greetings. You are to say, "All good wishes for the year ahead! Prosperity to yourself, your household, and all that is yours! I hear that you are shearing. Your shepherds have been with us lately and we did not molest them; nothing of theirs was missing all the time they were in Carmel. Ask your own men and they will tell you. Receive my men kindly, for this is an auspicious day with us, and give what you can to David your son and your servant."'

David's servants came and delivered this message to Nabal in David's name. When they paused, Nabal answered, 'Who is David? Who is this son of Jesse? In these days there are many slaves who break away from their masters. Am I to take my food and my wine and the meat I have provided for my shearers, and give it to men who come from I know not where?' David's servants turned and made their way back to him and told him all this. He said to his followers, 'Buckle on your swords, all of you.' So they buckled on their swords, as did David, and they followed him, four hundred of them, while two hundred stayed behind with the baggage.

One of Nabal's servants said to Abigail, Nabal's wife, 'David sent messengers from the wilderness to ask our master politely for a present, and he flared up at them. The men have been very good to us and have not molested us, nor did we miss anything all the time we were going about with them in the open country. They were as good as a wall round us, night and day, while we were minding the flocks. Consider carefully what you had better do, for it is certain ruin for our master and his whole house; he is such a wretched fellow that it is no good talking to him.'

Abigail hastily collected two hundred loaves and two skins of wine, five sheep ready dressed, five measures of roasted grain, a hundred bunches of raisins, and two hundred cakes of dried figs, and loaded them on donkeys, but told her husband nothing about it. She said to her servants, 'Go on ahead, I shall follow you.' As she made her way on her donkey, hidden by the hill, there were David and his men coming down towards her, and she met them. David had said, 'It was a waste of time to protect this fellow's property in the wilderness so well that nothing of his was missing. He has repaid me evil for good.' David swore a solemn oath: 'God do the same to me and more if I leave him a single mother's son alive by morning!'

When Abigail saw David she dismounted in haste and prostrated herself before him, bowing low to the ground at his feet, and said, 'Let me take the blame, my lord, but allow your humble servant to speak out, and let my lord give me a hearing. How can you take any notice of this wretched fellow? He is just what his name Nabal means: "Churl" is his name, and churlish his behaviour. Sir, I did not myself see the men you sent. And now, sir, the Lord has restrained you from starting a blood feud and from striking a blow for yourself. As the Lord lives, your life upon it, your enemies and all who want to see you ruined will be like Nabal. Here is the present which I, your humble servant, have brought; give it to the young men under your command. Forgive me, my lord, if I am presuming; for the Lord will establish your family for ever, because you have fought his battles. No calamity will overtake you as long as you live. If anyone tries to pursue you and take your life, the Lord your God will wrap your life up and put it with his own treasure, but the lives of your enemies he will hurl away like stones from a sling. When the Lord has made good all his promises to you, and has made you ruler of Israel, there will be no reason why you should stumble or your courage should falter because you have shed innocent blood or struck a blow for yourself. Then when the Lord makes all you do prosper, remember me, your servant.'

David said to Abigail, 'Blessed be the Lord the God of Israel who today has sent you to meet me. A blessing on your good sense, a blessing on you because you have saved me today from the guilt of bloodshed and from striking a blow for myself. For I swear by the life of the Lord the God of Israel who has kept me from doing you wrong: if you had not come at once to meet me, not a man of Nabal's household, not a single mother's son, would have been left alive by morning.' Then David accepted from her what she had brought him and said, 'Go home in peace; I have listened to you and I grant your request.'

On her return she found Nabal holding a right royal banquet in his house. He grew merry and became very drunk, so drunk that his wife said nothing at all to him till daybreak. In the morning, when the wine had worn off, she told him everything, and he had a seizure and lay there like a log. Some ten days later the Lord struck him and he died.

When David heard that Nabal was dead he said, 'Blessed be the Lord, who has himself punished Nabal for his insult, and has kept me his servant from doing wrong. The Lord has made Nabal's wrongdoing recoil on his own head.' David then sent a message to Abigail proposing that she should become his wife. His servants came to her at Carmel and said, 'David has sent us to fetch you to be his wife.' She rose and prostrated herself with her face to the ground, and said, 'I am his slave to command; I would wash the feet of my lord's servants.' Abigail made her preparations with all speed and, with her five maids in attendance and accompanied by David's messengers, she set out on a donkey; and she became David's wife. David had also married Ahinoam of Jezreel; both these women became his wives. Saul meanwhile had given his daughter Michal, David's wife, to Palti son of Laish from Gallim.

## DAVID SPARES SAUL'S LIFE
### 1 Samuel 26:1–25

The Ziphites came to Saul at Gibeah with the news that David was in hiding on the hill of Hachilah overlooking Jeshimon. Saul went down at once to the wilderness of Ziph, taking with him three thousand picked men, to search for David there. He encamped beside the road on the hill of Hachilah overlooking Jeshimon, while David was still in the wilderness. As soon as David learnt that Saul had come to the wilderness in pursuit of him, he sent out scouts and found that Saul had reached such and such a place. He went at once to the place where Saul had pitched his camp, and observed where Saul and Abner son of Ner, the commander-in-chief, were lying. Saul lay within the lines with his troops encamped in a circle round him. David turned to Ahimelech the Hittite and Abishai son of Zeruiah, Joab's brother, and said, 'Who will venture with me into the camp to Saul?' Abishai answered, 'I will.'

David and Abishai entered the camp at night, and there was Saul lying asleep within the lines with his spear thrust into the ground beside his head. Abner and the army were asleep all around him. Abishai said to David, 'God has put your enemy into your power today. Let me strike him and pin him to the ground with one thrust of the spear. I shall not have to strike twice.' David said to him, 'Do him no harm. Who has ever lifted his hand against the Lord's anointed and gone unpunished? As the Lord lives,' David went on, 'the Lord will strike him down; either his time will come and he will die, or he will go down to battle and meet his end. God forbid that I should lift my hand against the Lord's anointed! But now let us take the spear which is by his head, and the water-jar, and go.' So David took the spear and the water-jar from beside Saul's head, and they left. The whole camp was asleep; no one saw him, no one knew anything, no one woke. A deep sleep sent by the Lord had fallen on them.

Then David crossed over to the other side and stood on the top of a hill at some distance; there was a wide stretch between them. David shouted across to the army and hailed Abner son of Ner, 'Answer me, Abner!' He answered, 'Who are you to shout to the king?' David said to Abner, 'Do you call yourself a man? Is there anyone like you in Israel? Why, then, did you not keep watch over your lord the king, when someone came to harm your lord the king? This was not well done. As the Lord lives, you deserve to die, all of you, because you have not kept watch over your master the Lord's anointed. Look! Where are the king's spear and the water-jar that were by his head?'

Saul recognized David's voice and said, 'Is that you, David my son?' 'Yes, your majesty, it is,' said David. 'Why must my lord pursue me? What have I done? What mischief am I plotting? Listen, my lord king, to what I have to say. If it is the Lord who has set you against me, may an offering be acceptable to him; but if it is mortals, a curse on them in the Lord's name! For they have ousted me today from my share in the Lord's possession and have banished me to serve other gods! Do not let my blood be shed on foreign soil, far from the presence of the Lord, just because the king of Israel came out to look for a flea, as one might hunt a partridge over the hills.'

Saul said, 'I have done wrong; come back, David my son. You have held my life precious this day, and I will never harm you again. I have been a fool, I have been sadly in the wrong.' David answered, 'Here is the king's spear; let one of your men come across and fetch it. The Lord who rewards uprightness and loyalty will reward the man into whose power he put you today, for I refused to lift my hand against the Lord's anointed. As I held your life precious today, so may the Lord hold mine precious and deliver me from every distress.' Saul said to David, 'A blessing on you, David my son! You will do great things and be triumphant.' With that David went on his way and Saul returned home.

## DAVID THE MERCENARY
### 1 Samuel 27:1 – 28:2

David thought to himself, 'One of these days I shall be killed by Saul. The best thing for me to do will be to escape into Philistine territory;

then Saul will give up all further hope of finding me anywhere in Israel, search as he may, and I shall escape his clutches.' So David and his six hundred men set out and crossed the frontier to Achish son of Maoch, king of Gath. David settled in Gath with Achish, taking with him his men and their families and his two wives, Ahinoam of Jezreel and Abigail of Carmel, Nabal's widow. Saul was told that David had escaped to Gath, and he abandoned the search.

David said to Achish, 'If I stand well in your opinion, grant me a place in one of your country towns where I may settle. Why should I remain in the royal city with your majesty?' Achish granted him Ziklag on that day: that is why Ziklag still belongs to the kings of Judah.

David spent a year and four months in Philistine country. He and his men would sally out and raid the Geshurites, the Gizrites, and the Amalekites, for it was they who inhabited the country from Telaim all the way to Shur and Egypt. When David raided any territory he left no one alive, man or woman; he took flocks and herds, donkeys and camels, and clothes too, and then came back again to Achish. Achish would ask, 'Where was your raid today?' and David would answer, 'The Negeb of Judah' or 'The Negeb of the Jerahmeelites' or 'The Negeb of the Kenites'. He let neither man nor woman survive to be brought back to Gath, for fear that they might denounce him and his men for what they had done. This was his practice as long as he remained with the Philistines. Achish trusted him, thinking that David had made himself so obnoxious among his own people the Israelites that he would remain his vassal all his life.

At that time the Philistines mustered their army for an attack on Israel, and Achish said to David, 'You know that you and your men must take the field with me.' David answered, 'Good, you will learn what your servant can do.' Achish said, 'I will make you my bodyguard for life.'

## SAUL AND THE WITCH OF ENDOR
### 1 Samuel 28:3–25

By this time Samuel was dead, and all Israel had mourned for him and buried him in Ramah, his own town; and Saul had banished from the land all who trafficked with ghosts and spirits. The Philistines mustered and encamped at Shunem, and Saul mustered all the Israelites and encamped at Gilboa. At the sight of the Philistine forces, Saul was afraid, indeed struck to the heart by terror. He enquired of the Lord, but the Lord did not answer him, neither by dreams, nor by Urim, nor by prophets. So he said to his servants, 'Find a woman who has a familiar spirit, and I will go and enquire through her.' They told him that there was such a woman at En-dor.

Saul put on different clothes and went in disguise with two of his men. He came to the woman by night and said, 'Tell me my fortune by consulting the dead, and call up the man I name to you.' The woman answered, 'Surely you know what Saul has done, how he has made away with those who call up ghosts and spirits; why do you press me to do what will lead to my death?' Saul swore her an oath: 'As the Lord lives, no harm shall come to you for this.' The woman asked whom she should call up, and Saul answered, 'Samuel.' When the woman saw Samuel appear, she shrieked and said to Saul, 'Why have you deceived me? You are Saul!' The king said to her, 'Do not be afraid. What do you see?' The woman answered, 'I see a ghostly form coming up from the earth.' 'What is it like?' he asked; she answered, 'Like an old man coming up, wrapped in a cloak.' Then Saul knew it was Samuel, and he bowed low with his face to the ground, and prostrated himself.

Samuel said to Saul, 'Why have you disturbed me and raised me?' Saul answered, 'I am in great trouble; the Philistines are waging war against me, and God has turned away; he no longer answers me through prophets or through dreams, and I have summoned you to tell me what I should do.' Samuel said, 'Why do you ask me, now that the Lord has turned from you and become your adversary? He has done what he foretold through me. He has wrested the kingdom from your hand and given it to another, to David. You have not obeyed the Lord, or executed the judgment of his fierce anger against the Amalekites; that is why he has done this to you today. For the same reason the Lord will let your people Israel fall along with you into the hands of the Philistines. What is more, tomorrow you and your sons will be with me. I tell you again: the Lord will give the Israelite army into the power of the Philistines.' Saul was overcome, and terrified by

Samuel's words he fell full length to the ground. He had no strength left, for he had eaten nothing all day and all night.

The woman went to Saul and, seeing how deeply shaken he was, she said, 'I listened to what you said and I risked my life to obey you. Now listen to me: let me set before you a little food to give you strength for your journey.' He refused to eat anything, but when his servants joined the woman in pressing him, he yielded, rose from the ground, and sat on the couch. The woman had a fattened calf at home, which she quickly slaughtered; she also took some meal, kneaded it, and baked unleavened loaves. She set the food before Saul and his servants, and when they had eaten they set off that same night.

## DAVID'S VICTORY OVER THE AMALEKITES
### 1 Samuel 29:1 – 30:25

The Philistines mustered their entire army at Aphek; the Israelites encamped at En-harod in Jezreel. While the Philistine lords were advancing with their troops in units of a hundred and a thousand, David and his men were in the rear of the column with Achish. The Philistine commanders asked, 'What are those Hebrews doing here?' Achish answered, 'This is David, the servant of King Saul of Israel who has been with me now for a year or more. Ever since he came over to me I have had no fault to find with him.' The commanders were indignant and said, 'Send the man back to the place you allotted to him. He must not fight side by side with us, for he may turn traitor in the battle. What better way to buy his master's favour, than at the price of our lives? This is that David of whom they sang, as they danced:

"Saul struck down thousands,
but David tens of thousands."'

Achish summoned David and said to him, 'As the Lord lives, you are an upright man and your service on my campaigns has well satisfied me. I have had no fault to find with you ever since you joined me, but the lords are not willing to accept you. Now go home in peace, and you will then be doing nothing that they can regard as wrong.' David protested, 'What have I done, or what fault have you found in me from the day I first entered your service till now, that I should not come and fight against the enemies of my lord the king?' Achish answered, 'I agree that you have been as true to me as an angel of God, but the Philistine commanders insist that you are not to fight alongside them. Now rise early tomorrow with those of your lord's subjects who have followed you, and go to the town which I allotted to you; harbour no resentment, for I am well satisfied with you. Be up early and start as soon as it is light.' So in the morning David and his men made an early start to go back to the land of the Philistines, while the Philistines went on to Jezreel.

On the third day David and his men reached Ziklag. In the mean time the Amalekites had made a raid into the Negeb, attacked Ziklag, and set it on fire. They had taken captive all the women, young and old. They did not put any to death, but carried them off as they continued their march. When David and his men came to the town, they found it destroyed by fire, and their wives, their sons, and their daughters taken captive. David and the people with him wept aloud until they could weep no more. David's two wives, Ahinoam of Jezreel and Abigail widow of Nabal of Carmel, were among the captives. David was in a desperate position because the troops, embittered by the loss of their sons and daughters, threatened to stone him.

David sought strength in the Lord his God, and told Abiathar the priest, son of Ahimelech, to bring the ephod. When Abiathar had brought the ephod, David enquired of the Lord, 'Shall I pursue these raiders? And shall I overtake them?' The answer came, 'Pursue them: you will overtake them and rescue everyone.' David and his six hundred men set out and reached the wadi of Besor. Two hundred of them who were too exhausted to cross the wadi stayed behind, and David with four hundred pressed on in pursuit.

In the open country they came across an Egyptian and took him to David. They gave him food to eat and water to drink, also a lump of dried figs and two bunches of raisins. When he had eaten he revived; for he had had nothing to eat or drink for three days and nights. David asked him, 'Whose slave are you, and where have you come from?' 'I am an Egyptian,' he answered, 'the slave of an

Amalekite, but my master left me behind because three days ago I fell ill. We had raided the Negeb of the Kerethites, part of Judah, and the Negeb of Caleb; we also burned down Ziklag.' David asked, 'Can you guide me to the raiders?' 'Swear to me by God', he answered, 'that you will not put me to death or hand me back to my master, and I shall guide you to them.' He led him down, and there they found the Amalekites scattered everywhere, eating and drinking and celebrating the great mass of spoil taken from the Philistine and Judaean territories.

David attacked from dawn to dusk and continued till next day; only four hundred young men mounted on camels got away. David rescued all those whom the Amalekites had taken captive, including his two wives. No one was missing, young or old, sons or daughters, nor was any of the spoil missing, anything they had seized for themselves: David recovered everything. They took all the flocks and herds, drove the cattle before him and said, 'This is David's spoil.'

When David returned to the two hundred men who had been too exhausted to follow him and whom he had left behind at the wadi of Besor, they came forward to meet him and his men. David greeted them all, enquiring how things were with them. But some of those who had gone with David, rogues and scoundrels, broke in and said, 'These men did not go with us; we will not allot them any of the spoil that we have recaptured, except that each of them may take his wife and children and go.' 'That', said David, 'you must not do, considering what the Lord has given us, and how he has kept us safe and given the raiding party into our hands. Who could agree with what you propose? Those who stayed with the stores are to have the same share as those who went into battle. All must share and share alike.' From that time onwards, this has been the established custom in Israel down to this day.


## THE DEATH OF SAUL AND JONATHAN
1 Samuel 31:1–13


The Philistines engaged Israel in battle, and the Israelites were routed, leaving their dead on Mount Gilboa. The Philistines closely pursued

Saul and his sons, and Jonathan, Abinadab, and Malchishua, the sons of Saul, were killed. The battle went hard for Saul, and when the archers caught up with him they wounded him severely. He said to his armour-bearer, 'Draw your sword and run me through, so that these uncircumcised brutes may not come and taunt me and make sport of me.' But the armour-bearer refused; he dared not do it. Thereupon Saul took his own sword and fell on it. When the armour-bearer saw that Saul was dead, he too fell on his sword and died with him. So they died together on that day, Saul, his three sons, and his armour-bearer, as well as all his men. When the Israelites in the neighbourhood of the valley and of the Jordan saw that the other Israelites had fled and that Saul and his sons had perished, they fled likewise, abandoning their towns; and the Philistines moved in and occupied them.

Next day, when the Philistines came to strip the slain, they found Saul and his three sons lying dead on Mount Gilboa. They cut off his head and stripped him of his armour; then they sent messengers through the length and breadth of their land to carry the good news to idols and people alike. They deposited his armour in the temple of Ashtoreth and nailed his body on the wall of Beth-shan. When the inhabitants of Jabesh-gilead heard what the Philistines had done to Saul, all the warriors among them set out and journeyed through the night to recover the bodies of Saul and his sons from the wall of Beth-shan. They brought them back to Jabesh and burned them; they took the bones and buried them under the tamarisk tree in Jabesh, and for seven days they fasted.

## Part Two

# David the King

### DAVID'S LAMENT OVER SAUL AND JONATHAN
2 Samuel 1:1–27

After Saul's death David returned from his victory over the Amalekites and spent two days in Ziklag. On the third day a man came from Saul's camp; his clothes were torn and there was dust on his head. Coming into David's presence he fell to the ground and did obeisance. David asked him where he had come from, and he replied, 'I have escaped from the Israelite camp.' David said, 'What is the news? Tell me.' 'The army has been driven from the field,' he answered, 'many have fallen in battle, and Saul and Jonathan his son are dead.' David said to the young man who brought the news, 'How do you know that Saul and Jonathan are dead?' He answered, 'It so happened that I was on Mount Gilboa and saw Saul leaning on his spear with the chariots and horsemen closing in on him. He turned and, seeing me, called to me. I said, "What is it, sir?" He asked me who I was, and I said, "An Amalekite." He said to me, "Come and stand over me and dispatch me. I still live, but the throes of death have seized me." So I stood over him and dealt him the death blow, for I knew that, stricken as he was, he could not live. Then I took the crown from his head and the armlet from his arm, and I have brought them here to you, my lord.' At that David and all the men with him took hold of their clothes and tore them. They mourned and wept, and they fasted till evening because Saul and Jonathan his son and the army of the Lord and the house of Israel had fallen in battle.

David said to the young man who brought him the news, 'Where do you come from?' and he answered, 'I am the son of an alien, an Amalekite.' 'How is it', said David, 'that you were not afraid to raise your hand to kill the Lord's anointed?' Summoning one of his own young men he ordered him to fall upon the Amalekite. The young man struck him down and he died. David said, 'Your blood be on your own head; for out of your own mouth you condemned yourself by saying, "I killed the Lord's anointed."'

David raised this lament over Saul and Jonathan his son; and he ordered that this dirge over them should be taught to the people of Judah. It was written down and may be found in the Book of Jashar:

Israel, upon your heights your beauty lies slain!
How are the warriors fallen!

Do not tell it in Gath
or proclaim it in the streets of Ashkelon,
in case the Philistine maidens rejoice,
and the daughters of the uncircumcised exult.

Hills of Gilboa, let no dew or rain fall on you,
no showers on the uplands!
For there the shields of the warriors lie tarnished,
and the shield of Saul, no longer bright with oil.
The bow of Jonathan never held back
from the breast of the foeman, from the blood of the slain;
the sword of Saul never returned empty to the scabbard.

Beloved and lovely were Saul and Jonathan;
neither in life nor in death were they parted.
They were swifter than eagles, stronger than lions.

Daughters of Israel, weep for Saul,
who clothed you in scarlet and rich embroideries,
who spangled your attire with jewels of gold.

How are the warriors fallen on the field of battle!
Jonathan lies slain on your heights.

I grieve for you, Jonathan my brother;
you were most dear to me;
your love for me was wonderful,
surpassing the love of women.

How are the warriors fallen,
and their armour abandoned on the battlefield!

## DAVID KING OF JUDAH
### 2 Samuel 2:1–7

Afterwards David enquired of the Lord, 'Shall I go up into one of the towns of Judah?' The Lord answered, 'Go.' David asked, 'Where shall I go?' and the answer was, 'To Hebron.' So David went up there with his two wives, Ahinoam of Jezreel and Abigail widow of Nabal of Carmel. David also brought the men who had joined him, with their families, and they settled in Hebron and the neighbouring towns. The men of Judah came, and there they anointed David king over the house of Judah.

It was reported to David that the men of Jabesh-gilead had buried Saul, and he sent them this message: 'The Lord bless you because you kept faith with Saul your lord and buried him. For this may the Lord keep faith and truth with you, and I for my part will show you favour too, because you have done this. Be strong, be valiant, now that Saul your lord is dead, and the people of Judah have anointed me to be king over them.'

## ISHBOSHETH KING OF ISRAEL
### 2 Samuel 2:8–10

Meanwhile Saul's commander-in-chief, Abner son of Ner, had taken Saul's son Ishbosheth, brought him across to Mahanaim, and made him king over Gilead, the Asherites, Jezreel, Ephraim, and Benjamin, and all Israel. Ishbosheth was forty years old when he became king over Israel, and he reigned for two years. The tribe of Judah, however, followed David.

## WAR BETWEEN THE HOUSES OF SAUL AND DAVID
### 2 Samuel 2:11 – 3:6

David's rule over Judah in Hebron lasted seven and a half years.

Abner son of Ner, with the troops of Saul's son Ishbosheth, marched out from Mahanaim to Gibeon, and Joab son of Zeruiah marched out with David's troops from Hebron. They met at the pool of Gibeon and took up their positions, one force on one side of the pool and the other on the opposite side. Abner said to Joab, 'Let the young men come forward and join in single combat before us.' Joab agreed. So they came up, one by one, and took their places, twelve for Benjamin and Ishbosheth and twelve from David's men. Each man seized his opponent by the head and thrust his sword into his opponent's side; and thus they fell together. That is why that place, which lies in Gibeon, was called the Field of Blades.

There ensued a very hard-fought battle that day, and Abner and the men of Israel were defeated by David's troops. All three sons of Zeruiah were there, Joab, Abishai, and Asahel. Asahel, who was swift as a gazelle of the plains, chased after Abner, swerving to neither right nor left in his pursuit. Abner glanced back and said, 'Is it you, Asahel?' Asahel answered, 'It is.' Abner said, 'Turn aside to right or left; tackle one of the young men and win his belt for yourself.' But Asahel would not abandon the pursuit. Abner again urged him to give it up. 'Why should I kill you?' he said. 'How could I look Joab your brother in the face?' When he still refused to turn away, Abner struck him in the belly with a back-thrust of his spear so that the spear came out through his back, and he fell dead in his tracks. All who came to the place where Asahel lay dead stopped there. But Joab and Abishai kept up the pursuit of Abner, until, at sunset, they reached the hill of Ammah, opposite Giah on the road leading to the pastures of Gibeon.

The Benjamites rallied to Abner and, forming themselves into a single group, took their stand on the top of a hill. Abner called to Joab, 'Must the slaughter go on for ever? Can you not see the bitterness that will result? How long before you recall the troops from the pursuit of their kinsmen?' Joab answered, 'As God lives, if you had not spoken, they would not have given up the pursuit till morning.' Then Joab sounded the trumpet, and the troops all halted; they abandoned the pursuit of the Israelites, and the fighting ceased.

Abner and his men moved along the Arabah all that night, crossed the Jordan, and continued all morning till they reached Mahanaim. After Joab returned from the pursuit of Abner, he mustered his troops and found that, besides Asahel, nineteen of David's men were missing. David's forces had routed the Benjamites and the followers of Abner, killing three hundred and sixty of them. They took up Asahel and buried him in his father's tomb at Bethlehem. Joab and his men marched all night, and as day broke they reached Hebron.

The war between the house of Saul and the house of David was long drawn out, David growing steadily stronger while the house of Saul became weaker.

Sons were born to David at Hebron. His eldest was Amnon, whose mother was Ahinoam from Jezreel; his second Cileab, whose mother was Abigail widow of Nabal from Carmel; the third Absalom, whose mother was Maacah daughter of Talmai king of Geshur; the fourth Adonijah, whose mother was Haggith; the fifth Shephatiah, whose mother was Abital; and the sixth Ithream, whose mother was David's wife Eglah. These were born to David at Hebron.

As the war between the houses of Saul and David went on, Abner gradually strengthened his position in the house of Saul.

## THE DEATH OF ABNER
### 2 Samuel 3:7–39

Now Saul had had a concubine named Rizpah daughter of Aiah. Ishbosheth challenged Abner, 'Why have you slept with my father's concubine?' Abner, angered by this, exclaimed, 'Do you take me for a Judahite dog? Up to now I have been loyal to the house of your father Saul, to his brothers and friends, and I have not betrayed you into David's hands; yet you choose this moment to charge me with an offence over a woman. But now, so help me God, I shall do all I can to bring about what the Lord swore to do for David: I shall set to work to overthrow the house of Saul and to establish David's throne over Israel and Judah from Dan to Beersheba.' Ishbosheth dared not say another word; he was too much afraid of Abner.

Abner sent envoys on his own behalf to David with the message, 'Who is to control the land? Let us come to terms, and you will have my support in bringing the whole of Israel over to you.' David's answer was: 'Good, I will come to terms with you, but on one condition: that you do not come into my presence without bringing

143

Saul's daughter Michal to me.' David also sent messengers to Saul's son Ishbosheth with the demand: 'Hand over to me my wife Michal for whom I gave a hundred Philistine foreskins as the bride-price.' Thereupon Ishbosheth sent and took her from her husband, Paltiel son of Laish. Her husband followed her as far as Bahurim, weeping all the way, until Abner ordered him back, and he went.

Abner conferred with the elders of Israel: 'For some time past', he said, 'you have wanted David for your king. Now is the time to act, for this is the word of the Lord about David: "By the hand of my servant David I shall deliver my people Israel from the Philistines and from all their enemies."' Abner spoke also to the Benjamites and then went to report to David at Hebron all that the Israelites and the Benjamites had agreed. When Abner, attended by twenty men, arrived, David gave a feast for him and his men. Abner said to David, 'I shall now go and bring the whole of Israel over to your majesty. They will make a covenant with you, and you will be king over a realm after your own heart.' David dismissed Abner, granting him safe conduct.

Just then David's men and Joab returned from a raid, bringing a great quantity of plunder with them. Abner, having been dismissed, was no longer with David in Hebron. Joab and the whole force with him were greeted on their arrival with the news that Abner son of Ner had been with the king and had departed under safe conduct.

Joab went in to the king and said, 'What have you done? You have had Abner here with you. How could you let him go and get clean away? You know Abner son of Ner: his purpose in coming was to deceive you, to learn about your movements, and to find out everything you are doing.'

Leaving David's presence, Joab sent messengers after Abner, and they brought him back from the Pool of Sirah; but David knew nothing of this. On Abner's return to Hebron, Joab drew him aside in the gateway, as though to speak privately with him, and there, in revenge for his brother Asahel, he stabbed him in the belly, and he died.

When David heard the news he said, 'In the sight of the Lord I and my kingdom are for ever innocent of the blood of Abner son of Ner. May it recoil on the head of Joab and on all his family! May the house of Joab never be free from running sore or foul disease, nor lack a son fit only to ply the distaff or doomed to die by the sword or beg his bread!' Joab and Abishai his brother slew Abner because he had killed their brother Asahel in battle at Gibeon. Then David ordered Joab and all the troops with him to tear their clothes, put on sackcloth, and mourn for Abner, and the king himself walked behind the bier. They buried Abner in Hebron and the king wept aloud at the tomb, while all the people wept with him. The king made this lament for Abner:

> Must Abner die so base a death?
> Your hands were not bound,
> your feet not fettered;
> you fell as one who falls at the hands of a criminal.

The people all wept again for him.

They came to urge David to eat something; but it was still day and he took an oath, 'So help me God! I refuse to touch food of any kind before sunset.' The people noted this with approval; indeed, everything the king did pleased them all. It was then known throughout Israel that the king had had no hand in the murder of Abner son of Ner. The king said to his servants, 'You must know that a warrior, a great man, has fallen this day in Israel. Anointed king though I am, I feel weak and powerless in face of these ruthless sons of Zeruiah; they are too much for me. May the Lord requite the wrongdoer as his wrongdoing deserves.'

## THE DEATH OF ISHBOSHETH
### 2 Samuel 4:1–12

When Saul's son Ishbosheth heard that Abner had met his death in Hebron, his courage failed him, and all Israel was alarmed. Ishbosheth had two officers, who were captains of raiding parties, and whose names were Baanah and Rechab; they were Benjamites, sons of Rimmon of Beeroth, Beeroth being reckoned part of Benjamin; but the Beerothites had sought refuge in Gittaim, where they have lived as aliens ever since.

(Saul's son Jonathan had a son lame in both feet. He was five years old when word of the death of Saul and Jonathan came from Jezreel. His nurse had picked him up and fled, but as she hurried to get away he fell and was crippled. His name was Mephibosheth.)

Rechab and Baanah, the sons of Rimmon of Beeroth, came to Ishbosheth's house in the heat of the day, while he was taking his midday rest. The door-keeper had been sifting wheat, but she had grown drowsy and fallen asleep, so Rechab and his brother Baanah slipped past, found their way to the room where Ishbosheth was asleep on the bed, and attacked and killed him. They cut off his head and took it with them and, making their way along the Arabah all night, came to Hebron. They brought Ishbosheth's head to David there and said to the king, 'Here is the head of Ishbosheth son of Saul, your enemy, who sought your life. The Lord has avenged your majesty today on Saul and on his family.' David answered Rechab and his brother Baanah: 'As the Lord lives, who has delivered me from all my troubles, I seized the man who brought me word that Saul was dead and thought he was bringing good news; I killed him in Ziklag. That was how I rewarded him for his news! How much more shall I reward wicked men who have killed an innocent man on his bed in his own house! Am I not to take vengeance on you now for the blood you have shed, and rid the earth of you?' David gave the word, and the young men killed them; they cut off their hands and feet and hung them up beside the pool in Hebron; but the head of Ishbosheth they took and buried in Abner's tomb at Hebron.

## DAVID KING OF ALL ISRAEL
### 2 Samuel 5:1–13

All the tribes of Israel came to David at Hebron and said to him, 'We are your own flesh and blood. In the past, while Saul was still king over us, it was you that led the forces of Israel on their campaigns. To you the Lord said, "You are to be shepherd of my people Israel; you are to be their prince."' The elders of Israel all came to the king at Hebron; there David made a covenant with them before the Lord, and they anointed David king over Israel.

David came to the throne at the age of thirty and reigned for forty years. In Hebron he had ruled over Judah for seven and a half years, and in Jerusalem he reigned over Israel and Judah combined for thirty-three years.

The king and his men went to Jerusalem to attack the Jebusites, the inhabitants of that region. The Jebusites said to David, 'You will never come in here, not till you have disposed of the blind and the lame,' stressing that David would never come in. None the less David did capture the stronghold of Zion, and it is now known as the City of David. On that day David had said, 'Everyone who is eager to attack the Jebusites, let him get up the water-shaft to reach the lame and the blind, David's bitter enemies.' That is why they say, 'No one who is blind or lame is to come into the Lord's house.'

David took up his residence in the stronghold and called it the City of David. He built up the city around it, starting at the Millo and working inwards. David steadily grew more and more powerful, for the Lord the God of Hosts was with him.

King Hiram of Tyre sent envoys to David with cedar logs, and with them carpenters and stonemasons, who built David a house. David knew by now that the Lord had confirmed him as king over Israel and had enhanced his royal power for the sake of his people Israel.

After he had moved from Hebron he took more concubines and wives in Jerusalem, and more sons and daughters were born to him.

## DAVID DANCES BEFORE THE ARK
2 Samuel 6:1–23

David again summoned the picked men of Israel, thirty thousand in all, and went with the whole army that was then with him to Baalath-judah to fetch from there the Ark of God which bore the name of the Lord of Hosts, who is enthroned upon the cherubim. They mounted the Ark of God on a new cart and conveyed it from Abinadab's house on the hill, with Uzzah and Ahio, sons of Abinadab, guiding the cart. They led it with the Ark of God upon it from Abinadab's house on the hill, with Ahio walking in front. David and all Israel danced for joy before the Lord with all their might to the sound of singing, of lyres, lutes, tambourines, castanets, and cymbals.

When they came to a certain threshing-floor, the oxen stumbled, and Uzzah reached out and held the Ark of God. The Lord was angry with Uzzah and struck him down for his imprudent action, and he died there beside the Ark of God. David was vexed because the Lord's anger had broken out on Uzzah, and he called the place Perez-uzzah, the name it still bears.

David was afraid of the Lord that day and said, 'How can the Ark of the Lord come to me?' He felt he could not take the Ark of the Lord with him to the City of David; he turned aside and carried it to the house of Obed-edom the Gittite. The Ark of the Lord remained at Obed-edom's house for three months, and the Lord blessed Obed-edom and his whole household.

When David was informed that the Lord had blessed Obed-edom's family and all that he possessed because of the Ark of God, he went and brought the Ark of God from the house of Obed-edom up to the City of David amid rejoicing. When the bearers of the Ark of the Lord had gone six steps he sacrificed a bull and a buffalo. He was wearing a linen ephod, and he danced with abandon before the Lord, as he and all the Israelites brought up the Ark of the Lord with acclamation and blowing of trumpets. As the Ark of the Lord was entering the City of David, Saul's daughter Michal looked down from a window and saw King David leaping and whirling before the Lord, and she despised him in her heart.

After they had brought the Ark of the Lord, they put it in its place inside the tent that David had set up for it, and David offered whole-offerings and shared-offerings before the Lord. Having completed these sacrifices, David blessed the people in the name of the Lord of Hosts, and distributed food to them all, a flat loaf of bread, a portion of meat, and a cake of raisins, to every man and woman in the whole gathering of the Israelites. Then all the people went home.

David returned to greet his household, and Michal, Saul's daughter, came out to meet him. She said, 'What a glorious day for the king of Israel, when he made an exhibition of himself in the sight of his servants' slave-girls, as any vulgar clown might do!' David answered her, 'But it was done in the presence of the Lord, who chose me instead of your father and his family and appointed me prince over Israel, the people of the Lord. Before the Lord I shall dance for joy, yes, and I shall earn yet more disgrace and demean myself still more in your eyes; but those slave-girls of whom you speak, they will hold me in honour for it.'

To her dying day Michal, Saul's daughter, was childless.

## GOD'S PROMISE TO DAVID
### 2 Samuel 7

Once the king was established in his palace and the Lord had given him security from his enemies on all sides, he said to Nathan the prophet, 'Here I am living in a house of cedar, while the Ark of God is housed in a tent.' Nathan answered, 'Do whatever you have in mind, for the Lord is with you.' But that same night the word of the Lord came to Nathan: 'Go and say to David my servant, This is the word of the Lord: Are you to build me a house to dwell in? Down to this day I have never dwelt in a house since I brought Israel up from Egypt; I lived in a tent and a tabernacle. Wherever I journeyed with Israel, did I ever ask any of the judges whom I appointed shepherds of my people Israel why they had not built me a cedar house?

'Then say this to my servant David: This is the word of the Lord of Hosts: I took you from the pastures and from following the sheep to be prince over my people Israel. I have been with you wherever you have gone, and have destroyed all the enemies in your path. I shall bring you fame like the fame of the great ones of the earth. I shall assign a place for my people Israel; there I shall plant them to dwell in their own land. They will be disturbed no more; never again will the wicked oppress them as they did in the past, from the day when I appointed judges over my people Israel; and I shall give you peace from all your enemies.

'The Lord has told you that he would build up your royal house. When your life ends and you rest with your forefathers, I shall set up one of your family, one of your own children, to succeed you, and I shall establish his kingdom. It is he who is to build a house in honour of my name, and I shall establish his royal throne for all time. I shall be a father to him, and he will be my son. When he does wrong, I shall punish him as any father might, and not spare the rod. But my love will never be withdrawn from him as I withdrew it from Saul, whom I removed from your path. Your family and your kingdom will be established for ever in my sight; your throne will endure for all time.'

Nathan recounted to David all that had been said to him and all that had been revealed. Then King David went into the presence of the Lord and, taking his place there, said, 'Who am I, Lord God, and what is my family, that you have brought me thus far? It was a small thing in your sight, Lord God, to have planned for your servant's house in days long past. What more can I say? Lord God, you yourself know your servant David. For the sake of your promise and in accordance with your purpose you have done all this great thing to reveal it to your servant.

'Lord God, you are great. There is none like you; there is no God but you, as everything we have heard bears witness. And your people Israel, to whom can they be compared? Is there any other nation on earth whom you, God, have set out to redeem from slavery to be your people? You have won renown for yourself by great and awesome deeds, driving out other nations and their gods to make way for your people whom you redeemed from Egypt. You have established your people Israel as your own for ever, and you, Lord, have become their God.

'Now, Lord God, perform for all time what you have promised for your servant and his house; make good what you have promised. May your fame be great for evermore, and let people say, "The Lord of Hosts is God over Israel"; and may the house of your servant David be established before you. Lord of Hosts, God of Israel, you have shown me your purpose, in saying to your servant, "I shall build up your house"; and therefore I have made bold to offer this prayer to you. Now, Lord God, you are God and your promises will come true; you have made these noble promises to your servant. Be pleased now to bless your servant's house so that it may continue always before you; you, Lord God, have promised, and may your blessing rest on your servant's house for ever.'

## DAVID'S KINDNESS TO SAUL'S FAMILY
2 Samuel 9:1–13

David enquired, 'Is any member of Saul's family left, to whom I can show kindness for Jonathan's sake?' A servant of Saul's family named Ziba was summoned to David, who asked, 'Are you Ziba?' He answered, 'Your servant, sir.' The king asked, 'Is there any member of Saul's family still alive to whom I may show the kindness that God requires?' 'Yes,' said Ziba, 'there is still a son of Jonathan alive; he is a cripple, lame in both feet.' 'Where is he?' said the king, and Ziba answered, 'He is staying with Machir son of Ammiel in Lo-debar.'

The king had him fetched from Lodebar, from the house of Machir son of Ammiel, and when Mephibosheth, son of Jonathan and grandson of Saul, entered David's presence, he prostrated himself and did obeisance. David said to him, 'Mephibosheth!' and he answered, 'Your servant, sir.' Then David said, 'Do not be afraid; I mean to show you kindness for your father Jonathan's sake; I shall restore to you the whole estate of your grandfather Saul and you will have a regular place at my table.' Mephibosheth prostrated himself again and said, 'Who am I that you should spare a thought for a dead dog like me?'

David summoned Saul's servant Ziba and said, 'I assign to your master's grandson all the property that belonged to Saul and his family. You and your sons and your slaves must cultivate the land and bring in the harvest to provide for your master's household, but Mephibosheth your master's grandson shall have a regular place at my table.' Ziba, who had fifteen sons and twenty slaves, answered: 'I shall do all that your majesty commands.' So Mephibosheth took his place in the royal household like one of the king's sons. He had a young son, named Mica; and the members of Ziba's household were all Mephibosheth's servants, while Mephibosheth lived in Jerusalem and had his regular place at the king's table, crippled as he was in both feet.

## DAVID AND BATHSHEBA
2 Samuel 11:1 – 12:24

At the turn of the year, when kings go out to battle, David sent Joab out with his other officers and all the Israelite forces, and they ravaged

Ammon and laid siege to Rabbah. David remained in Jerusalem, and one evening, as he got up from his couch and walked about on the roof of the palace, he saw from there a woman bathing, and she was very beautiful. He made enquiries about the woman and was told, 'It must be Bathsheba daughter of Eliam and wife of Uriah the Hittite.' He sent messengers to fetch her, and when she came to him, he had intercourse with her, though she was still purifying herself after her period, and then she went home. She conceived, and sent word to David that she was pregnant.

David ordered Joab to send Uriah the Hittite to him. Joab did so, and when Uriah arrived, David asked him for news of Joab and the troops and how the campaign was going, and then said to him, 'Go down to your house and wash your feet after your journey.' As he left the palace, a present from the king followed him. Uriah, however, did not return to his house; he lay down by the palace gate with all the king's servants. David, learning that Uriah had not gone home, said to him, 'You have had a long journey; why did you not go home?' Uriah answered, 'Israel and Judah are under canvas, and so is the Ark, and my lord Joab and your majesty's officers are camping in the open; how can I go home to eat and drink and to sleep with my wife? By your life, I cannot do this!' David then said to Uriah, 'Stay here another day, and tomorrow I shall let you go.' So Uriah stayed in Jerusalem that day. On the following day David invited him to eat and drink with him and made him drunk. But in the evening Uriah went out to lie down in his blanket among the king's servants and did not go home.

In the morning David wrote a letter to Joab and sent it with Uriah. In it he wrote, 'Put Uriah opposite the enemy where the fighting is fiercest and then fall back, and leave him to meet his death.' So Joab, during the siege of the city, stationed Uriah at a point where he knew the enemy had expert troops. The men of the city sallied out and engaged Joab, and some of David's guards fell; Uriah the Hittite was also killed. Joab sent David a dispatch with all the news of the battle and gave the messenger these instructions: 'When you have finished your report to the king, he may be angry and ask, "Why did you go so near the city during the fight? You must have known there would be shooting from the wall. Remember who killed Abimelech son of Jerubbesheth. Was it not a woman who threw down an upper millstone on him from the wall of Thebez and killed him? Why did you go near the wall?" – if he asks this, then tell him, "Your servant Uriah the Hittite also is dead."'

The messenger set out and, when he came to David, he made his report as Joab had instructed him. David, angry with Joab, said to the messenger, 'Why did you go so near the city during the fight? You must have known you would be struck down from the wall. Remember who killed Abimelech son of Jerubbesheth. Was it not a woman who threw down an upper millstone on him from the wall of Thebez and killed him? Why did you go near the wall?' He answered, 'The enemy massed against us and sallied out into the open; we drove them back as far as the gateway. There the archers shot down at us from the wall and some of your majesty's men fell; and your servant Uriah the Hittite is dead.' David told the messenger to say this to Joab: 'Do not let the matter distress you – there is no knowing where the sword will strike. Press home your attack on the city, take it, and raze it to the ground'; and to tell him to take heart.

When Uriah's wife heard that her husband was dead, she mourned for him. Once the period of mourning was over, David sent for her and brought her into the palace; she became his wife and bore him a son. But what David had done was wrong in the eyes of the Lord.

The Lord sent Nathan the prophet to David, and when he entered the king's presence, he said, 'In a certain town there lived two men, one rich, the other poor. The rich man had large flocks and herds; the poor man had nothing of his own except one little ewe lamb he had bought. He reared it, and it grew up in his home together with his children. It shared his food, drank from his cup, and nestled in his arms; it was like a daughter to him. One day a traveller came to the rich man's house, and he, too mean to take something from his own flock or herd to serve to his guest, took the poor man's lamb and served that up.'

David was very angry, and burst out, 'As the Lord lives, the man who did this deserves to die! He shall pay for the lamb four times over, because he has done this and shown no pity.'

Nathan said to David, 'You are the man! This is the word of the

Lord the God of Israel to you: I anointed you king over Israel, I rescued you from the power of Saul, I gave you your master's daughter and his wives to be your own, I gave you the daughters of Israel and Judah; and, had this not been enough, I would have added other favours as well. Why then have you flouted the Lord's word by doing what is wrong in my eyes? You have struck down Uriah the Hittite with the sword; the man himself you murdered by the sword of the Ammonites, and you have stolen his wife. Now, therefore, since you have despised me and taken the wife of Uriah the Hittite to be your own wife, your family will never again have rest from the sword. This is the word of the Lord: I shall bring trouble on you from within your own family. I shall take your wives and give them to another man before your eyes, and he will lie with them in broad daylight. What you did was done in secret; but I shall do this in broad daylight for all Israel to see.' David said to Nathan, 'I have sinned against the Lord.' Nathan answered, 'The Lord has laid on another the consequences of your sin: you will not die, but, since by this deed you have shown your contempt for the Lord, the child who will be born to you shall die.'

After Nathan had gone home, the Lord struck the boy whom Uriah's wife had borne to David, and he became very ill. David prayed to God for the child; he fasted and went in and spent the nights lying in sackcloth on the ground. The older men of his household tried to get him to rise, but he refused and would eat no food with them. On the seventh day the child died, and David's servants were afraid to tell him. 'While the boy was alive', they said, 'we spoke to him, and he did not listen to us; how can we now tell him that the boy is dead? He may do something desperate.' David saw his servants whispering among themselves and realized that the boy was dead. He asked, 'Is the child dead?' and they answered, 'Yes, he is dead.'

David then rose from the ground, bathed and anointed himself, and put on fresh clothes; he entered the house of the Lord and prostrated himself there. Afterwards he returned home; he ordered food to be brought and, when it was set before him, ate it. His servants asked him, 'What is this? While the boy lived you fasted and wept for him, but now that he is dead you rise and eat.' 'While the boy was still alive', he answered, 'I fasted and wept, thinking, "It may be that the Lord will be gracious to me, and the boy will live." But now that he is dead, why should I fast? Can I bring him back again? I shall go to him; he will not come back to me.' David consoled Bathsheba his wife; he went to her and had intercourse with her, and she gave birth to a son and called him Solomon.

# THE RAPE OF TAMAR
## 2 Samuel 13:1–22

David's son Absalom had a beautiful sister named Tamar, and David's son Amnon fell in love with her. Amnon was so tormented that he became ill with love for his half-sister; for he thought it an impossible thing to approach her since she was a virgin. But Amnon had a friend, a very shrewd man named Jonadab, son of David's brother Shimeah, and he said to Amnon, 'Why are you, the king's son, so low-spirited morning after morning? Will you not tell me?' Amnon told him that he was in love with Tamar, his brother Absalom's sister. Jonadab said to him, 'Take to your bed and pretend to be ill. When your father comes to visit you, say to him, "Please let my sister Tamar come and give me my food. Let her prepare it in front of me, so that I may watch her and then take it from her own hands."' So Amnon lay down and pretended to be ill. When the king came to visit him, he said, 'Sir, let my sister Tamar come and make a few bread-cakes in front of me, and serve them to me with her own hands.'

David sent a message to Tamar in the palace: 'Go to your brother Amnon's quarters and prepare a meal for him.' Tamar came to her brother and found him lying down. She took some dough, kneaded it, and made cakes in front of him; having baked them, she took the pan and turned them out before him. But Amnon refused to eat and ordered everyone out of the room. When they had all gone, he said to Tamar, 'Bring the food over to the recess so that I may eat from your own hands.' Tamar took the cakes she had made and brought them to Amnon her brother in the recess. When she offered them to him, he caught hold of her and said, 'Sister, come to bed with me.' She answered, 'No, my brother, do not dishonour me. Such things are not done in Israel; do not behave so infamously. Where could I go and hide my disgrace? You would sink as low as the most infamous in Israel. Why not speak to the king for me? He will not refuse you leave to marry me.' But he would not listen; he overpowered and raped her.

Then Amnon was filled with intense revulsion; his revulsion for her was stronger than the love he had felt; he said to her, 'Get up and go.' She answered, 'No, this great wrong, your sending me away, is worse than anything else you have done to me.' He would not listen to her; he summoned the servant who attended him and said, 'Rid me of this woman; put her out and bolt the door after her.' The servant turned her out and bolted the door. She had on a long robe with sleeves, the usual dress of unmarried princesses. Tamar threw ashes over her head, tore the robe that she was wearing, put her hand on her head, and went away, sobbing as she went.

Her brother Absalom asked her, 'Has your brother Amnon been with you? Keep this to yourself; he is your brother. Do not take it to heart.' Forlorn and desolate, Tamar remained in her brother Absalom's house. When King David heard the whole story he was very angry; but he would not hurt Amnon because he was his eldest son and he loved him. Absalom did not speak a single word to Amnon, friendly or unfriendly, but he hated him for having dishonoured his sister Tamar.

## THE DEATH OF AMNON
### 2 Samuel 13:23–39

Two years later Absalom invited all the king's sons to his sheep-shearing at Baal-hazor, near Ephron. He approached the king and said, 'Sir, I am shearing; will your majesty and your servants come?' The king answered, 'No, my son, we must not all come and be a burden to you.' Absalom pressed him, but David was still unwilling to go and dismissed him with his blessing. Absalom said, 'If you will not come, may my brother Amnon come with us?' 'Why should he go with you?' the king asked; but Absalom pressed him again, so he let Amnon and all the other princes go with him.

Absalom prepared a feast fit for a king, and gave this order to his servants: 'Watch your chance, and when Amnon is merry with wine and I say to you, "Strike Amnon," then kill him. You have nothing to fear; these are my orders. Be bold and resolute.' Absalom's servants did to Amnon as Absalom had ordered, whereupon all the king's sons immediately mounted their mules and fled.

While they were on their way, a rumour reached David that Absalom had murdered all the royal princes and that not one was left alive. The king stood up and tore his clothes and then threw himself on the ground; all his servants were standing round him with their clothes torn. Then Jonadab, son of David's brother Shimeah, said, 'My lord must not think that all the young princes have been murdered; only Amnon is dead. Absalom has gone about with a scowl on his face ever since Amnon ravished his sister Tamar. Your majesty must not pay attention to what is no more than a rumour that all the princes are dead; only Amnon is dead.' Absalom meanwhile had made good his escape.

The sentry on duty saw a crowd of people coming down the hill from the direction of Horonaim. He came and reported to the king, 'I see men coming down the hill from Horonaim.' Jonadab said to the king, 'Here come the royal princes, just as I said they would.' As he finished speaking, the princes came in and broke into loud lamentations; the king and all his servants also wept bitterly.

Absalom went to take refuge with Talmai son of Ammihud king of Geshur; and for a long while the king mourned for Amnon. Absalom, having escaped to Geshur, stayed there for three years; and David's heart went out to him with longing, as he became reconciled to the death of Amnon.

## ABSALOM RETURNS TO JERUSALEM
### 2 Samuel 14:1–33

Joab son of Zeruiah saw that the king longed in his heart for Absalom, so he sent for a wise woman from Tekoa and said to her, 'Pretend to be a mourner; put on mourning garb, go without anointing yourself, and behave like a woman who has been bereaved these many days. Then go to the king and repeat what I tell you.' He told her exactly what she was to say.

When the woman from Tekoa came into the king's presence,

she bowed to the ground in homage and cried, 'Help, your majesty!' The king asked, 'What is it?' She answered, 'Sir, I am a widow; my husband is dead. I had two sons; they came to blows out in the country where there was no one to part them, and one struck the other and killed him. Now, sir, the kinsmen have confronted me with the demand, "Hand over the one who killed his brother, so that we can put him to death for taking his brother's life, and so cut off the succession." If they do this, they will stamp out my last live ember and leave my husband without name or descendant on the earth.' 'Go home,' said the king to the woman, 'and I shall settle your case.'

But the woman continued, 'The guilt be on me, your majesty, and on my father's house; let the king and his throne be blameless.' The king said, 'If anyone says anything more to you, bring him to me and he will not trouble you again.' Then the woman went on, 'Let your majesty call upon the Lord your God, to prevent the next-of-kin from doing their worst and destroying my son.' The king swore, 'As the Lord lives, not a hair of your son's head shall fall to the ground.'

The woman then said, 'May I add one word more, your majesty?' 'Say on,' said the king. So she continued, 'How then could it enter your head to do this same wrong to God's people? By the decision you have pronounced, your majesty, you condemn yourself in that you have refused to bring back the one you banished. We shall all die; we shall be like water that is spilt on the ground and lost; but God will spare the man who does not set himself to keep the outlaw in banishment.

'I came to say this to your majesty because the people have threatened me: I thought, "If I can only speak to the king, perhaps he will attend to my case; for he will listen, and he will save me from anyone who is seeking to cut off me and my son together from God's own possession." I thought too that the words of my lord the king would be a comfort to me; for your majesty is like the angel of God and can decide between right and wrong. May the Lord your God be with you!'

The king said to the woman, 'Tell me no lies: I shall now ask you a question.' 'Let your majesty speak,' she said. The king asked, 'Is the hand of Joab behind you in all this?' 'Your life upon it, sir!' she answered. 'When your majesty asks a question, there is no way round it, right or left. Yes, your servant Joab did prompt me; it was he who put the whole story into my mouth. He did it to give a new turn to this affair. Your majesty is as wise as the angel of God and knows all that goes on in the land.'

The king said to Joab, 'You have my consent; go and bring back the young man Absalom.' Then Joab humbly prostrated himself, took leave of the king with a blessing, and said, 'Now I know that I have found favour with your majesty, because you have granted my humble petition.' Joab went at once to Geshur and brought Absalom to Jerusalem. But the king said, 'Let him go to his own quarters; he shall not come into my presence.' So Absalom repaired to his own quarters and did not enter the king's presence.

In all Israel no man was so much admired for his beauty as Absalom; from the crown of his head to the sole of his foot he was without flaw. When he cut his hair (as had to be done every year, for he found it heavy), it weighed two hundred shekels by the royal standard. Three sons were born to Absalom, and a daughter named Tamar, who became a very beautiful woman.

Absalom lived in Jerusalem for two whole years without entering the king's presence. Then he summoned Joab, intending to send a message by him to the king, but Joab refused to come; he sent for him a second time, but he still refused. Absalom said to his servants, 'You know that Joab has a field next to mine with barley growing in it; go and set fire to it.' When Absalom's servants set fire to the field, Joab promptly came to Absalom in his own quarters and demanded, 'Why have your servants set fire to my field?' Absalom answered, 'I had sent for you to come here, so that I could ask you to give the king this message from me: "Why did I leave Geshur? It would be better for me if I were still there. Let me now come into your majesty's presence and, if I have done any wrong, put me to death."' When Joab went to the king and told him, he summoned Absalom, who came and prostrated himself humbly, and the king greeted him with a kiss.

## ABSALOM'S REBELLION
### 2 Samuel 15:1–15

After this Absalom provided himself with a chariot and horses and fifty outrunners. He made it a practice to rise early and stand by the road leading through the city gate, and would hail everyone who had a case to bring before the king for judgment and ask him which town he came from. When he answered, 'I come, sir, from such and such a tribe of Israel,' Absalom would say to him, 'I can see that you have a very good case, but you will get no hearing from the king.' He would add, 'If only I were appointed judge in the land, it would be my business to see that everyone with a lawsuit or a claim got justice from me.' Whenever a man approached to prostrate himself, Absalom would stretch out his hand, take hold of him, and kiss him. By behaving like this to every Israelite who sought justice from the king, Absalom stole the affections of the people.

At the end of four years, Absalom said to the king, 'Give me leave to go to Hebron to fulfil a vow there that I made to the Lord. When I lived at Geshur in Aram, I vowed, "If the Lord brings me back to Jerusalem, I shall worship the Lord in Hebron."' The king answered, 'You may go'; so he set off and went to Hebron.

Absalom sent runners through all the tribes of Israel with this message: 'As soon as you hear the sound of the trumpet, then say, "Absalom has become king in Hebron."' Two hundred men accompanied Absalom from Jerusalem; they were invited as guests and went in all innocence, knowing nothing of the affair. Absalom also sent to summon Ahithophel the Gilonite, David's counsellor, from Giloh his town, where he was offering the customary sacrifices. The conspiracy gathered strength, and Absalom's supporters increased in number.

A messenger brought the news to David that the men of Israel had transferred their allegiance to Absalom. The king said to those who were with him in Jerusalem, 'We must get away at once, or there will be no escape from Absalom for any of us. Make haste, or else he will soon be upon us, bringing disaster and putting the city to the sword.' The king's servants said to him, 'Whatever your majesty thinks best; we are ready.'

## DAVID FLEES FROM JERUSALEM
2 Samuel 15:16 – 16:14

The king set out, and all his household followed him except ten concubines whom he left in charge of the palace.

At the Far House the king and all the people who were with him halted. His own servants then stood at his side, while the Kerethite and Pelethite guards and Ittai with the six hundred Gittites under him marched past the king. The king said to Ittai the Gittite, 'Why should you come with us? Go back and stay with the new king, for you are a foreigner and, what is more, an exile from your own country. You came only yesterday, and must you today be compelled to share my wanderings when I do not know where I am going? Go back home and take your countrymen with you; and may the Lord ever be your steadfast friend.' Ittai answered, 'As the Lord lives, your life upon it, wherever you may be whether for life or death, I, your servant, shall be there.' David said to Ittai, 'It is well, march on!' And Ittai the Gittite marched on with his whole company and all the dependants who were with him. The whole countryside resounded with their weeping. The king remained standing while all the people crossed the wadi of the Kidron before him, by way of the olive tree in the wilderness.

Zadok also was there and all the Levites with him, carrying the Ark of the Covenant of God. They set it down beside Abiathar until all the army had passed out of the city. The king said to Zadok, 'Take the Ark of God back into the city. If I find favour with the Lord, he will bring me back and let me see the Ark and its dwelling-place again. But if he says he does not want me, then here I am; let him do what he pleases with me.' The king went on to say to Zadok the priest, 'Are you not a seer? You may safely go back to the city, you and Abiathar, and take with you the two young men, Ahimaaz your son and Abiathar's son Jonathan. I shall wait at the Fords of the Wilderness until you can send word to me.' Then Zadok and Abiathar took the Ark of God back to Jerusalem and remained there.

David wept as he went up the slope of the mount of Olives; he was bareheaded and went barefoot. The people with him all had their heads uncovered and wept as they went. David had been told that Ahithophel was among the conspirators with Absalom, and he prayed, 'Lord, frustrate the counsel of Ahithophel.'

As David was approaching the top of the ridge where it was the custom to prostrate oneself to God, Hushai the Archite was there to meet him with his tunic torn and dust on his head. David said to him, 'If you come with me you will only be a hindrance; but you can help me to frustrate Ahithophel's plans if you go back to the city and say to Absalom, "I shall be your majesty's servant. In the past I was your father's servant; now I shall be yours." You will have with you, as you know, the priests Zadok and Abiathar; report to them everything that you hear in the royal palace. They have with them Zadok's son Ahimaaz and Abiathar's son Jonathan, and through them you may pass on to me everything you hear.' So Hushai, David's friend, came to the city as Absalom was entering Jerusalem.

When David had moved on a little from the top of the ridge, he was met by Ziba the servant of Mephibosheth, who had with him a pair of donkeys saddled and loaded with two hundred loaves of bread, a hundred clusters of raisins, a hundred bunches of summer fruit, and a skin of wine. The king asked, 'What are you doing with these?' Ziba answered, 'The donkeys are for the king's family to ride on, the bread and the summer fruit are for his servants to eat, and the wine for anyone who becomes exhausted in the wilderness.' The king asked, 'Where is your master's grandson?' 'He is staying in Jerusalem,' said Ziba, 'for he thought that the Israelites might now restore to him his grandfather's kingdom.' The king said to Ziba, 'You shall have everything that belongs to Mephibosheth.' Ziba said, 'I am your humble servant, sir; may I always find favour with your majesty.'

As King David approached Bahurim, a man of Saul's family, whose name was Shimei son of Gera, came out, cursing all the while. He showered stones right and left on David and on all the king's servants and on everyone, soldiers and people alike. With curses Shimei shouted: 'Get out, get out, you murderous scoundrel! The Lord has taken vengeance on you for the blood of the house of Saul whose throne you took, and he has given the kingdom to your son Absalom. You murderer, see how your crimes have overtaken you!'

Abishai son of Zeruiah said to the king, 'Why let this dead dog curse your majesty? I will go across and strike off his head.' But the king said, 'What has this to do with us, you sons of Zeruiah? If he curses because the Lord has told him to curse David, who can question it?' David said to Abishai and to all his servants, 'If my very own son is out to kill me, who can wonder at this Benjamite? Let him be, let him curse; for the Lord has told him to. Perhaps the Lord will mark my sufferings and bestow a blessing on me in place of the curse laid on me this day.' David and his men continued on their way, and Shimei kept abreast along the ridge of the hill parallel to David's path, cursing as he went and hurling stones across the valley at him and covering him with dust. When the king and all the people with him reached the Jordan, they rested there, for they were worn out.

## THE LORD FRUSTRATES
## THE COUNSEL OF AHITHOPHEL
### 2 Samuel 16:15 – 17:23

By now Absalom and all his Israelites had reached Jerusalem, and Ahithophel was with him. When Hushai the Archite, David's Friend, met Absalom he said, 'Long live the king! Long live the king!' But Absalom retorted, 'Is this your loyalty to your friend? Why did you not go with him?' Hushai answered, 'Because I mean to attach myself to the man chosen by the Lord and by this people and by all the men of Israel, and with him I shall stay. After all, whom ought I to serve? Should I not serve the son? I shall serve you as I have served your father.'

Absalom said to Ahithophel, 'Give us your advice: how shall we act?' Ahithophel answered, 'Lie with your father's concubines whom he left in charge of the palace. Then all Israel will come to hear that you have given great cause of offence to your father, and this will confirm the resolution of your followers.' So they set up a tent for Absalom on the roof, and he lay with his father's concubines in the sight of all Israel.

In those days a man would seek counsel of Ahithophel as if he were making an enquiry of the word of God; that was how Ahithophel's counsel was esteemed by both David and Absalom. Ahithophel said to Absalom, 'Let me pick twelve thousand men to go in pursuit of David tonight. If I overtake him when he is tired and dispirited I shall cut him off from his people and they will all scatter; I shall kill no one but the king. I shall bring all the people over to you as a bride is brought to her husband. It is only one man's life that you are seeking; the rest of the people will be unharmed.' Absalom and all the elders of Israel approved of Ahithophel's advice; but Absalom said, 'Now summon Hushai the Archite and let us also hear what he has to say.' When Hushai came, Absalom told him what Ahithophel had said and asked him, 'Shall we do as he advises? If not, speak up.'

Hushai said to Absalom, 'For once the counsel that Ahithophel has given is not good. You know', he went on, 'that your father and the men with him are hardened warriors and savage as a bear in the wilds robbed of her cubs. Your father is an old campaigner and will not spend the night with the main body; even now he will be lying hidden in a pit or in some such place. Then if any of your men are killed at the outset, whoever hears the news will say, "Disaster has overtaken Absalom's followers." The courage of the most resolute and lion-hearted will melt away, for all Israel knows that your father is a man of war and has seasoned warriors with him.

'Here is my advice. Wait until the whole of Israel, from Dan to Beersheba, is gathered about you, countless as grains of sand on the seashore, and then march to battle with them in person. When we come on him somewhere, wherever he may be, and descend on him like dew falling on the ground, not a man of his family or of his followers will be left alive. If he retreats into a town, all Israel will bring ropes to that town, and we shall drag it into a ravine until not a stone can be found on the site.' Absalom and all the Israelites said, 'Hushai the Archite has given us better advice than Ahithophel.' It was the Lord's purpose to frustrate Ahithophel's good advice and so bring disaster on Absalom.

Hushai told Zadok and Abiathar the priests all the advice that Ahithophel had given to Absalom and the elders of Israel, and also what he himself had advised. 'Now send quickly to David', he said, 'and warn him not to spend the night at the Fords of the Wilderness but to cross the river at once, before an overwhelming blow can be launched at the king and his followers.' Jonathan and Ahimaaz were waiting at En-rogel, and a servant-girl used to go and tell them what happened and they would pass it on to King David; for they dared not risk being seen entering the city. But a lad saw them and told Absalom; so the two of them hurried to Bahurim to the house of a man who had a cistern in his courtyard, and they climbed down into it. The man's wife took a covering, spread it over the mouth of the cistern, and scattered grain over it, so that nothing would be noticed.

Absalom's servants came to the house and asked the woman, 'Where are Ahimaaz and Jonathan?' She answered, 'They went past the pool.' The men searched, but not finding them they returned to Jerusalem. As soon as they had gone the two climbed out of the cistern and went off to report to King David. They said to him, 'Get over the water at once, and with all speed!' and they told him Ahithophel's plan against him. So David and all his company began at once to cross the Jordan; by daybreak there was not one who had not reached the other bank.

When Ahithophel saw that his advice had not been taken he saddled his donkey, went straight home to his own town, gave his last instructions to his household, and then hanged himself. So he died and was buried in his father's grave.

## THE DEATH OF ABSALOM
### 2 Samuel 17:24 – 19:4

By the time that Absalom had crossed the Jordan with the Israelites, David was already at Mahanaim. Absalom had appointed Amasa as commander-in-chief in Joab's place; he was the son of a man named Ithra, an Ishmaelite, by Abigal daughter of Nahash and sister to Joab's mother Zeruiah. The Israelites and Absalom camped in the district of Gilead.

When David came to Mahanaim, he was met by Shobi son of Nahash from the Ammonite town Rabbah, Machir son of Ammiel from Lo-debar, and Barzillai the Gileadite from Rogelim, bringing mattresses and blankets, bowls, and jugs. They brought also wheat and barley, flour and roasted grain, beans and lentils, honey and curds, sheep and fat cattle, and offered them to David and his people to eat, knowing that the people must be hungry and thirsty and weary in the wilderness.

David reviewed the troops who were with him, and appointed officers over units of a thousand and of a hundred. He divided his army in three, one division under the command of Joab, one under Joab's brother Abishai son of Zeruiah, and the third under Ittai the Gittite. The king announced to the troops that he himself was coming out with them. But they said, 'No, you must not; if we take to flight, no one will care, nor will they even if half of us are killed; but you are worth ten thousand of us, and it would be better now for you to remain in the town in support.' The king answered, 'I shall do what you think best.' He stood beside the gate, while all the army marched past by hundreds and by thousands, and he gave this order to Joab, Abishai, and Ittai: 'Deal gently with the young man Absalom for my sake.' The whole army heard the king giving each of the officers the order about Absalom.

The army took the field against the Israelites, and a battle was fought in the forest of Ephron. There the Israelites were routed before the onslaught of David's men, and the loss of life was great, for twenty thousand fell. The fighting spread over the whole countryside, and the forest took toll of more people that day than the sword.

Some of David's men caught sight of Absalom; he was riding his mule and, as it passed beneath a large oak, his head was caught in its boughs; he was left in mid-air, while the mule went on from under him. One of the men who saw this told Joab, 'I saw Absalom hanging from an oak.' While the man was telling him, Joab broke in, 'You saw him? Why did you not strike him to the ground then and there? I would have given you ten pieces of silver and a belt.' The man answered, 'If you were to put into my hands a thousand pieces of silver, I would not lift a finger against the king's son; we all heard the king giving orders to you and Abishai and Ittai to take care of the young man Absalom. If I had dealt him a treacherous blow, the king would soon have known, and you would have kept well out of it.' 'That is a lie!' said Joab. 'I will make a start and show you.' He picked up three javelins and drove them into Absalom's chest while he was held fast in the tree and still alive. Then ten young men who were Joab's armour-bearers closed in on Absalom, struck at him, and killed him. Joab sounded the trumpet, and the army came back from the pursuit of Israel, because he had called on them to halt. They took Absalom's body and flung it into a large pit in the forest, and raised over it a great cairn of stones. The Israelites all fled to their homes.

The pillar in the King's Valley had been set up by Absalom in his lifetime, for he said, 'I have no son to carry on my name.' He had named the pillar after himself, and to this day it is called Absalom's Monument.

Ahimaaz son of Zadok said, 'Let me run and take the news to the king that the Lord has avenged him and delivered him from his enemies.' But Joab replied, 'This is no day for you to be the bearer of news. Another day you may have news to carry, but not today, because the king's son is dead.' Joab told a Cushite to go and report to the king what he had seen. The Cushite bowed to Joab and set off running. Ahimaaz pleaded again with Joab, 'Come what may,' he said, 'let me run after the Cushite.' 'Why should you, my son?' asked Joab. 'You will get no reward for your news.' 'Come what may,' he said, 'let me run.' 'Go, then,' said Joab. So Ahimaaz ran by the road through the plain of the Jordan and outstripped the Cushite.

David was sitting between the inner and outer gates and the watchman had gone up to the roof of the gatehouse by the wall of the town. Looking out and seeing a man running alone, the watchman called to the king and told him. 'If he is alone,' said the king, 'then he is bringing news.' The man continued to approach, and then the watchman saw another man running. He called down into the gate, 'Look, there is another man running alone.' The king said, 'He too brings news.' The watchman said, 'I see by the way he runs that the first runner is Ahimaaz son of Zadok.' The king said, 'He is a good man and shall earn the reward for good news.'

Ahimaaz called out to the king, 'All is well!' He bowed low before him and said, 'Blessed be the Lord your God who has given into your hands the men who rebelled against your majesty.' The king asked, 'Is all well with the young man Absalom?' Ahimaaz answered, 'Sir, when your servant Joab sent me, I saw a great commotion, but I did not know what had happened.' The king told him to stand on one side; so he turned aside and waited there.

Then the Cushite came in and said, 'Good news for my lord the king! The Lord has avenged you this day on all those who rebelled against you.' The king said to the Cushite, 'Is all well with the young man Absalom?' The Cushite answered, 'May all the king's enemies and all rebels intent on harming you be as that young man is.' The king was deeply moved and went up to the roof-chamber over the gate and wept, crying out as he went, 'O, my son! Absalom my son, my son Absalom! Would that I had died instead of you! O Absalom, my son, my son.'

Joab was told that the king was weeping and mourning for Absalom; and that day's victory was turned for the whole army into mourning, because the troops heard how the king grieved for his son; they stole into the city like men ashamed to show their faces after fleeing from a battle. The king covered his face and cried aloud, 'My son Absalom; O Absalom, my son, my son.'

## DAVID RETURNS TO JERUSALEM
### 2 Samuel 19:5–43

Joab came into the king's quarters and said to him, 'All your servants, who have saved you and your sons and daughters, your wives and your concubines, you have covered with shame this day by showing love for those who hate you and hate for those who love you. Today you have made it clear to officers and men alike that we are nothing to you; I realize that if Absalom were still alive and all of us dead, you would be content. Now go at once and give your servants some encouragement; if you refuse, I swear by the Lord that by nightfall not a man will remain with you, and that would be a worse disaster than any you have suffered since your earliest days.' At that the king rose and took his seat by the gate; and when the army was told that the king was sitting at the gate, they assembled before him there.

Meanwhile the Israelites had scattered to their homes. Throughout all the tribes of Israel people were discussing it among themselves and saying, 'The king has saved us from our enemies and freed us from the power of the Philistines, and now he has fled the country because of Absalom. But Absalom, whom we anointed king, has fallen in battle; so now why have we no plans for bringing the king back?'

What all Israel was saying came to the king's ears, and he sent word to Zadok and Abiathar the priests: 'Ask the elders of Judah why they should be the last to bring the king back to his palace. Tell them, "You are my brothers, my own flesh and blood; why are you last to bring me back?" And say to Amasa, "You are my own flesh and blood. So help me God, you shall be my commander-in-chief for the rest of your life in place of Joab."' Thus David swayed the hearts of all in

Judah, and one and all they sent to the king, urging him and his men to return.

When on his way back the king reached the Jordan, the men of Judah came to Gilgal to meet him and escort him across the river. Shimei son of Gera the Benjamite from Bahurim hastened down among the men of Judah to meet King David with a thousand men from Benjamin; Ziba was there too, the servant of Saul's family, with his fifteen sons and twenty servants. They rushed into the Jordan under the king's eyes and crossed to and fro conveying his household in order to win his favour. Shimei son of Gera, when he had crossed the river, threw himself down before the king and said, 'I beg your majesty not to remember how disgracefully your servant behaved when your majesty left Jerusalem; do not hold it against me. I humbly acknowledge that I did wrong, and today I am the first of all the house of Joseph to come down to meet your majesty.' Abishai son of Zeruiah objected. 'Ought not Shimei to be put to death', he said, 'because he cursed the Lord's anointed prince?' David answered, 'What right have you, you sons of Zeruiah, to oppose me today? Should anyone be put to death this day in Israel? I know now that I am king of Israel.' The king said to Shimei, 'You shall not die,' and he confirmed it with an oath.

Saul's grandson Mephibosheth also went down to meet the king. He had not bathed his feet, trimmed his beard, or washed his clothes, from the day the king went away until he returned victorious. When he came from Jerusalem to meet the king, David said to him, 'Why did you not go with me, Mephibosheth?' He answered, 'Sir, my servant deceived me; I did intend to harness my donkey and ride with the king, for I am lame, but his stories set your majesty against me. Your majesty is like the angel of God; you must do what you think right. My father's whole family, one and all, deserved to die at your majesty's hands, but you gave me, your servant, my place at your table. What further favour can I expect of the king?' The king answered, 'You have said enough. My decision is that you and Ziba are to share the estate.' Mephibosheth said, 'Let him have it all, now that your majesty has come home victorious.'

Barzillai the Gileadite too had come down from Rogelim, and he went as far as the Jordan with the king to escort him on his way.

Barzillai was very old, eighty years of age; it was he who had provided for the king while he was at Mahanaim, for he was a man of great wealth. The king said to Barzillai, 'Cross over with me and I shall provide for you in my household in Jerusalem.' Barzillai answered, 'Your servant is far too old to go up with your majesty to Jerusalem. I am now eighty years old. I cannot tell what is pleasant and what is not; I cannot taste what I eat or drink; I can no longer listen to the voices of men and women singing. Why should I be a further burden on your majesty? Your servant will attend the king for a short way across the Jordan; and why should the king reward me so handsomely? Let me go back and end my days in my own town near the grave of my father and mother. Here is my son Kimham; let him cross over with your majesty, and do for him what you think best.' The king answered, 'Let Kimham cross with me, and I shall do for him whatever you think best; and I shall do for you whatever you ask.'

All the people crossed the Jordan while the king waited. The king then kissed Barzillai and gave him his blessing. Barzillai returned home; the king crossed to Gilgal, Kimham with him.

The whole army of Judah had escorted the king over the river, as had also half the army of Israel. But the Israelites all kept coming to the king and saying, 'Why should our brothers of Judah have got possession of the king's person by joining King David's own men and then escorting him and his household across the Jordan?' The answer of all the men of Judah to the Israelites was, 'Because his majesty is our near kinsman. Why should you resent it? Have we eaten at the king's expense? Have we received any gifts?' The men of Israel answered, 'We have ten times your interest in the king and, what is more, we are senior to you; why do you disparage us? Were we not the first to speak of bringing the king back?' The men of Judah used language even fiercer than the men of Israel.

## SHEBA'S REBELLION
### 2 Samuel 20:1–22

A scoundrel named Sheba son of Bichri, a man of Benjamin, happened to be there. He sounded the trumpet and cried out:

'We have no share in David,
no lot in the son of Jesse.
Every man to his tent, O Israel!'

All the men of Israel deserted David to follow Sheba son of Bichri, but
the men of Judah stood by their king and followed him from the
Jordan to Jerusalem.

When David went up to his palace in Jerusalem he took the ten
concubines whom he had left in charge of the palace and put them in
a house under guard; he maintained them but did not have
intercourse with them. They were kept in seclusion, living as if they
were widows until the day of their death.

The king said to Amasa, 'Call up the men of Judah and appear
before me again in three days' time.' Amasa went to call up the men
of Judah, but he took longer than the time fixed by the king. David
said to Abishai, 'Sheba son of Bichri will give us more trouble than
Absalom; take the royal bodyguard and follow him closely in case he
occupies some fortified cities and escapes us.' Joab, along with the
Kerethite and Pelethite guards and all the fighting men, marched out
behind Abishai, and left Jerusalem in pursuit of Sheba son of Bichri.

When they reached the great stone in Gibeon, Amasa came to
meet them. Joab was wearing his tunic and over it a belt supporting a
sword in its scabbard. He came forward, concealing his treachery, and
said to Amasa, 'I hope you are well, my brother,' and with his right
hand he grasped Amasa's beard to kiss him. Amasa was not on his
guard against the sword in Joab's hand. Joab struck him with it in the
belly and his entrails poured out to the ground; he did not have to
strike a second blow, for Amasa was dead. Joab with his brother
Abishai went on in pursuit of Sheba son of Bichri. One of Joab's men
stood over Amasa and called out, 'Follow Joab, all who are for Joab
and for David!' Amasa's body lay soaked in blood in the middle of the
road, and when the man saw how all the people stopped, he rolled
him off the road into the field and threw a cloak over him; for
everyone who came by stopped at the sight of the body. When it had
been removed from the road, they all went on and followed Joab in
pursuit of Sheba son of Bichri.

Sheba passed through all the tribes of Israel until he came to

Abel-beth-maacah, and all the clan of Bichri rallied to him and followed him into the city. Joab's forces came up and besieged him in Abel-beth-maacah, raised a siege-ramp against it, and began undermining the wall to bring it down. Then a wise woman stood on the rampart and called from the city, 'Listen, listen! Tell Joab to come here and let me speak with him.' When he came forward the woman said, 'Are you Joab?' He answered, 'I am.' 'Listen to what I have to say, sir,' she said. 'I am listening,' he replied. 'In the old days', she went on, 'there was a saying, "Go to Abel for the answer," and that settled the matter. My town is known to be one of the most peaceable and loyal in Israel; she is like a watchful mother in Israel, and you are seeking to kill her. Would you destroy the Lord's own possession?' Joab answered, 'God forbid, far be it from me to ruin or destroy! That is not our aim; but a man from the hill-country of Ephraim named Sheba son of Bichri has raised a revolt against King David. Surrender this one man, and I shall retire from the city.' The woman said to Joab, 'His head will be thrown over the wall to you.' Then the woman went to the people, who, persuaded by her wisdom, cut off Sheba's head and threw it to Joab. He then sounded the trumpet, and the whole army withdrew from the town; they dispersed to their homes, while Joab went back to the king in Jerusalem.

## THE GIBEONITES' REVENGE
## ON THE HOUSE OF SAUL
2 Samuel 21:1–14

In David's reign there was a famine that lasted for three successive years. David consulted the Lord, who answered, 'Blood-guilt rests on Saul and on his family because he put the Gibeonites to death.' (The Gibeonites were not of Israelite descent; they were a remnant of Amorite stock whom the Israelites had sworn that they would spare. Saul, however, in his zeal for Israel and Judah had sought to exterminate them.) King David summoned the Gibeonites, therefore, and said to them, 'What can be done for you? How can I make expiation, so that you may have cause to bless the Lord's own people?' The Gibeonites answered, 'Our feud with Saul and his family cannot be settled in silver or gold, and there is no other man in Israel whose death would content us.' 'Then what do you want me to do for you?' asked David. They answered, 'Let us make an end of the man who caused our undoing and ruined us, so that he will never again have his place within the borders of Israel. Hand over to us seven of that man's descendants, and we shall hurl them down to their death before the Lord in Gibeah of Saul, the Lord's chosen one.' The king agreed to hand them over. He spared Mephibosheth son of Jonathan, son of Saul, because of the oath that had been taken in the Lord's name by David and Saul's son Jonathan, but the king took the two sons whom Rizpah daughter of Aiah had borne to Saul, Armoni and Mephibosheth, and the five sons whom Merab, Saul's daughter, had borne to Adriel son of Barzillai of Meholah. He handed them over to the Gibeonites, and they flung them down from the mountain before the Lord; the seven of them fell together. They were put to death in the first days of harvest at the beginning of the barley harvest.

Rizpah daughter of Aiah took sackcloth and spread it out as a bed for herself on the rock, from the beginning of harvest until the rains came and fell from the heavens on the bodies. She kept the birds away from them by day and the wild beasts by night. When David was told what Rizpah the concubine of Saul had done, he went and got the bones of Saul and his son Jonathan from the citizens of Jabesh-gilead, who had carried them off from the public square at Beth-shan, where the Philistines had hung them on the day they defeated Saul at Gilboa. He removed the bones of Saul and Jonathan from there and gathered up the bones of the men who had been hurled to death. They buried the bones of Saul and his son Jonathan at Zela in Benjamin, in the grave of his father Kish. Everything was done as the king ordered, and thereafter the Lord was willing to accept prayers offered for the country.

## DAVID TAKES A CENSUS
### 2 Samuel 24:1–25

Once again the Israelites felt the Lord's anger, when he incited David against them and instructed him to take a census of Israel and Judah.

The king commanded Joab and the officers of the army with him to go round all the tribes of Israel, from Dan to Beersheba, and make a record of the people and report back the number to him. Joab answered, 'Even if the Lord your God should increase the people a hundredfold and your majesty should live to see it, what pleasure would that give your majesty?' But Joab and the officers, being overruled by the king, left his presence in order to take the census.

They crossed the Jordan and began at Aroer and the town at the wadi, proceeding towards Gad and Jazer. They came to Gilead and to the land of the Hittites, to Kadesh, and then to Dan and Iyyon and so round towards Sidon. They went as far as the walled city of Tyre and all the towns of the Hivites and Canaanites, and then went on to the Negeb of Judah at Beersheba. They covered the whole country and arrived back at Jerusalem after nine months and twenty days. Joab reported to the king the numbers recorded: the number of able-bodied men, capable of bearing arms, was eight hundred thousand in Israel and five hundred thousand in Judah.

After he had taken the census, David was overcome with remorse, and said to the Lord, 'I have acted very wickedly: I pray you, Lord, remove your servant's guilt, for I have been very foolish.' When he rose next morning, the command of the Lord had come to the prophet Gad, David's seer, to go and tell David: 'This is the word of the Lord: I offer you three things; choose one and I shall bring it upon you.' Gad came to David and reported this to him and said, 'Is it to be three years of famine in your land, or three months of flight with the enemy in close pursuit, or three days of pestilence in your land? Consider carefully now what answer I am to take back to him who sent me.' David said to Gad, 'This is a desperate plight I am in; let us fall into the hands of the Lord, for his mercy is great; and let me not fall into the hands of men.'

The Lord sent a pestilence throughout Israel from the morning till the end of the appointed time; from Dan to Beersheba seventy thousand of the people died. The angel stretched out his arm towards Jerusalem to destroy it; but the Lord repented of the evil and said to the angel who was destroying the people, 'Enough! Stay your hand.' At that moment the angel of the Lord was at the threshing-floor of Araunah the Jebusite.

When David saw the angel who was striking down the people, he said to the Lord, 'It is I who have sinned, I who committed the wrong; but these poor sheep, what have they done? Let your hand fall on me and on my family.'

Gad came to David that day and said, 'Go and set up an altar to the Lord on the threshing-floor of Araunah the Jebusite.' David obeyed Gad's instructions, and went up as the Lord had commanded. When Araunah looked down and saw the king and his servants coming towards him, he went out and, prostrating himself before the king, said, 'Why has your majesty come to visit his servant?' David answered, 'To buy the threshing-floor from you so that I may build an altar to the Lord, and the plague which has attacked the people may be stopped.' Araunah answered, 'I beg your majesty to take it and sacrifice what you think fit. See, here are the oxen for the whole-offering, and the threshing-sledges and the ox-yokes for fuel.' Araunah gave it all to the king for his own use and said to him, 'May the Lord your God accept you.' But the king said to Araunah, 'No, I shall buy it from you; I am not going to offer up to the Lord my God whole-offerings that have cost me nothing.' So David bought the threshing-floor and the oxen for fifty shekels of silver. He built an altar to the Lord there and offered whole-offerings and shared-offerings. Then the Lord yielded to his prayer for the land, and the plague in Israel stopped.

## ADONIJAH CLAIMS THE THRONE
### 1 Kings 1:1–37

King David was now a very old man, and, though they wrapped clothes round him, he could not keep warm. His attendants said to him, 'Let us find a young virgin for your majesty, to attend you and take care of you; and let her lie in your arms, sir, and make you warm.' After searching throughout Israel for a beautiful maiden, they found Abishag, a Shunammite, and brought her to the king. She was a very beautiful girl. She took care of the king and waited on him, but he did not have intercourse with her.

Adonijah, whose mother was Haggith, was boasting that he was to be king. He provided himself with chariots and horses and fifty outrunners. His father never corrected him or asked why he behaved as he did. He was next in age to Absalom, and was a very handsome man too. He took counsel with Joab son of Zeruiah and with Abiathar the priest, and they assured him of their support; but Zadok the priest, Benaiah son of Jehoiada, Nathan the prophet, Shimei, Rei, and David's bodyguard of heroes did not take his side. Adonijah then held a sacrifice of sheep, oxen, and buffaloes at the stone Zoheleth beside En-rogel; he invited all his royal brothers and all those officers of the household who were of the tribe of Judah, but he did not invite Nathan the prophet, Benaiah and the bodyguard, or Solomon his brother.

Nathan said to Bathsheba, Solomon's mother, 'Have you not heard that Adonijah son of Haggith has become king, without the knowledge of our lord David? Now come, let me advise you what to do for your own safety and for the safety of your son Solomon. Go in at once to the king and say to him, "Did not your majesty swear to me, your servant, that my son Solomon should succeed you as king, and that it was he who should sit on your throne? Why then has Adonijah become king?" While you are still there speaking to the king, I shall come in after you and confirm your words.'

Bathsheba went to the king in his private chamber; he was now very old, and Abishag the Shunammite was waiting on him. Bathsheba bowed before the king and did obeisance. 'What is your request?' asked the king. She answered, 'My lord, you yourself swore to me your servant, by the Lord your God, that my son Solomon should succeed you as king and sit on your throne. But now, here is Adonijah become king, all unknown to your majesty. He has sacrificed great numbers of oxen, buffaloes, and sheep, and has invited to the feast all the king's sons, with Abiathar the priest and Joab the commander-in-chief, but he has not invited your servant Solomon. Your majesty, all Israel is now looking to you to announce your successor on the throne. Otherwise, when you, sir, rest with your forefathers, my son Solomon and I will be treated as criminals.'

Bathsheba was still addressing the king when Nathan the prophet arrived. The king was informed that Nathan was there; he came into the king's presence and prostrated himself. 'My lord,' he said, 'has your majesty declared that Adonijah should succeed you and sit on your throne? He has today gone down and sacrificed great numbers of oxen, buffaloes, and sheep, and has invited to the feast all the king's sons, the commanders of the army, and Abiathar the priest; and at this very moment they are eating and drinking in his presence and shouting, "Long live King Adonijah!" But he has not invited me your servant, Zadok the priest, Benaiah son of Jehoiada, or your servant Solomon. Has this been done by your majesty's authority? You have not told us your servants who should succeed you on the throne.'

King David said, 'Call Bathsheba,' and when she came into his presence and stood before him, the king swore an oath to her: 'As the Lord lives, who has delivered me from all my troubles, I swore by the Lord the God of Israel that Solomon your son should succeed me and that he should sit on my throne; this day I give effect to my oath.' Bathsheba bowed low to the king, did obeisance, and said, 'May my lord King David live for ever!'

King David said, 'Summon Zadok the priest, Nathan the prophet, and Benaiah son of Jehoiada,' and, when they came into the king's presence, he gave them this order: 'Take the officers of the household with you; mount my son Solomon on the king's mule and escort him down to Gihon. There let Zadok the priest and Nathan the prophet anoint him king over Israel. Then sound the trumpet and shout, "Long live King Solomon!' When you escort him home again let him come and sit on my throne and reign in my place; for he is the man that I have designated to be prince over Israel and Judah.' Benaiah son of Jehoiada answered the king, 'It will be done. And may the Lord, the God of my lord the king, confirm it! As the Lord has been with your majesty, so may he be with Solomon; may he make his throne even greater than the throne of my lord King David.'

## ZADOK THE PRIEST ANOINTS THE NEW KING
1Kings 1:38–53

Zadok the priest, Nathan the prophet, and Benaiah son of Jehoiada, together with the Kerethite and Pelethite guards, went down and, mounting Solomon on King David's mule, they escorted him to Gihon. Zadok the priest took the horn of oil from the Tent of the Lord and anointed Solomon; they sounded the trumpet and all the people shouted, 'Long live King Solomon!' Then all the people escorted him home in procession, with great rejoicing and playing of pipes, so that the very earth split with the noise.

Adonijah and his guests had just finished their banquet when the noise reached their ears. On hearing the sound of the trumpet, Joab exclaimed, 'What is the meaning of this uproar in the city?' Even as he was speaking, Jonathan son of Abiathar the priest arrived. 'Come in,' said Adonijah. 'You are an honourable man and must be a bringer of good news.''Far from it,' Jonathan replied; 'our lord King David has made Solomon king. He has sent with him Zadok the priest, Nathan the prophet, and Benaiah son of Jehoiada, together with the Kerethite and Pelethite guards, and they have mounted Solomon on the king's mule, and Zadok the priest and Nathan the prophet have anointed him king at Gihon. They have now escorted him home rejoicing, and the city is in an uproar. That was the noise you heard. More than that, Solomon has taken his seat on the royal throne. Yes, and the officers of the household have been to our lord, King David, and greeted him in this fashion: "May your God make the name of Solomon your son more famous than your own and his throne even greater than yours," and the king bowed upon his couch. What is more, he said this: "Blessed be the Lord the God of Israel who has set a successor on my throne this day while I am still alive to see it."'

Adonijah's guests all rose in panic and dispersed. Adonijah himself, in fear of Solomon, went at once to the altar and grasped hold of its horns. A message was sent to Solomon: 'Adonijah, in his fear of King Solomon, is clinging to the horns of the altar; he says, "Let King Solomon swear to me here and now that he will not put his servant to the sword."' Solomon said, 'If he proves himself an honourable man, not a hair of his head will fall to the ground; but if he is found making trouble, he must die.' Then King Solomon sent and had him brought down from the altar. He came in and prostrated himself before the king, and Solomon said to him, 'Go to your house.'

# THE LAST WORDS OF DAVID

1 Kings 2:1–9, 1 Chronicles 29:10–14, 19–20, 1 Kings 2:10–12

As the time of David's death drew near, he gave this charge to his son Solomon: 'I am about to go the way of all the earth. Be strong and show yourself a man. Fulfil your duty to the Lord your God; conform to his ways, observe his statutes and his commandments, his judgments and his solemn precepts, as they are written in the law of Moses, so that you may prosper in whatever you do and whichever way you turn, and that the Lord may fulfil this promise that he made about me: "If your descendants are careful to walk faithfully in my sight with all their heart and with all their soul, you shall never lack a successor on the throne of Israel."

'You know how Joab son of Zeruiah treated me and what he did to two commanders-in-chief in Israel, Abner son of Ner and Amasa son of Jether. He killed them both, breaking the peace by bloody acts of war; and with that blood he stained the belt about his waist and the sandals on his feet. Act as your wisdom prompts you, and do not let his grey hairs go down to the grave in peace. Show constant friendship to the family of Barzillai of Gilead; let them have their place at your table; they rallied to me when I was a fugitive from your brother Absalom. Do not forget Shimei son of Gera, the Benjamite from Bahurim, who cursed me bitterly the day I went to Mahanaim. True, he came down to meet me at the Jordan, and I swore by the Lord that I would not put him to death. But you do not need to let him go unpunished now; you are a wise man and will know how to deal with him; bring down his grey hairs in blood to the grave.'...

David blessed the Lord in the presence of all the assembly, saying:

'Blessed are you, Lord God of our father Israel,
from of old and for ever.
Yours, Lord, is the greatness and the power,
the glory, the splendour, and the majesty;
for everything in heaven and on earth is yours;
yours, Lord, is the sovereignty,
and you are exalted over all as head.

Wealth and honour come from you; you rule over all;
might and power are of your disposing;
yours it is to give power and strength to all.
Now, our God, we give you thanks
and praise your glorious name.

'But who am I, and who are my people, that we should be able to give willingly like this? For everything comes from you, and it is only of your gifts that we give to you... Grant that Solomon my son may loyally keep your commandments, your solemn charge, and your statutes, that he may fulfil them all, and build the palace for which I have made provision.'

Turning to the whole assembly, David said, 'Now bless the Lord your God.' Then all the assembly blessed the Lord the God of their forefathers, bowing low and prostrating themselves before the Lord and the king...

So David rested with his forefathers and was buried in the city of David, having reigned over Israel for forty years, seven in Hebron and thirty-three in Jerusalem; and Solomon succeeded his father David as king and was firmly established on the throne.

# Part Three

# The Golden Age of Solomon

## SOLOMON SECURES THE THRONE
### 1 Kings 2:13–46

Adonijah son of Haggith came to Bathsheba, Solomon's mother. 'Do you come as a friend?' she asked. 'As a friend,' he answered; 'I have something to discuss with you.' 'Tell me,' she said. 'You know', he went on, 'that the throne was mine and that all Israel was looking to me to be king; but I was passed over and the throne has gone to my brother; it was his by the will of the Lord. Now I have one request to make of you; do not refuse me.' 'What is it?' she said. He answered, 'Will you ask King Solomon (he will never refuse you) to give me Abishag the Shunammite in marriage?' 'Very well,' said Bathsheba, 'I shall speak to the king on your behalf.'

When Bathsheba went in to King Solomon to speak for Adonijah, the king rose to meet her and do obeisance to her. Then he seated himself on his throne, and a throne was set for the king's mother at his right hand. She said, 'I have one small request to make of you; do not refuse me.' 'What is it, mother?' he replied. 'I will not refuse you.' 'It is this,' she said, 'that Abishag the Shunammite be given in marriage to your brother Adonijah.' At that King Solomon answered, 'Why do you ask that Abishag the Shunammite be given to Adonijah? You might as well ask the kingdom for him; he is my elder brother and has both Abiathar the priest and Joab son of Zeruiah on his side.' Then he swore by the Lord: 'So help me God, Adonijah must pay for this with his life. As the Lord lives, who has established me and set me on the throne of David my father and has founded a house for me as he promised, this very day Adonijah must be put to death!' King Solomon sent Benaiah son of Jehoiada with orders to strike him down; so Adonijah died.

Abiathar the priest was told by the king to go to Anathoth to his estate. 'You deserve to die,' he said, 'but in spite of this day's work I shall not put you to death, for you carried the Ark of the Lord God before my father David, and you shared in all the hardships he endured.' Solomon deposed Abiathar from his office as priest of the Lord, so fulfilling the sentence pronounced by the Lord against the house of Eli in Shiloh.

When news of all this reached Joab, he fled to the Tent of the Lord and laid hold of the horns of the altar; for he had sided with Adonijah, though not with Absalom. When King Solomon was told that Joab had fled to the Tent of the Lord and was beside the altar, he sent Benaiah son of Jehoiada with orders to strike him down. Benaiah came to the Tent of the Lord and ordered Joab in the king's name to come away. But he said, 'No, I will die here.' Benaiah reported Joab's answer to the king, and the king said, 'Let him have his way; strike him down and bury him, and so rid me and my father's house of the guilt for the blood that he wantonly shed. The Lord will hold him responsible for his own death, because he struck down two innocent men who were better men than he, Abner son of Ner, commander of the army of Israel, and Amasa son of Jether, commander of the army of Judah, and ran them through with the sword, without my father David's knowledge. Let the guilt of their blood recoil on Joab and his descendants for all time; but may David and his descendants, his house and his throne, enjoy perpetual prosperity from the Lord.' Benaiah son of Jehoiada went up to the altar and struck Joab down and killed him, and he was buried at his house out in the country. The king appointed Benaiah to command the army in place of Joab, and installed Zadok the priest in the place of Abiathar.

Next the king sent for Shimei and said to him, 'Build yourself a house in Jerusalem and stay there; you are not to leave the city for any other place. If ever you leave and cross the wadi Kidron, know for certain that you will die. Your blood will be on your own head.' Shimei replied, 'I accept your sentence; I shall do as your majesty commands.'

For a long time Shimei remained in Jerusalem. But when three years later two of his slaves ran away to Achish son of Maacah, king of Gath, and this was reported to Shimei, he at once saddled his donkey and went to Achish in search of his slaves; he reached Gath and brought them back. When King Solomon was informed that Shimei had gone from Jerusalem to Gath and back, he sent for him and said, 'Did I not require you to swear by the Lord? Did I not give you this solemn warning: "If ever you leave this city for any other place, know for certain that you will die"? You said, "I accept your sentence; I shall obey." Why then have you not kept the oath which you swore by the Lord, and the order which I gave you? Shimei, you know in your heart what mischief you did to my father David; the Lord is now making that mischief recoil on your own head. But King Solomon is blessed, and the throne of David will be secure before the Lord for all time.' The king then gave orders to Benaiah son of Jehoiada, who went out and struck Shimei down, and he died. Thus Solomon's royal power was securely established.

## SOLOMON ASKS FOR WISDOM
1 Kings 3:1–15

Solomon allied himself to Pharaoh king of Egypt by marrying his daughter. He brought her to the City of David, until he had finished building his palace and the house of the Lord and the wall round Jerusalem. The people however continued to sacrifice at the shrines, for up to that time no house had been built for the name of the Lord. Solomon himself loved the Lord, conforming to the precepts laid down by his father David; but he too slaughtered and burnt sacrifices at the shrines.

The king went to Gibeon to offer a sacrifice, for that was the chief shrine, where he used to offer a thousand whole-offerings on the altar. That night the Lord appeared to Solomon there in a dream. God said, 'What shall I give you? Tell me.' He answered, 'You have shown great and constant love to your servant David my father, because he walked before you in loyalty, righteousness, and integrity of heart; and you have maintained this great and constant love towards him and now you have given him a son to succeed him on the throne.

'Now, Lord my God, you have made your servant king in place of my father David, though I am a mere child, unskilled in leadership. Here I am in the midst of your people, the people of your choice, too many to be numbered or counted. Grant your servant, therefore, a heart with skill to listen, so that he may govern your people justly and distinguish good from evil. Otherwise who is equal to the task of governing this great people of yours?'

The Lord was well pleased that this was what Solomon had asked for, and God said, 'Because you have asked for this, and not for long life, or for wealth, or for the lives of your enemies, but have asked for discernment in administering justice, I grant your request; I give you a heart so wise and so understanding that there has been none like you before your time, nor will there be after you. What is more, I give you those things for which you did not ask, such wealth and glory as no king of your time can match. If you conform to my ways and observe my ordinances and commandments, as your father David did, I will also give you long life.' Then Solomon awoke, and realized it was a dream.

Solomon came to Jerusalem and stood before the Ark of the Covenant of the Lord, where he sacrificed whole-offerings and brought shared-offerings, and gave a banquet for all his household.

## THE JUDGMENT OF SOLOMON
### 1 Kings 3:16–28

Two women who were prostitutes approached the king at that time, and as they stood before him one said, 'My lord, this woman and I share a house, and I gave birth to a child when she was there with me. On the third day after my baby was born she too gave birth to a child. We were alone; no one else was with us in the house; only the two of us were there. During the night this woman's child died because she lay on it, and she got up in the middle of the night, took my baby from my side while I, your servant, was asleep, and laid it on her bosom, putting her dead child on mine. When I got up in the morning to feed my baby, I found him dead; but when I looked at him closely, I found that it was not the child that I had borne.' The other woman broke in, 'No, the living child is mine; yours is the dead one,' while the first insisted, 'No, the dead child is yours; mine is the living one.' So they went on arguing before the king.

The king thought to himself, 'One of them says, "This is my child, the living one; yours is the dead one." The other says, "No, it is your child that is dead and mine that is alive."' Then he said, 'Fetch me a sword.' When a sword was brought, the king gave the order: 'Cut the living child in two and give half to one woman and half to the other.' At this the woman who was the mother of the living child, moved with love for her child, said to the king, 'Oh, sir, let her have the baby! Whatever you do, do not kill it.' The other said, 'Let neither of us have it; cut it in two.' The king then spoke up: 'Give the living baby to the first woman,' he said; 'do not kill it. She is its mother.' When Israel heard the judgment which the king had given, they all stood in awe of him; for they saw that he possessed wisdom from God for administering justice.

## SOLOMON'S WEALTH AND FAME
### 1 Kings 4:20–34

The people of Judah and Israel were countless as the sands of the sea; they ate and drank and enjoyed life. Solomon ruled over all the kingdoms from the river Euphrates to Philistia and as far as the frontier of Egypt; they paid tribute and were subject to him all his life.

Solomon's provisions for one day were thirty kor of flour and sixty kor of meal, ten fat oxen and twenty oxen from the pastures and a hundred sheep, as well as stags, gazelles, roebucks, and fattened fowl. For he was paramount over all the region west of the Euphrates from Tiphsah to Gaza, ruling all the kings west of the river; and he enjoyed peace on all sides. All through his reign the people of Judah and Israel lived in peace, everyone from Dan to Beersheba under his own vine and his own fig tree.

Solomon had forty thousand chariot-horses in his stables and twelve thousand cavalry horses.

The regional governors, each for a month in turn, supplied provisions for King Solomon and all who came to his table; they never fell short in their deliveries. They provided also barley and straw, each according to his duty, for the horses and chariot-horses where it was required.

God gave Solomon deep wisdom and insight, and understanding as wide as the sand on the seashore, so that Solomon's wisdom surpassed that of all the men of the east and of all Egypt. For he was wiser than any man, wiser than Ethan the Ezrahite, and Heman, Calcol, and Darda, the sons of Mahol; his fame spread among all the surrounding nations. He propounded three thousand proverbs, and his songs numbered a thousand and five. He discoursed of trees, from the cedar of Lebanon down to the marjoram that grows out of the wall, of beasts and birds, of reptiles and fish. People of all races came to listen to the wisdom of Solomon, and he received gifts from all the kings in the world who had heard of his wisdom.

## SOLOMON BUILDS THE TEMPLE
2 Chronicles 2:1 – 3:17, 4:19–22

Solomon resolved to build a house for the name of the Lord and a royal palace for himself. He engaged seventy thousand bearers and eighty thousand quarrymen, and three thousand six hundred men to superintend them. He sent this message to King Huram of Tyre: 'You were so good as to send my father David cedar-wood to build his royal residence. Now I am about to build a house for the name of the Lord my God and to consecrate it to him, so that I may burn fragrant incense in it before him, and present the rows of the Bread of the Presence regularly, and whole-offerings morning and evening, on the sabbaths and at the new moons and appointed festivals of the Lord our God; for this is a duty laid on Israel for ever. The house I am about to build must be great, because our God is greater than all gods. But who is able to build a house for him when heaven itself, the highest heaven, cannot contain him? Who am I that I should build him a house, except to burn sacrifices before him? Send me now a skilled craftsman, one able to work in gold and silver, bronze, and iron, and in purple, crimson, and violet yarn, one who is also an expert engraver and will work in Judah and in Jerusalem with my skilled workmen who were provided by David my father. Send me also cedar, pine, and algum timber from Lebanon, for I know that your men are expert at felling the trees of Lebanon; my men will work with yours to get an ample supply of timber ready for me, for the house which I shall build will be great and wonderful. I shall supply provisions for your servants, the woodmen who fell the trees: twenty thousand kor of wheat and twenty thousand kor of barley, with twenty thousand bath of wine and twenty thousand bath of oil.'

King Huram of Tyre sent this letter in reply: 'It is because of the love which the Lord has for his people that he has made you king over them.' The letter continued, 'Blessed be the Lord the God of Israel, maker of heaven and earth, who has given to King David a wise son, endowed with insight and understanding, to build a house for the Lord and a royal palace for himself.

'I now send you my expert Huram, a skilful and experienced craftsman. He is the son of a Danite woman and a Tyrian father; he is an experienced worker in gold and silver, bronze and iron, stone and wood, as well as in purple, violet, and crimson yarn, and in fine linen; he is also a trained engraver who will be able to work with your own skilled craftsmen and those of my lord David your father, to any design submitted to him. Now let my lord send his servants the wheat and the barley, the oil and the wine, which he promised; we shall fell all the timber in Lebanon that you need and float it as rafts to the roadstead at Joppa; you can convey it up to Jerusalem.'

Solomon took a census of all the aliens resident in Israel, similar to the census which David his father had taken; these were found to be a hundred and fifty-three thousand six hundred. He made seventy thousand of them bearers, and eighty thousand quarrymen, and three thousand six hundred superintendents to make the people work.

Then Solomon began to build the house of the Lord in Jerusalem on Mount Moriah, where the Lord had appeared to his father David; it was the site which David had prepared on the threshing-floor of Ornan the Jebusite. He began to build in the second month of the fourth year of his reign. These are the foundations which Solomon laid for building the house of God: according to the old standard of measurement the length was sixty cubits and the breadth twenty. The vestibule in front of the house was twenty cubits long, spanning the whole breadth of the house, and its height was twenty; on the inside he overlaid it with pure gold. He panelled the large chamber with pine, covered it with fine gold, and carved on it palm trees and chain-work. He adorned the house with precious stones for decoration and with gold from Parvaim. He overlaid the whole house with gold, its rafters and frames, its walls and doors; and he carved cherubim on the walls.

He made the Most Holy Place twenty cubits long, corresponding to the breadth of the house, and twenty cubits broad. He overlaid it all with six hundred talents of fine gold, and the weight of the gold nails was fifty shekels. He also covered the upper chambers with gold.

In the Most Holy Place he carved two images of cherubim and overlaid them with gold. The total span of the wings of the cherubim was twenty cubits. A wing of one cherub extended five cubits to touch the wall of the house, while its other wing reached out five cubits to meet a wing of the other cherub. Similarly, a wing of the second cherub extended five cubits to touch the other wall of the house, while its other wing met a wing of the first cherub. The wings of these cherubim extended twenty cubits; they stood with their feet on the ground, facing the outer chamber. He made the veil of violet, purple, and crimson yarn, and fine linen, and embroidered cherubim on it.

In front of the house he erected two pillars eighteen cubits high, with a capital five cubits high on top of each. He made chain-work like a necklace and set it round the tops of the pillars, and he carved a hundred pomegranates and set them in the chain-work. He erected the pillars in front of the temple, one on the right and one on the left; the one on the right he named Jachin and the one on the left Boaz...

Solomon made also all the furnishings for the house of God: the golden altar, the tables upon which was set the Bread of the Presence, the lampstands of red gold whose lamps burned before the inner shrine in the prescribed manner, the flowers, lamps, and tongs of solid gold, the snuffers, tossing-bowls, saucers, and firepans of red gold, and, at the entrance to the house, the inner doors leading to the Most Holy Place and those leading to the sanctuary, of gold.

## THE COMPLETION OF THE TEMPLE
2 Chronicles 5:1–14

When all the work which Solomon did for the house of the Lord was completed, he brought in the treasures dedicated by his father David, the silver, the gold, and the vessels, and deposited them in the treasuries of the house of God.

Then Solomon summoned the elders of Israel, and all the heads of the tribes who were chiefs of families in Israel, to assemble in Jerusalem, in order to bring up the Ark of the Covenant of the Lord from the City of David, which is called Zion. All the men of Israel were assembled in the king's presence at the pilgrim-feast in the seventh month. When the elders of Israel had all arrived, the Levites lifted the Ark and carried it up; the Tent of Meeting and all the sacred furnishings of the Tent were carried by the priests and the Levites. King Solomon and the whole congregation of Israel assembled with him before the Ark sacrificed sheep and oxen in numbers past counting or reckoning.

The priests brought in the Ark of the Covenant of the Lord to its place, in the inner shrine of the house, the Most Holy Place, beneath the wings of the cherubim. The cherubim, whose wings were spread over the place of the Ark, formed a canopy above the Ark and its poles. The poles projected, and their ends were visible from the Holy Place immediately in front of the inner shrine, but from nowhere else outside; they are there to this day. There was nothing inside the Ark but the two tablets which Moses had put there at Horeb, when the Lord made the covenant with the Israelites after they left Egypt.

When the priests came out of the Holy Place (for all the priests who were present had hallowed themselves without keeping to their divisions), all the levitical singers, Asaph, Heman, and Jeduthun, their sons, and their kinsmen, attired in fine linen, stood with cymbals, lutes, and lyres to the east of the altar, together with a hundred and twenty priests who blew trumpets. Now the trumpeters and the singers joined in unison to sound forth praise and thanksgiving to the Lord, and the song was raised with trumpets, cymbals, and musical instruments, in praise of the Lord, because 'it is good, for his love endures for ever'; and the house was filled with the cloud of the glory of the Lord. The priests could not continue to minister because of the cloud, for the glory of the Lord filled the house of God.

## SOLOMON'S PRAYER OF DEDICATION
2 Chronicles 6:1–3, 13–23, 36 – 7:10

Then Solomon said:

> 'The Lord has caused the sun to shine in the heavens;
> but he has said he would dwell in thick darkness.
> I have built you a lofty house,
> a dwelling-place for you to occupy for ever.'

While the whole assembly of Israelites stood, the king turned and...
spreading out his hands towards heaven, he said, 'Lord God of Israel,
there is no God like you in heaven or on earth, keeping covenant with
your servants and showing them constant love while they continue
faithful to you with all their heart. You have kept your promise to your
servant David my father; by your deeds this day you have fulfilled
what you said to him in words. Now, therefore, Lord God of Israel,
keep this promise of yours to your servant David my father, when you
said: "You will never want for a man appointed by me to sit on the
throne of Israel, if only your sons look to their ways and conform to
my law, as you have walked before me." Lord God of Israel, let the
promise which you made to your servant David be now confirmed.

'But can God indeed dwell with mortals on earth? Heaven itself,
the highest heaven, cannot contain you; how much less this house
that I have built! Yet attend, Lord my God, to the prayer and the
supplication of your servant; listen to the cry and the prayer which
your servant makes before you, that your eyes may ever be on this
house day and night, this place where you said you would set your
name. Hear your servant when he prays towards this place. Hear the
supplications of your servant and of your people Israel when they pray
towards this place. Hear from heaven your dwelling and, when you
hear, forgive.

'Should anyone wrong a neighbour and be adjured to take an
oath, and come to take the oath before your altar in this house, then
hear from heaven and take action: be your servants' judge, requiting
the guilty person and bringing his deeds on his own head, acquitting
the innocent and rewarding him as his innocence may deserve...

'Should they sin against you (and who is free from sin?) and should you in your anger give them over to an enemy who carries them captive to a land far or near; and should they then in the land of their captivity have a change of heart and turn back and make supplication to you there and say, "We have sinned and acted perversely and wickedly," and turn back to you wholeheartedly in the land of their captivity to which they have been taken, and pray, turning towards their land which you gave to their forefathers and towards this city which you chose and this house which I have built for your name; then from heaven your dwelling-place hear their prayer and supplications and maintain their cause. Forgive your people their sins against you. Now, my God, let your eyes be open and your ears attentive to the prayer made in this place.

> 'Arise now, Lord God, and come to your resting-place,
> you and your powerful Ark.
> Let your priests, Lord God, be clothed with salvation
> and your loyal servants rejoice in prosperity.
> Lord God, do not reject your anointed one;
> remember the loyal service of David your servant.'

As Solomon finished this prayer, fire came down from heaven and consumed the whole-offering and the sacrifices, while the glory of the Lord filled the house. The priests were unable to enter the house of the Lord because the glory of the Lord had filled it. All the Israelites witnessed the fire coming down with the glory of the Lord on the house, and where they were on the paved court they bowed low to the ground and worshipped and gave thanks to the Lord, because 'it is good, for his love endures for ever'.

The king and all the people offered sacrifice before the Lord; King Solomon offered a sacrifice of twenty-two thousand oxen and a hundred and twenty thousand sheep. Thus the king and all the people dedicated the house of God. The priests stood at their appointed posts; so too the Levites with their musical instruments for the Lord's service, which King David had made for giving thanks to the Lord – 'for his love endures for ever' – whenever he rendered praise with their help; opposite them, the priests sounded their trumpets, while all the Israelites were standing. Then Solomon consecrated the centre of the court which lay in front of the house of the Lord; there he offered the whole-offerings and the fat portions of the shared-offerings, because the bronze altar which he had made could not accommodate the whole-offering, the grain-offering, and the fat portions.

So Solomon and with him all Israel, a very great assembly from Lebo-hamath to the wadi of Egypt, celebrated the pilgrim-feast at that time for seven days. On the eighth day they held a closing ceremony; for they had celebrated the dedication of the altar for seven days, and the pilgrim-feast lasted seven days. On the twenty-third day of the seventh month he dismissed the people to their homes, happy and glad at heart for all the prosperity granted by the Lord to David, to Solomon, and to his people Israel.

## THE VISIT OF THE QUEEN OF SHEBA
### 1 Kings 10:1–13

The queen of Sheba heard of Solomon's fame and came to test him with enigmatic questions. She arrived in Jerusalem with a very large retinue, camels laden with spices, gold in vast quantity, and precious stones. When she came to Solomon, she talked to him about everything she had on her mind. Solomon answered all her questions; not one of them was too hard for the king to answer. When the queen of Sheba observed all the wisdom of Solomon, the palace he had built, the food on his table, the courtiers sitting around him, and his attendants standing behind in their livery, his cupbearers, and the whole-offerings which he used to offer in the house of the Lord, she was overcome with amazement. She said to the king, 'The account which I heard in my own country about your achievements and your wisdom was true, but I did not believe what they told me until I came and saw for myself. Indeed I was not told half of it; your wisdom and your prosperity far surpass all I had heard of them. Happy are your wives, happy these courtiers of yours who are in attendance on you every day and hear your wisdom! Blessed be the Lord your God who has delighted in you and has set you on the throne of Israel; because he loves Israel unendingly, he has made you king to maintain law and justice.' She presented the king with a hundred and twenty talents of gold, spices in great abundance, and precious stones. Never again did such a quantity of spices come as the queen of Sheba gave to King Solomon.

Besides all this, Hiram's fleet of ships, which had brought gold from Ophir, brought also from Ophir huge cargoes of almug wood and precious stones. The king used the wood to make stools for the house of the Lord and for the palace, as well as lyres and lutes for the singers. No such quantities of almug wood have ever been imported or even seen since that time.

King Solomon gave the queen of Sheba whatever she desired and asked for, in addition to all that he gave her of his royal bounty. Then she departed with her retinue and went back to her own land.

## SOLOMON'S APOSTASY
### 1 Kings 11:1–13

King Solomon loved many foreign women; in addition to Pharaoh's daughter there were Moabite, Ammonite, Edomite, Sidonian, and Hittite women, from the nations with whom the Lord had forbidden the Israelites to intermarry, 'because', he said, 'they will entice you to serve their gods'. But Solomon was devoted to them and loved them dearly. He had seven hundred wives, all princesses, and three hundred concubines, and they influenced him, for as he grew old, his wives turned his heart to follow other gods, and he did not remain wholly loyal to the Lord his God as his father David had been. He followed Ashtoreth, goddess of the Sidonians, and Milcom, the loathsome god of the Ammonites. Thus Solomon did what was wrong in the eyes of the Lord, and was not wholehearted in his loyalty to the Lord as his father David had been. He built a shrine for Kemosh, the loathsome god of Moab, on the heights to the east of Jerusalem, and one for Milcom, the loathsome god of the Ammonites. These things he did for the gods to whom all his foreign wives burnt offerings and made sacrifices.

The Lord was angry with Solomon because his heart had turned away from the Lord the God of Israel, who had appeared to him twice and had strictly commanded him not to follow other gods; but he disobeyed the Lord's command. The Lord therefore said to Solomon, 'Because you have done this and have not kept my covenant and my statutes as I commanded you, I will tear the kingdom from you and give it to your servant. Nevertheless, for the sake of your father David I will not do this in your day; I will tear it out of your son's hand. Even so not the whole kingdom; I will leave him one tribe for the sake of my servant David and for the sake of Jerusalem, my chosen city.'

## AHIJAH FORETELLS JEROBOAM'S REBELLION
### 1 Kings 11:26–43

Jeroboam son of Nebat, one of Solomon's courtiers, an Ephrathite from Zeredah, whose widowed mother was named Zeruah, rebelled against the king. This is the story of his rebellion. When Solomon built the Millo and closed the breach in the wall of the city of his father David, he saw how the young man worked, for Jeroboam was a man of great ability, and the king put him in charge of all the labour-gangs in the tribal district of Joseph. On one occasion when Jeroboam left Jerusalem, the prophet Ahijah from Shiloh met him on the road. The prophet was wearing a new cloak and, when the two of them were alone out in the open country, Ahijah, taking hold of the new cloak he was wearing, tore it into twelve pieces, and said to Jeroboam, 'Take for yourself ten pieces, for the Lord the God of Israel has declared that he is about to tear the kingdom from the hand of Solomon and give you ten tribes. But, says the Lord, one tribe will remain Solomon's, for the sake of my servant David and for the sake of Jerusalem, the city I have chosen out of all the tribes of Israel. I shall do this because Solomon has forsaken me; he has bowed down before Ashtoreth goddess of the Sidonians, Kemosh god of Moab, and Milcom god of the Ammonites, and has not conformed to my ways. He has not done what is right in my eyes or observed my statutes and judgments as David his father did.

'Nevertheless I shall not take the whole kingdom from him, but shall maintain his rule as long as he lives, for the sake of my chosen servant David, who did observe my commandments and statutes. But I shall take the kingdom, that is the ten tribes, from his son and give it to you. To his son I shall give one tribe, that my servant David may always have a lamp burning before me in Jerusalem, the city which I chose to receive my name. I shall appoint you to rule over all that you can desire, and to be king over Israel. If you pay heed to all my commands, if you conform to my ways and do what is right in my eyes, observing my statutes and commandments as my servant David did, then I shall be with you. I shall establish your family for ever as I did for David; I shall give Israel to you, and punish David's descendants as they have deserved, but not for ever.'

After this Solomon sought to kill Jeroboam, but he fled to King Shishak in Egypt and remained there till Solomon's death.

The other acts and events of Solomon's reign, and all his wisdom, are recorded in the annals of Solomon. The reign of King Solomon in Jerusalem over the whole of Israel lasted forty years. Then he rested with his forefathers and was buried in the city of David his father; he was succeeded by his son Rehoboam.

## THE KINGDOM IS DIVIDED
1 Kings 12:1–19

Rehoboam went to Shechem, for all Israel had gone there to make him king. When Jeroboam son of Nebat, who was still in Egypt, heard of it, he remained there, having taken refuge in Egypt to escape King Solomon. The people now recalled him, and he and all the assembly of Israel came to Rehoboam and said, 'Your father laid a harsh yoke upon us; but if you will now lighten the harsh labour he imposed and the heavy yoke he laid on us, we shall serve you.' 'Give me three days,' he said, 'and then come back.'

When the people had gone, King Rehoboam consulted the elders who had been in attendance during the lifetime of his father Solomon: 'What answer do you advise me to give to this people?' They said, 'If today you are willing to serve this people, show yourself their servant now and speak kindly to them, and they will be your servants ever after.' But he rejected the advice given him by the elders, and consulted the young men who had grown up with him, and were now in attendance; he asked them, 'What answer do you advise me to give to this people's request that I should lighten the yoke which my father laid on them?' The young men replied, 'Give this answer to the people who say that your father made their yoke heavy and ask you to lighten it; tell them: "My little finger is thicker than my father's loins. My father laid a heavy yoke on you, but I shall make it heavier. My father whipped you, but I shall flay you."'

Jeroboam and the people all came to Rehoboam on the third day, as the king had ordered. The king gave them a harsh answer; he rejected the advice which the elders had given him and spoke to the people as the young men had advised: 'My father made your yoke heavy, but I shall make it heavier. My father whipped you, but I shall flay you.' The king would not listen to the people; for the Lord had given this turn to the affair in order that the word he had spoken by Ahijah of Shiloh to Jeroboam son of Nebat might be fulfilled.

When all Israel saw that the king would not listen to them, they answered:

'What share have we in David?
We have no lot in the son of Jesse.
Away to your tents, Israel!
Now see to your own house, David!'

With that Israel went off to their homes. Rehoboam ruled only over those Israelites who lived in the cities and towns of Judah.

King Rehoboam sent out Adoram, the commander of the forced levies, but when the Israelites stoned him to death, the king hastily mounted his chariot and fled to Jerusalem. From that day to this Israel has been in rebellion against the house of David.

# Part Four
# The Kings of Israel

## JEROBOAM I
### 1 Kings 12:20, 25 – 13:6, 33 – 14:20

When the men of Israel heard that Jeroboam had returned, they sent and called him to the assembly and made him king over the whole of Israel. The tribe of Judah alone stayed loyal to the house of David...

Jeroboam rebuilt Shechem in the hill-country of Ephraim and took up residence there; from there he went out and built Penuel. 'As things now stand', he said to himself, 'the kingdom will revert to the house of David. If these people go up to sacrifice in the house of the Lord in Jerusalem, it will revive their allegiance to their lord King Rehoboam of Judah, and they will kill me and return to King Rehoboam.' After taking counsel about the matter he made two calves of gold and said to the people, 'You have gone up to Jerusalem long enough; here are your gods, Israel, that brought you up from Egypt.' One he set up at Bethel and the other he put at Dan, and this thing became a sin in Israel; the people went to Bethel to worship the one, and all the way to Dan to worship the other. He also erected temple buildings at shrines and appointed priests who did not belong to the Levites, from every class of the people. He instituted a pilgrim-feast on the fifteenth day of the eighth month like that in Judah, and he offered sacrifices on the altar. This he did at Bethel, sacrificing to the calves that he had made and compelling the priests of the shrines, which he had set up, to serve at Bethel. He went up on the fifteenth day of the eighth month to the altar that he had made at Bethel; there, in a month of his own choosing, he instituted for the Israelites a pilgrim-feast and himself went up to the altar to burn the sacrifice.

As Jeroboam stood by the altar to burn the sacrifice, a man of God from Judah, moved by the word of the Lord, appeared at Bethel. He inveighed against the altar in the Lord's name, crying out, 'O altar,

altar! This is the word of the Lord: Listen! To the house of David a child shall be born named Josiah. On you he will sacrifice the priests of the shrines who make offerings on you, and he will burn human bones on you.' He gave a sign the same day: 'This is the sign which the Lord has ordained: This altar will be split asunder and the ashes on it will be scattered.' When King Jeroboam heard the sentence which the man of God pronounced against the altar at Bethel, he pointed to him from the altar and cried, 'Seize him!' Immediately the hand which he had pointed at him became paralysed, so that he could not draw it back. The altar too was split asunder and the ashes were scattered, in fulfilment of the sign that the man of God had given at the Lord's command. The king appealed to the man of God to placate the Lord his God and pray for him that his hand might be restored. The man of God did as he asked; the king's hand was restored and became as it had been before.

After this Jeroboam still did not abandon his evil ways, but went on appointing priests for the shrines from all classes of the people; any man who offered himself he would consecrate to be priest of a shrine. By doing this he brought guilt on his own house and doomed it to utter destruction.

At that time Jeroboam's son Abijah fell ill, and Jeroboam said to his wife, 'Go at once to Shiloh, but disguise yourself so that people will not recognize you as my wife. Ahijah the prophet is there, he who said I was to be king over this people. Take with you ten loaves, some raisins, and a jar of honey. Go to him and he will tell you what will happen to the boy.' Jeroboam's wife did so; she set off at once for Shiloh and came to Ahijah's house. Now as Ahijah could not see, for his eyes were fixed in the blindness of old age, the Lord had said to him, 'Jeroboam's wife is on her way to consult you about her son, who is ill; you are to give her such and such an answer.'

When she came in, concealing who she was, and Ahijah heard her footsteps at the door, he said, 'Come in, wife of Jeroboam. Why conceal who you are? I have heavy news for you. Go, tell Jeroboam: "This is the word of the Lord the God of Israel: I raised you out of the people and appointed you prince over my people Israel; I tore the kingdom from the house of David and gave it to you. But you have not been like my servant David, who kept my commands and followed me with his whole heart, doing only what was right in my eyes. You have outdone all your predecessors in wickedness; you have provoked me to anger by making for yourself other gods and images of cast metal; and you have turned your back on me. For this I am going to bring disaster on the house of Jeroboam; I shall destroy them all, every mother's son, whether still under the protection of the family or not, and I shall sweep away the house of Jeroboam in Israel, as one sweeps away dung until none is left. Those of that house who die in the town shall be food for the dogs, and those who die in the country shall be food for the birds. It is the word of the Lord."

'Go home now; the moment you set foot in the town, the child will die. All Israel will mourn for him and bury him; he alone of all Jeroboam's family will have proper burial, because in him alone could the Lord the God of Israel find anything good.

'The Lord will set up a king over Israel who will put an end to the house of Jeroboam. This first; and what next? The Lord will strike Israel, till it trembles like a reed in the water; he will uproot its people from this good land which he gave to their forefathers and scatter them beyond the Euphrates, because they have made their sacred poles, thus provoking the Lord's anger. He will abandon Israel because of the sins that Jeroboam has committed and has led Israel to commit.'

Jeroboam's wife went away back to Tirzah and, as she crossed the threshold of the house, the boy died. They buried him, and all Israel mourned over him; and thus the word of the Lord was fulfilled which he had spoken through his servant Ahijah the prophet.

The other events of Jeroboam's reign, in war and peace, are recorded in the annals of the kings of Israel. After reigning for twenty-two years, he rested with his forefathers and was succeeded by his son Nadab.

# NADAB
## 1 Kings 15:25–29

Nadab son of Jeroboam became king of Israel in the second year of King Asa of Judah, and he reigned for two years. He did what was wrong in the eyes of the Lord and followed in his father's footsteps, repeating the sin which Jeroboam had led Israel to commit. Baasha son of Ahijah, of the house of Issachar, conspired against him and attacked him at Gibbethon, a Philistine town which Nadab was besieging with all his forces. Baasha slew him and usurped the throne in the third year of King Asa of Judah.

As soon as he became king, he struck down the whole family of Jeroboam, destroying every living soul and leaving not one survivor. Thus the word of the Lord was fulfilled which he spoke through his servant Ahijah the Shilonite.

## BAASHA
### 1 Kings 15:33 – 16:4

Baasha son of Ahijah became king of all Israel in Tirzah and reigned for twenty-four years. He did what was wrong in the eyes of the Lord and followed in Jeroboam's footsteps, repeating the sin which Jeroboam had led Israel to commit.

This word of the Lord against Baasha came to Jehu son of Hanani: 'I raised you from the dust and made you a prince over my people Israel, but you have followed in the footsteps of Jeroboam and have led my people Israel into sin, so provoking me to anger with their sins. Therefore I am about to sweep away Baasha and his house and deal with it as I dealt with the house of Jeroboam son of Nebat. Those of Baasha's family who die in a town will be food for the dogs, and those who die in the country will be food for the birds.'

## ELAH
### 1 Kings 16:8–12

Elah son of Baasha became king of Israel and he reigned in Tirzah for two years. Zimri, who was in his service commanding half the chariotry, plotted against him. The king was in Tirzah drinking himself into insensibility in the house of Arza, comptroller of the household there, when Zimri broke in, attacked and assassinated him, and made himself king...

As soon as Zimri had become king and was enthroned, he struck down all the household of Baasha; he left him not a single mother's son alive, neither kinsman nor friend. By destroying the whole household of Baasha he fulfilled the word of the Lord concerning Baasha, spoken through the prophet Jehu.

## ZIMRI
### 1 Kings 16:15–18

Zimri reigned in Tirzah for seven days. At the time the army was investing the Philistine city of Gibbethon. When the Israelite troops in the camp heard of Zimri's conspiracy and the murder of the king, there and then they made their commander Omri king of Israel by common consent.

Omri and his whole force then withdrew from Gibbethon and laid siege to Tirzah. As soon as Zimri saw that the city had fallen, he retreated to the keep of the royal palace, set the whole of it on fire over his head, and so perished.

## OMRI
### 1 Kings 16:21–26

Thereafter the people of Israel were split into two factions: one supported Tibni son of Ginath, determined to make him king; the other supported Omri. Omri's party proved the stronger; Tibni lost his life, and Omri became king...

He reigned for twelve years, six of them in Tirzah. He bought the hill of Samaria from Shemer for two talents of silver, and built a city on it which he named Samaria after Shemer the owner of the hill. Omri did what was wrong in the eyes of the Lord; he outdid all his predecessors in wickedness. He followed in the footsteps of Jeroboam son of Nebat, repeating the sins which he had led Israel to commit, so that they provoked the anger of the Lord their God with their worthless idols.

# AHAB
## 1 Kings 16:29–34

Ahab son of Omri... reigned over Israel in Samaria for twenty-two years. More than any of his predecessors he did what was wrong in the eyes of the Lord. As if it were not enough for him to follow the sinful ways of Jeroboam son of Nebat, he took as his wife Jezebel daughter of King Ethbaal of Sidon, and went and served Baal; he prostrated himself before him and erected an altar to him in the temple of Baal which he built in Samaria. He also set up a sacred pole; indeed he did more to provoke the anger of the Lord the God of Israel than all the kings of Israel before him.

During Ahab's reign Hiel of Bethel rebuilt Jericho; laying its foundations cost him his eldest son Abiram, and the setting up of its gates cost him Segub his youngest son. Thus was fulfilled what the Lord had spoken through Joshua son of Nun.

# THE PROPHET ELIJAH
## 1 Kings 17:1–24

Elijah the Tishbite from Tishbe in Gilead said to Ahab, 'I swear by the life of the Lord the God of Israel, whose servant I am, that there will be neither dew nor rain these coming years unless I give the word.' Then the word of the Lord came to him: 'Leave this place, turn eastwards, and go into hiding in the wadi of Kerith east of the Jordan. You are to drink from the stream, and I have commanded the ravens to feed you there.' Elijah did as the Lord had told him: he went and stayed in the wadi of Kerith east of the Jordan, and the ravens brought him bread and meat morning and evening, and he drank from the stream.

After a while the stream dried up, for there had been no rain in the land. Then the word of the Lord came to him: 'Go now to Zarephath, a village of Sidon, and stay there; I have commanded a widow there to feed you.' He went off to Zarephath, and when he reached the entrance to the village, he saw a widow gathering sticks. He called to her, 'Please bring me a little water in a pitcher to drink.'

As she went to fetch it, he called after her, 'Bring me, please, a piece of bread as well.' But she answered, 'As the Lord your God lives, I have no food baked, only a handful of flour in a jar and a little oil in a flask. I am just gathering two or three sticks to go and cook it for my son and myself before we die.' 'Have no fear,' said Elijah; 'go and do as you have said. But first make me a small cake from what you have and bring it out to me, and after that make something for your son and yourself. For this is the word of the Lord the God of Israel: The jar of flour will not give out, nor the flask of oil fail, until the Lord sends rain on the land.' She went and did as Elijah had said, and there was food for him and for her and her family for a long time. The jar of flour did not give out, nor did the flask of oil fail, as the word of the Lord foretold through Elijah.

Afterwards the son of the woman, the owner of the house, fell ill and was in a very bad way, until at last his breathing stopped. The woman said to Elijah, 'What made you interfere, you man of God? You came here to bring my sins to light and cause my son's death!' 'Give me your son,' he said. He took the boy from her arms and carried him up to the roof-chamber where his lodging was, and laid him on his bed. He called out to the Lord, 'Lord my God, is this your care for the widow with whom I lodge, that you have been so cruel to her son?' Then he breathed deeply on the child three times and called to the Lord, 'I pray, Lord my God, let the breath of life return to the body of this child.' The Lord listened to Elijah's cry, and the breath of life returned to the child's body, and he revived.

Elijah lifted him and took him down from the roof-chamber into the house, and giving him to his mother he said, 'Look, your son is alive.' She said to Elijah, 'Now I know for certain that you are a man of God and that the word of the Lord on your lips is truth.'

## ELIJAH AND THE PROPHETS OF BAAL
### 1 Kings 18:1–2, 17–46

Time went by, and in the third year the word of the Lord came to Elijah: 'Go, appear before Ahab, and I shall send rain on the land.' So Elijah went to show himself to Ahab...

As soon as Ahab saw Elijah, he said to him, 'Is it you, you troubler of Israel?' 'It is not I who have brought trouble on Israel,' Elijah replied, 'but you and your father's family, by forsaking the commandments of the Lord and following Baal. Now summon all Israel to meet me on Mount Carmel, including the four hundred and fifty prophets of Baal and the four hundred prophets of the goddess Asherah, who are attached to Jezebel's household.' So Ahab sent throughout the length and breadth of Israel and assembled the prophets on Mount Carmel.

Elijah stepped forward towards all the people there and said, 'How long will you sit on the fence? If the Lord is God, follow him; but if Baal, then follow him.' Not a word did they answer. Then Elijah said, 'I am the only prophet of the Lord still left, but there are four hundred and fifty prophets of Baal. Bring two bulls for us. Let them choose one for themselves, cut it up, and lay it on the wood without setting fire to it, and I shall prepare the other and lay it on the wood without setting fire to it. Then invoke your god by name and I shall invoke the Lord by name; the god who answers by fire, he is God.' The people all shouted their approval.

Elijah said to the prophets of Baal, 'Choose one of the bulls and offer it first, for there are more of you; invoke your god by name, but do not set fire to the wood.' They took the bull provided for them and offered it, and they invoked Baal by name from morning until noon, crying, 'Baal, answer us'; but there was no sound, no answer. They danced wildly by the altar they had set up. At midday Elijah mocked them: 'Call louder, for he is a god. It may be he is deep in thought, or engaged, or on a journey; or he may have gone to sleep and must be woken up.' They cried still louder and, as was their custom, gashed themselves with swords and spears until the blood flowed. All afternoon they raved and ranted till the hour of the regular offering, but still there was no sound, no answer, no sign of attention.

Elijah said to the people, 'Come here to me,' and they all came to him. He repaired the altar of the Lord which had been torn down. He took twelve stones, one for each tribe of the sons of Jacob, him who was named Israel by the word of the Lord. With these stones he built an altar in the name of the Lord, and dug a trench round it big enough to hold two measures of seed; he arranged the wood, cut up the bull, and laid it on the wood. Then he said, 'Fill four jars with water and pour it on the whole-offering and on the wood.' They did so; he said, 'Do it again.' They did it again; he said, 'Do it a third time.' They did it a third time, and the water ran all round the altar and even filled the trench.

At the hour of the regular offering the prophet Elijah came forward and prayed, 'Lord God of Abraham, of Isaac, and of Israel, let it be known today that you are God in Israel and that I am your servant and have done all these things at your command. Answer me, Lord, answer me and let this people know that you, Lord, are God and that it is you who have brought them back to their allegiance.' The fire of the Lord fell, consuming the whole-offering, the wood, the stones, and the earth, and licking up the water in the trench. At the sight the people all bowed with their faces to the ground and cried, 'The Lord is God, the Lord is God.' Elijah said to them, 'Seize the prophets of Baal; let not one of them escape.' They were seized, and Elijah took them down to the Kishon and slaughtered them there in the valley.

Elijah said to Ahab, 'Go back now, eat and drink, for I hear the sound of heavy rain.' He did so, while Elijah himself climbed to the crest of Carmel, where he bowed down to the ground and put his face between his knees. He said to his servant, 'Go and look toward the west.' He went and looked; 'There is nothing to see,' he said. Seven times Elijah ordered him back, and seven times he went. The seventh time he said, 'I see a cloud no bigger than a man's hand, coming up from the west.' 'Now go', said Elijah, 'and tell Ahab to harness his chariot and be off, or the rain will stop him.' Meanwhile the sky grew black with clouds, the wind rose, and heavy rain began to fall. Ahab mounted his chariot and set off for Jezreel; and the power of the Lord was on Elijah: he tucked up his robe and ran before Ahab all the way to Jezreel.

## ELIJAH IN THE WILDERNESS
### 1 Kings 19:1–18

When Ahab told Jezebel all that Elijah had done and how he had put all the prophets to the sword, she sent this message to Elijah, 'The gods do the same to me and more, unless by this time tomorrow I have taken your life as you took theirs.' In fear he fled for his life, and when he reached Beersheba in Judah he left his servant there, while he himself went a day's journey into the wilderness. He came to a broom bush, and sitting down under it he prayed for death: 'It is enough,' he said; 'now, Lord, take away my life, for I am no better than my fathers before me.' He lay down under the bush and, while he slept, an angel touched him and said, 'Rise and eat.' He looked, and there at his head was a cake baked on hot stones, and a pitcher of water. He ate and drank and lay down again. The angel of the Lord came again and touched him a second time, saying, 'Rise and eat; the journey is too much for you.' He rose and ate and drank and, sustained by this food, he went on for forty days and forty nights to Horeb, the mount of God. There he entered a cave where he spent the night.

The word of the Lord came to him: 'Why are you here, Elijah?' 'Because of my great zeal for the Lord the God of Hosts,' he replied. 'The people of Israel have forsaken your covenant, torn down your altars, and put your prophets to the sword. I alone am left, and they seek to take my life.' To this the answer came: 'Go and stand on the mount before the Lord.' The Lord was passing by: a great and strong wind came, rending mountains and shattering rocks before him, but the Lord was not in the wind; and after the wind there was an earthquake, but the Lord was not in the earthquake; and after the earthquake fire, but the Lord was not in the fire; and after the fire a faint murmuring sound. When Elijah heard it, he wrapped his face in his cloak and went out and stood at the entrance to the cave. There came a voice: 'Why are you here, Elijah?' 'Because of my great zeal for the Lord the God of Hosts,' he replied. 'The people of Israel have forsaken your covenant, torn down your altars, and put your prophets to the sword. I alone am left, and they seek to take my life.'

The Lord said to him, 'Go back by way of the wilderness of Damascus, enter the city, and anoint Hazael to be king of Aram; anoint also Jehu son of Nimshi to be king of Israel, and Elisha son of Shaphat of Abel-meholah to be prophet in your place. Whoever escapes the sword of Hazael Jehu will slay, and whoever escapes the sword of Jehu Elisha will slay. But I shall leave seven thousand in Israel, all who have not bowed the knee to Baal, all whose lips have not kissed him.'

# THE CALL OF ELISHA
## 1 Kings 19:19–21

Elijah departed and found Elisha son of Shaphat ploughing; there were twelve pair of oxen ahead of him, and he himself was with the last of them. As Elijah passed, he threw his cloak over him. Elisha, leaving his oxen, ran after Elijah and said, 'Let me kiss my father and mother goodbye, and then I shall follow you.' 'Go back,' he replied; 'what have I done to prevent you?' He followed him no farther but went home, took his pair of oxen, slaughtered them, and burnt the wooden yokes to cook the flesh, which he gave to the people to eat. He then followed Elijah and became his disciple.

# NABOTH'S VINEYARD
## 1 Kings 21

Some time later there occurred an incident involving Naboth of Jezreel, who had a vineyard in Jezreel adjoining the palace of King Ahab of Samaria. Ahab made a proposal to Naboth: 'Your vineyard is close to my palace; let me have it for a garden, and I shall give you a better vineyard in exchange for it or, if you prefer, I shall give you its value in silver.' But Naboth answered, 'The Lord forbid that I should surrender to you land which has always been in my family.' Ahab went home sullen and angry because Naboth had refused to let him have his ancestral holding. He took to his bed, covered his face, and refused to eat. When his wife Jezebel came in to him and asked, 'Why this sullenness, and why do you refuse to eat?' he replied, 'I proposed that Naboth of Jezreel should let me have his vineyard at its value or, if he liked, in exchange for another; but he refused to let me have it.' 'Are you or are you not king in Israel?' retorted Jezebel. 'Come, eat and take heart; I shall make you a gift of the vineyard of Naboth of Jezreel.'

She wrote letters in Ahab's name, sealed them with his seal, and sent them to the elders and notables of Naboth's city, who sat in council with him. She wrote: 'Proclaim a fast and give Naboth the seat of honour among the people. Opposite him seat two unprincipled rogues to charge him with cursing God and the king; then take him out and stone him to death.' The elders and notables of Naboth's city carried out the instructions Jezebel had sent them in her letter: they proclaimed a fast and gave Naboth the seat of honour. The two unprincipled rogues came in, sat opposite him, and charged him publicly with cursing God and the king. He was then taken outside the city and stoned, and word was sent to Jezebel that Naboth had been stoned to death.

As soon as Jezebel heard of the death of Naboth, she said to Ahab, 'Get up and take possession of the vineyard which Naboth refused to sell you, for he is no longer alive; Naboth of Jezreel is dead.' On hearing that Naboth was dead, Ahab got up and went to the vineyard to take possession.

The word of the Lord came to Elijah the Tishbite: 'Go down at once to King Ahab of Israel, who is in Samaria; you will find him in Naboth's vineyard, where he has gone to take possession. Say to him, "This is the word of the Lord: Have you murdered and seized property?" Say to him, "This is the word of the Lord: Where dogs licked the blood of Naboth, there dogs will lick your blood."' Ahab said to Elijah, 'So you have found me, my enemy.' 'Yes,' he said, 'because you have sold yourself to do what is wrong in the eyes of the Lord. I shall bring disaster on you; I shall sweep you away and destroy every mother's son of the house of Ahab in Israel, whether under protection of the family or not. I shall deal with your house as I dealt with the house of Jeroboam son of Nebat and that of Baasha son of Ahijah, because you have provoked my anger and led Israel into sin.' The Lord went on to say of Jezebel, 'Jezebel will be eaten by dogs near the rampart of Jezreel. Of the house of Ahab, those who die in the city will be food for the dogs, and those who die in the country food for the birds.'

(Never was there a man who sold himself to do what is wrong in the Lord's eyes as Ahab did, and all at the prompting of Jezebel his wife. He committed gross abominations in going after false gods, doing everything that had been done by the Amorites, whom the Lord dispossessed in favour of Israel.)

When Ahab heard Elijah's words, he tore his clothes, put on sackcloth, and fasted; he lay down in his sackcloth and went about moaning. The word of the Lord came to Elijah the Tishbite: 'Have you seen how Ahab has humbled himself before me? Because he has thus humbled himself, I shall not bring disaster on his house in his own lifetime, but in that of his son.'

## THE DEATH OF AHAB
### 1 Kings 22:1–38

For three years there was no war between the Arameans and the Israelites. In the third year King Jehoshaphat of Judah went down to visit the king of Israel, who had said to his ministers, 'You know that Ramoth-gilead belongs to us, and yet we do nothing to recover it from the king of Aram'; and to Jehoshaphat he said, 'Will you join me in attacking Ramoth-gilead?' Jehoshaphat replied, 'What is mine is yours: myself, my people, and my horses,' but he said to the king of Israel, 'First let us seek counsel from the Lord.'

The king of Israel assembled the prophets, some four hundred of them, and asked, 'Shall I attack Ramoth-gilead or not?' 'Attack,' was the answer; 'the Lord will deliver it into your majesty's hands.' Jehoshaphat asked, 'Is there no other prophet of the Lord here through whom we may seek guidance?' 'There is one more', the king of Israel answered, 'through whom we may seek guidance of the Lord, but I hate the man, because he never prophesies good for me, never anything but evil. His name is Micaiah son of Imlah.' Jehoshaphat exclaimed, 'My lord king, let no such word pass your lips!' So the king of Israel called one of his eunuchs and told him to fetch Micaiah son of Imlah with all speed.

The king of Israel and King Jehoshaphat of Judah in their royal robes were seated on their thrones at the entrance to the gate of Samaria, and all the prophets were prophesying before them. One of them, Zedekiah son of Kenaanah, made himself iron horns and declared, 'This is the word of the Lord: With horns like these you will gore the Arameans and make an end of them.' In the same vein all the prophets prophesied, 'Attack Ramoth-gilead and win the day; the Lord will deliver it into your hands.'

The messenger sent to fetch Micaiah told him that the prophets had unanimously given the king a favourable answer. 'And mind you agree with them,' he added. 'As the Lord lives,' said Micaiah, 'I shall say only what the Lord tells me to say.' When he came into the king's presence, the king asked, 'Micaiah, shall I attack Ramoth-gilead, or shall I refrain?' 'Attack and win the day,' he replied; 'the Lord will deliver it into your hands.' 'How often must I adjure you', said the king, 'to tell me nothing but the truth in the name of the Lord?' Then Micaiah said,

> 'I saw all Israel scattered on the mountains,
> like sheep without a shepherd;
> and I heard the Lord say, "They have no master;
> let them go home in peace."'

The king of Israel said to Jehoshaphat, 'Did I not tell you that he never prophesies good for me, never anything but evil?' Micaiah went on, 'Listen now to the word of the Lord: I saw the Lord seated on his throne, with all the host of heaven in attendance on his right and on his left. The Lord said, "Who will entice Ahab to go up and attack Ramoth-gilead?" One said one thing and one said another, until a spirit came forward and, standing before the Lord, said, "I shall entice him." "How?" said the Lord. "I shall go out", he answered, "and be a lying spirit in the mouths of all his prophets." "Entice him; you will succeed," said the Lord. "Go and do it." You see, then, how the Lord has put a lying spirit in the mouths of all these prophets of yours, because he has decreed disaster for you.'

At that, Zedekiah son of Kenaanah came up to Micaiah and struck him in the face: 'And how did the spirit of the Lord pass from me to speak to you?' he demanded. Micaiah retorted, 'That you will find out on the day when you run into an inner room to hide.' The king of Israel ordered Micaiah to be arrested and committed to the custody of Amon the governor of the city and Joash the king's son. 'Throw this fellow into prison,' he said, 'and put him on a prison diet of bread and water until I come home in safety.' Micaiah declared, 'If you do return in safety, the Lord has not spoken by me.'

The king of Israel and King Jehoshaphat of Judah marched on Ramoth-gilead. The king of Israel went into battle in disguise, for he had said to Jehoshaphat, 'I shall disguise myself to go into battle, but you must wear your royal robes.' The king of Aram had ordered the thirty-two captains of his chariots not to engage all and sundry, but the king of Israel alone. When the captains saw Jehoshaphat, they thought he was the king of Israel and turned to attack him, but Jehoshaphat cried out, and when the captains saw that he was not the king of Israel, they broke off the attack on him. One man, however, drew his bow at random and hit the king of Israel where the breastplate joins the plates of the armour. The king said to his driver, 'Turn about and take me out of the line; I am wounded.' When the day's fighting reached its height, the king was facing the Arameans, propped up in his chariot, and the blood from his wound flowed down to the floor of the chariot; and in the evening he died. At sunset the herald went through the ranks, crying, 'Every man to his city, every man to his country.' Thus the king died. He was brought to Samaria and buried there. The chariot was swilled out at the pool of Samaria where the prostitutes washed themselves, and dogs licked up the blood, in fulfilment of the word the Lord had spoken.

## AHAZIAH
### 1 Kings 22:51–53, 2 Kings 1:1–17

Ahaziah son of Ahab became king of Israel in Samaria in the seventeenth year of King Jehoshaphat of Judah, and reigned over Israel for two years. He did what was wrong in the eyes of the Lord, following in the footsteps of his father and mother and in those of Jeroboam son of Nebat, who had led Israel into sin. He served Baal and worshipped him, and provoked the anger of the Lord the God of Israel, as his father had done.

After Ahab's death Moab rebelled against Israel.

When Ahaziah fell through a latticed window in his roof-chamber in Samaria and injured himself, he sent messengers to enquire of Baal-zebub the god of Ekron whether he would recover from this injury. The angel of the Lord ordered Elijah the Tishbite to go and meet the messengers of the king of Samaria and say to them, 'Is there no God in Israel, that you go to consult Baal-zebub the god of Ekron? For what you have done the word of the Lord to your master is this: You will not rise from the bed where you are lying; you will die.' With that Elijah departed.

When the messengers returned to the king, he asked them why they had come back. They answered that a man had come to meet them and had ordered them to return to the king who had sent them and say, 'This is the word of the Lord: Is there no God in Israel, that you send to enquire of Baal-zebub the god of Ekron? In consequence, you will not rise from the bed where you are lying; you will die.' The king asked them what kind of man it was who had come to meet them and given them this message. 'A hairy man', they answered, 'with a leather belt round his waist.' 'It is Elijah the Tishbite,' said the king.

The king sent a captain with his company of fifty men to Elijah. He went up to the prophet, who was sitting on a hilltop, and said, 'Man of God, the king orders you to come down.' Elijah answered, 'If I am a man of God, may fire fall from heaven and consume you and your company!' Fire fell from heaven and consumed the officer and his fifty men.

The king sent another captain of fifty with his company, and he went up and said to the prophet, 'Man of God, this is the king's command: Come down at once.' Elijah answered, 'If I am a man of God, may fire fall from heaven and consume you and your company!' Fire from God fell from heaven and consumed the man and his company.

The king sent the captain of a third company with his fifty men, and this third captain went up the hill to Elijah and knelt down before him. 'Man of God,' he pleaded, 'consider me and these fifty servants of yours, and have some regard for our lives. Fire fell from heaven and consumed the other two captains of fifty and their companies; but now have regard for my life.' The angel of the Lord said to Elijah, 'Go down with him; do not be afraid.' At that he rose and went down with him to the king, to whom he said, 'This is the word of the Lord: You have sent to consult Baal-zebub the god of Ekron. Is that because there is no God in Israel you could consult? For what you have done you will not rise from the bed where you are lying; you will die.' Ahaziah's death fulfilled the word of the Lord which Elijah had spoken. Because Ahaziah had no son, his brother Jehoram succeeded him.

# ELIJAH AND THE HEAVENLY CHARIOT
## 2 Kings 2:1–18

When the Lord was about to take Elijah up to heaven in a whirlwind, Elijah and Elisha had set out from Gilgal. Elijah said to Elisha, 'Stay here; for the Lord has sent me to Bethel.' Elisha replied, 'As the Lord lives, your life upon it, I shall not leave you.' They went down country to Bethel, and there a company of prophets came out to Elisha and said to him, 'Do you know that the Lord is going to take your lord and master from you today?' 'I do know,' he replied; 'say nothing.'

Elijah said to him, 'Stay here, Elisha; for the Lord has sent me to Jericho.' He replied, 'As the Lord lives, your life upon it, I shall not leave you.' So they went to Jericho, and there a company of prophets came up to Elisha and said to him, 'Do you know that the Lord is going to take your lord and master from you today?' 'I do know,' he replied; 'say nothing.'

Then Elijah said to him, 'Stay here; for the Lord has sent me to the Jordan.' The other replied, 'As the Lord lives, your life upon it, I shall not leave you.' So the two of them went on. Fifty of the prophets followed, and stood watching from a distance as the two of them stopped by the Jordan. Elijah took his cloak, rolled it up, and struck the water with it. The water divided to right and left, and both crossed over on dry ground.

While they were crossing, Elijah said to Elisha, 'Tell me what I can do for you before I am taken from you.' Elisha said, 'Let me inherit a double share of your spirit.' 'You have asked a hard thing,' said Elijah. 'If you see me taken from you, your wish will be granted; if you do not, it will not be granted.' They went on, talking as they went, and suddenly there appeared a chariot of fire and horses of fire, which separated them from one another, and Elijah was carried up to heaven in a whirlwind. At the sight Elisha cried out, 'My father, my father, the chariot and the horsemen of Israel!' and he saw him no more. He clutched hold of his mantle and tore it in two. He picked up the cloak which had fallen from Elijah, and went back and stood on the bank of the Jordan. There he struck the water with Elijah's cloak, saying as he did so, 'Where is the Lord, the God of Elijah?' As he too struck the water, it divided to right and left, and he crossed over.

The prophets from Jericho, who were watching, said, 'The spirit of Elijah has settled on Elisha.' They came to meet him, bowed to the ground before him, and said, 'Your servants have fifty stalwart men. Let them go and search for your master; perhaps the spirit of the Lord has lifted him up and cast him on some mountain or into some valley.' But he said, 'No, you must not send them.'

They pressed him, however, until he had not the heart to refuse. So they sent out the fifty men but, though they searched for three days, they did not find him. When they came back to Elisha, who had remained at Jericho, he said to them, 'Did I not tell you not to go?'

## THE PROPHET ELISHA
### 2 Kings 2:19–25

The people of the city said to Elisha, 'Lord, you can see how pleasantly situated our city is, but the water is polluted and the country is sterile.' He said, 'Fetch me a new, unused bowl and put salt in it.' When they had brought it, he went out to the spring and, throwing the salt into it, he said, 'This is the word of the Lord: I purify this water. It shall no longer cause death or sterility.' The water has remained pure till this day, in fulfilment of Elisha's word.

From there he went up to Bethel and, as he was on his way, some small boys came out of the town and jeered at him, saying, 'Get along with you, bald head, get along.' He turned round, looked at them, and cursed them in the name of the Lord; and two she-bears came out of a wood and mauled forty-two of them. From there he went on to Mount Carmel, and thence back to Samaria.

## JEHORAM
### 2 Kings 3

In the eighteenth year of King Jehoshaphat of Judah, Jehoram son of Ahab became king of Israel in Samaria, and he reigned for twelve years. He did what was wrong in the eyes of the Lord, though not as his father and his mother had done; he did remove the sacred pillar of the Baal which his father had made. Yet he persisted in the sins into which Jeroboam son of Nebat had led Israel, and did not give them up.

King Mesha of Moab was a sheep-breeder, and he had to supply the king of Israel regularly with the wool of a hundred thousand lambs and a hundred thousand rams. When Ahab died, the king of Moab rebelled against the king of Israel, and King Jehoram marched out from Samaria and mustered all Israel. He also sent this message to King Jehoshaphat of Judah: 'The king of Moab has rebelled against me. Will you join me in a campaign against Moab?' 'I will join you,' he replied; 'what is mine is yours: myself, my people, and my horses.' 'From which direction shall we attack?' he asked. 'Through the wilderness of Edom,' replied the other.

The king of Israel set out with the king of Judah and the king of Edom, and when they had been seven days on the indirect route they were following, they had no water left for the army or their pack-animals. The king of Israel cried, 'Alas, the Lord has brought together three kings, only to put us at the mercy of the Moabites.' Jehoshaphat said, 'Is there not a prophet of the Lord here through whom we may seek the Lord's guidance?' One of the officers of the king of Israel answered, 'Elisha son of Shaphat is here, the man who poured water on Elijah's hands.' 'The word of the Lord is with him,' said Jehoshaphat. When the king of Israel and Jehoshaphat and the king of Edom went down to Elisha, he said to the king of Israel, 'Why do you come to me? Go to your father's prophets or your mother's.' 'No,' answered the king of Israel; 'it is the Lord who has called us three kings out to put us at the mercy of the Moabites.' 'As the Lord of Hosts lives, whom I serve,' said Elisha, 'I would not spare a look or a glance for you, if it were not for my regard for King Jehoshaphat of Judah. But now fetch me a minstrel'; and while the minstrel played, the power of the Lord came on Elisha, and he said, 'This is the word of the Lord: Pools will form all over this wadi. The Lord has decreed that you will see neither wind nor rain, yet this wadi will be filled with water for you and your army and your pack-animals to drink. That is a mere trifle in the sight of the Lord; what he will also do is to put Moab at your mercy. You will raze to the ground every fortified town and every noble city; you will cut down all their fine trees; you will stop up all the springs of water; and you will spoil every good piece

215

of land by littering it with stones.' In the morning at the hour of the regular offering they saw water flowing in from the direction of Edom, and the land was flooded.

Meanwhile all Moab had heard that the kings had come up to wage war against them, and every man, young and old, who could bear arms was called out and stationed on the frontier. When they got up next morning and the sun was shining over the water, the Moabites saw the water in front of them red like blood and cried out, 'It is blood! The kings must have quarrelled and attacked one another. Now to the plunder, Moab!' But when they came to the Israelite camp, the Israelites sallied out and attacked them, driving the Moabites in headlong flight. The Israelites pushed forward into Moab, destroying as they went. They razed the towns to the ground; they littered every good piece of land with stones, each man casting a stone on it; they stopped up every spring of water; they cut down all the fine trees; and they harried Moab until only in Kir-hareseth were any buildings left standing, and even this city the slingers surrounded and attacked.

When the Moabite king saw that the war had gone against him, he took with him seven hundred men armed with swords to cut a way through to the king of Aram, but the attempt failed. Then he took his eldest son, who would have succeeded him, and offered him as a whole-offering on the city wall. There was such great consternation among the Israelites that they struck camp and returned to their own land.

## ELISHA AND THE SHUNAMITE WOMAN
### 2 Kings 4:8–37

It happened once that Elisha went over to Shunem. There was a well-to-do woman there who pressed him to accept hospitality, and afterwards whenever he came that way, he stopped there for a meal. One day she said to her husband, 'I know that this man who comes here regularly is a holy man of God. Why not build up the wall to make him a small roof-chamber, and put in it a bed, a table, a seat, and a lamp, and let him stay there whenever he comes to us?'

One time when he arrived there and went to this roof-chamber to lie down, he said to Gehazi, his servant, 'Call this Shunammite woman.' When he called her and she appeared before the prophet, Elisha said to his servant, 'Say to her, "You have taken all this trouble for us. What can I do for you? Shall I speak for you to the king or to the commander-in-chief?"' But she replied, 'I am content where I am, among my own people.' He said, 'Then what can be done for her?' Gehazi said, 'There is only this: she has no child and her husband is old.' 'Call her back,' Elisha said. When she was called and appeared in the doorway, he said, 'In due season, this time next year, you will have a son in your arms.' But she said, 'No, no, my lord, you are a man of God and would not lie to your servant.' Next year in due season the woman conceived and bore a son, as Elisha had foretold.

When the child was old enough, he went out one day to his father among the reapers. All of a sudden he cried out to his father, 'Oh, my head, my head!' His father told a servant to carry the child to his mother, and when he was brought to her, he sat on her lap till midday, and then he died. She went up, laid him on the bed of the man of God, shut the door, and went out. She called her husband and said, 'Send me one of the servants and a she-donkey; I must go to the man of God as fast as I can, and come straight back.' 'Why go to him today?' he asked. 'It is neither new moon nor sabbath.' 'Never mind that,' she answered. When the donkey was saddled, she said to her servant, 'Lead on and do not slacken pace unless I tell you.' So she set out and came to the man of God on Mount Carmel.

The man of God spied her in the distance and said to Gehazi, his servant, 'That is the Shunammite woman coming. Run and meet her, and ask, "Is all well with you? Is all well with your husband? Is all well with the boy?"' She answered, 'All is well.' When she reached the man of God on the hill, she clutched his feet. Gehazi came forward to push her away, but the man of God said, 'Let her alone; she is in great distress, and the Lord has concealed it from me and not told me.' 'My lord,' she said, 'did I ask for a son? Did I not beg you not to raise my hopes and then dash them?' Elisha turned to Gehazi: 'Hitch up your cloak; take my staff with you and run. If you meet anyone on the way, do not stop to greet him, if anyone greets you, do not answer. Lay my staff on the boy's face.' But the mother cried, 'As the Lord lives, your life upon it, I shall not leave you.' So he got up and followed her.

Gehazi went on ahead and laid the staff on the boy's face, but there was no sound or sign of life, so he went back to meet Elisha and told him that the boy had not stirred. When Elisha entered the house, there was the dead boy, where he had been laid on the bed. He went into the room, shut the door on the two of them, and prayed to the Lord. Then, getting on to the bed, he lay upon the child, put his mouth to the child's mouth, his eyes to his eyes, and his hands to his hands; as he crouched upon him, the child's body grew warm. Elisha got up and walked once up and down the room; getting on to the bed again, he crouched upon him and breathed into him seven times, and the boy opened his eyes. The prophet summoned Gehazi and said, 'Call the Shunammite woman.' She answered his call and the prophet said, 'Take up your child.' She came in and prostrated herself before him. Then she took up her son and went out.

# THE HEALING OF NAAMAN
## 2 Kings 5

Naaman, commander of the king of Aram's army, was a great man and highly esteemed by his master, because through him the Lord had given victory to Aram; he was a mighty warrior, but he was a leper. On one of their raids the Arameans brought back as a captive from the land of Israel a young girl, who became a servant to Naaman's wife. She said to her mistress, 'If only my master could meet the prophet who lives in Samaria, he would cure him of the leprosy.' Naaman went and reported to his master what the Israelite girl had said. 'Certainly you may go,' said the king of Aram, 'and I shall send a letter to the king of Israel.'

Naaman set off, taking with him ten talents of silver, six thousand shekels of gold, and ten changes of clothing. He delivered the letter to the king of Israel; it read: 'This letter is to inform you that I am sending to you my servant Naaman, and I beg you to cure him of his leprosy.' When the king of Israel read the letter, he tore his clothes and said, 'Am I God to kill and to make alive, that this fellow sends to me to cure a man of his disease? See how he picks a quarrel with me.' When Elisha, the man of God, heard how the king of Israel had torn his clothes, he sent him this message: 'Why did you tear your clothes? Let the man come to me, and he will know that there is a prophet in Israel.' When Naaman came with his horses and chariots and halted at the entrance to Elisha's house, Elisha sent out a messenger to say to him, 'If you go and wash seven times in the Jordan, your flesh will be restored and you will be clean.'

At this Naaman was furious and went away, saying, 'I thought he would at least have come out and stood and invoked the Lord his God by name, waved his hand over the place, and cured me of the leprosy. Are not Abana and Pharpar, rivers of Damascus, better than all the waters of Israel? Can I not wash in them and be clean?' So he turned and went off in a rage.

But his servants came to him and said, 'If the prophet had told you to do something difficult, would you not do it? How much more should you, then, if he says to you, "Wash and be clean"!' So he went down and dipped himself in the Jordan seven times as the man of God had told him, and his flesh was restored so that it was like a little child's, and he was clean.

Accompanied by his retinue he went back to the man of God and standing before him said, 'Now I know that there is no god anywhere in the world except in Israel. Will you accept a token of gratitude from your servant?' 'As the Lord lives, whom I serve,' said the prophet, 'I shall accept nothing.' Though pressed to accept, he refused. 'Then if you will not,' said Naaman, 'let me, sir, have two mules' load of earth, for I shall no longer offer whole-offering or sacrifice to any god but the Lord. In one matter only may the Lord pardon me: when my master goes to the temple of Rimmon to worship, leaning on my arm, and I worship in the temple of Rimmon when he worships there, for this let the Lord pardon me.' Elisha bade him go in peace.

Naaman had gone only a short distance on his way, when Gehazi, the servant of Elisha the man of God, said to himself, 'Has my master let this Aramaean, Naaman, go without accepting what he brought? As the Lord lives, I shall run after him and get something from him.' So Gehazi hurried after Naaman. When Naaman saw him running after him, he alighted from his chariot to meet him saying, 'Is anything wrong?' 'Nothing,' replied Gehazi, 'but my master sent me to say that two young men of the company of prophets from the hill-country of Ephraim have just arrived. Could you provide them with a talent of silver and two changes of clothing?' Naaman said, 'By all means; take two talents.' He pressed him to take them; then he tied up the two talents of silver in two bags, and the two changes of clothing, and gave them to two of his servants, and they walked ahead carrying them. When Gehazi came to the citadel he took them from the two servants, deposited them in the house, and dismissed the men; and they went away.

When he went in and stood before his master, Elisha said, 'Where have you been, Gehazi?' 'Nowhere,' said Gehazi. But he said to him, 'Was I not present in spirit when the man turned and got down from his chariot to meet you? Was it a time to get money and garments, olive trees and vineyards, sheep and oxen, slaves and slave-girls? Naaman's leprosy will fasten on you and on your descendants for ever.' Gehazi left Elisha's presence, his skin diseased, white as snow.

## THE AXE THAT FLOATED
### 2 Kings 6:1–7

The company of prophets who were with Elisha said to him, 'As you see, this place where we live with you is too cramped for us. Let us go to the Jordan and each fetch a log, and make ourselves a place to live in.' The prophet said, 'Yes, go.' One of them said, 'Please, sir, come with us.' 'I shall come,' he said, and he went with them. When they reached the Jordan and began cutting down trees it chanced that, as one of them was felling a trunk, the head of his axe flew off into the water. 'Oh, master!' he exclaimed. 'It was borrowed.' 'Where did it fall?' asked the man of God. When shown the place, he cut off a piece of wood and threw it into the water and made the iron float. Elisha said, 'Lift it out.' So he reached down and picked it up.

## ELISHA CAPTURES THE ARAMEAN SOLDIERS
### 2 Kings 6:8–23

Once, when the king of Aram was at war with Israel, he held a conference with his staff at which he said, 'I mean to attack in such and such a direction.' The man of God warned the king of Israel: 'Take care to avoid this place, for the Arameans are going down there.' The king of Israel sent word to the place about which the man of God had given him this warning; and the king took special precautions every time he found himself near that place. The king of Aram was greatly incensed at this and, summoning his staff, he said to them, 'Tell me, which of us is for the king of Israel?' 'There is no one, my lord king,' said one of his staff; 'but Elisha, the prophet in Israel, tells the king of Israel the very words you speak in your bedchamber.' 'Go, find out where he is,' said the king, 'and I shall send and seize him.' It was reported to him that the prophet was at Dothan, and he sent a strong force there with horses and chariots. They came by night and surrounded the town.

When the attendant of the man of God rose and went out early next morning, he saw a force with horses and chariots surrounding the town. 'Oh, master,' he said, 'which way are we to turn?' Elisha answered, 'Do not be afraid, for those on our side are more than those on theirs.' He offered this prayer: 'Lord, open his eyes and let him see.' The Lord opened the young man's eyes, and he saw the hills covered with horses and chariots of fire all around Elisha. As the Arameans came down towards him, Elisha prayed to the Lord: 'Strike this host, I pray, with blindness'; and they were struck blind as Elisha had asked. Elisha said to them, 'You are on the wrong road; this is not the town. Follow me and I will lead you to the man you are looking for.' And he led them to Samaria.

As soon as they had entered Samaria, Elisha prayed, 'Lord, open the eyes of these men and let them see again.' He opened their eyes, and they saw that they were inside Samaria. When the king of Israel saw them, he said to Elisha, 'My father, am I to destroy them?' 'No, you must not do that,' he answered. 'Would you destroy those whom you have not taken prisoner with your own sword and bow? As for these men, provide them with food and water, and let them eat and drink and go back to their master.' So he prepared a great feast for them; they ate and drank and then were sent back to their master. From that time Aramaean raids on Israel ceased.

## BEN-HADAD BESIEGES SAMARIA
### 2 Kings 6:24 – 7:19

But later, Ben-hadad king of Aram mustered his whole army and marched to the siege of Samaria. The city was near starvation, and they were besieging it so closely that a donkey's head was sold for eighty shekels of silver, and a quarter of a kab of locust-beans for five shekels. One day, as the king of Israel was walking along the city wall, a woman called to him, 'Help, my lord king!' He said, 'If the Lord does not bring you help, where can I find help for you? From threshing-floor or from winepress? What is your trouble?' She replied, 'This woman said to me, "Give up your child for us to eat today, and we will eat mine tomorrow." So we cooked my son and ate him; but when I said to her the next day, "Now give up your child for us to eat," she had hidden him.' When he heard the woman's story, the king tore his clothes. He was walking along the wall at the time, and, when the people looked, they saw that he had sackcloth underneath, next to his skin. He said, 'The Lord do the same to me and more, if the head of Elisha son of Shaphat stays on his shoulders today.'

Elisha was sitting at home, the elders with him. The king had dispatched one of those at court, but, before the messenger arrived, Elisha said to the elders, 'See how this son of a murderer has sent to behead me! When the messenger comes, be sure to close the door and hold it fast against him. Can you not hear his master following on his heels?' While he was still speaking, the king arrived and said, 'Look at our plight! This is the Lord's doing. Why should I wait any longer for him to help us?' Elisha answered, 'Hear this word from the Lord: By this time tomorrow a shekel will buy a measure of flour or two measures of barley at the gate of Samaria.' The officer on whose arm the king leaned said to the man of God, 'Even if the Lord were to open windows in the sky, such a thing could not happen!' He answered, 'You will see it with your own eyes, but you will not eat any of it.'

At the city gate were four lepers. They said to one another, 'Why should we stay here and wait for death? If we say we will go into the city, the famine is there, and we shall die; if we stay here, we shall die. Well then, let us go to the camp of the Arameans and give ourselves up: if they spare us, we shall live; if they put us to death, we can but die.'

At dusk they set out for the Aramaean camp, and when they reached the outskirts, they found no one there. The Lord had caused the Aramaean army to hear a sound like that of chariots and horses and a great host, so that the word went round: 'The king of Israel has hired the kings of the Hittites and the kings of Egypt to attack us.' They had taken to flight in the dusk, abandoning their tents, horses, and donkeys. Leaving the camp as it stood, they had fled for their lives. Those lepers came to the outskirts of the camp, where they went into a tent. They ate and drank, looted silver and gold and clothing, and made off and hid them. Then they came back, went into another tent and rifled it, and made off and hid the loot.

But they said to one another, 'What we are doing is not right. This is a day of good news and we are keeping it to ourselves. If we wait till morning, we shall be held to blame. We must go now and give the news to the king's household.' So they went and called to the watch at the city gate and described how they had gone to the Aramaean camp and found not one man in it and had heard no human voice: nothing but horses and donkeys tethered, and the tents left as they were. The watch called out and announced the news to the king's household in the palace.

The king rose in the night and said to his staff, 'I shall tell you what the Arameans have done. They know we are starving, so they have left their camp to go and hide in the open country, expecting us to come out, and then they can take us alive and enter the city.' One of his staff said, 'Send out a party of men with some of the horses that are left; if they live, they will be as well off as all the other Israelites who are still left; if they die, they will be no worse off than all those who have already perished. Let them go and see what has happened.' They picked two mounted men, and the king dispatched them in the track of the Aramaean army with the order to go and find out what had happened. Having followed as far as the Jordan and found the whole road littered with clothing and equipment which the Arameans had discarded in their haste, the messengers returned and made their report to the king.

The people went out and plundered the Aramaean camp, and a

223

measure of flour was sold for a shekel and two measures of barley for a shekel, so that the word of the Lord came true. The king had appointed the officer on whose arm he leaned to take charge of the gate, and the crowd trampled him to death there, just as the man of God had foretold when the king visited him. For when the man of God said to the king, 'By this time tomorrow a shekel will buy two measures of barley or one measure of flour at the gate of Samaria,' the officer had answered, 'Even if the Lord were to open windows in the sky, such a thing could not happen!' And the man of God had said, 'You will see it with your own eyes, but you will not eat any of it.'

## HAZAEL KILLS BEN-HADAD
### 2 Kings 8:7–15

Elisha came to Damascus, at a time when King Ben-hadad of Aram was ill; and when the king was told that the man of God had arrived, he ordered Hazael to take a gift with him and go to the man of God and through him enquire of the Lord whether he would recover from his illness. Hazael went, taking with him as a gift forty camel-loads of all kinds of Damascus wares. When he came into the prophet's presence, he said, 'Your son King Ben-hadad of Aram has sent me to you to ask whether he will recover from his illness.' 'Go and tell him that he will recover,' he answered; 'but the Lord has revealed to me that in fact he will die.' The man of God stood staring with set face until Hazael became disconcerted; then the man of God wept. 'Why do you weep, sir?' said Hazael. He answered, 'Because I know the harm you will do to the Israelites: you will set their fortresses on fire and put their young men to the sword; you will dash the children to the ground and rip open their pregnant women.' Hazael said, 'But I am a dog, a mere nobody; how can I do this great thing?' Elisha answered, 'The Lord has revealed to me that you will become king of Aram.' Hazael left Elisha and returned to his master, who asked what Elisha had said. 'He told me that you would recover,' he replied. But the next day he took a blanket and, after dipping it in water, laid it over the king's face, so that he died; and Hazael succeeded him.

# JEHU
## 2 Kings 9:1–21

Elisha the prophet summoned one of the company of prophets and said to him, 'Get ready for the road; take this flask of oil with you and go to Ramoth-gilead. When you arrive, look there for Jehu son of Jehoshaphat, son of Nimshi; go in and call him aside from his fellow-officers, and lead him through to an inner room. Take the flask and pour the oil on his head and say, "This is the word of the Lord: I anoint you king over Israel." After that open the door and flee for your life.'

The young prophet went to Ramoth-gilead, and when he arrived, he found the officers sitting together. He said, 'Sir, I have a word for you.' 'For which of us?' asked Jehu. 'For you, sir,' he said. Jehu rose and went into the house, where the prophet poured the oil on his head, saying, 'This is the word of the Lord the God of Israel: I anoint you king over Israel, the people of the Lord. You are to strike down the house of Ahab your master, and I shall take vengeance on Jezebel for the blood of my servants the prophets and for the blood of all the Lord's servants. The entire house of Ahab will perish; I shall destroy every mother's son of his house in Israel, whether under the protection of the family or not. I shall make Ahab's house like the house of Jeroboam son of Nebat and the house of Baasha son of Ahijah. Jezebel will be devoured by dogs in the plot of ground at Jezreel and no one will bury her.' With that he opened the door and fled.

When Jehu rejoined the king's officers, they said to him, 'Is all well? What did this crazy fellow want with you?' 'You know him and his ideas,' he said. 'That is no answer!' they replied. 'Tell us what happened.' 'I shall tell you exactly what he said: "This is the word of the Lord: I anoint you king over Israel."' They snatched up their cloaks and spread them under him at the top of the steps, and they sounded the trumpet and shouted, 'Jehu is king.'

Jehu son of Jehoshaphat, son of Nimshi, organized a conspiracy against Jehoram, while Jehoram and all the Israelites were defending Ramoth-gilead against King Hazael of Aram. King Jehoram had returned to Jezreel to recover from the wounds inflicted on him by the

Arameans in his battle against Hazael. Jehu said to his colleagues, 'If you are on my side, see that no one escapes from the city to carry the news to Jezreel.' He mounted his chariot and drove to Jezreel, for Jehoram was laid up there and King Ahaziah of Judah had gone down to visit him.

The watchman standing on the watch-tower in Jezreel saw Jehu's troops approaching and called out, 'I see a troop of men.' Jehoram said, 'Fetch a horseman and send to meet them and ask if they come peaceably.' The horseman went to meet him and said, 'The king asks, "Is it peace?"' Jehu said, 'Peace? What is that to do with you? Fall in behind me.' The watchman reported, 'The messenger has met them but is not coming back.' A second horseman was sent; when he met them, he also said, 'The king asks, "Is it peace?"' 'Peace?' said Jehu. 'What is that to do with you? Fall in behind me.' The watchman reported, 'He has met them but is not coming back. The driving is like the driving of Jehu son of Nimshi, for he drives furiously.'

'Harness my chariot,' said Jehoram. When it was ready King Jehoram of Israel and King Ahaziah of Judah went out each in his own chariot to meet Jehu, and they met him by the plot of Naboth of Jezreel.

## THE DEATH OF JEHORAM
### 2 Kings 9:22–26

When Jehoram saw Jehu, he said, 'Is it peace, Jehu?' He replied, 'Do you call it peace while your mother Jezebel keeps up her obscene idol-worship and monstrous sorceries?' Jehoram wheeled about and fled, crying out, 'Treachery, Ahaziah!' Jehu drew his bow and shot Jehoram between the shoulders; the arrow pierced his heart and he slumped down in his chariot. Jehu said to Bidkar, his lieutenant, 'Pick him up and throw him into the plot of land belonging to Naboth of Jezreel; remember how, when you and I were riding side by side behind Ahab his father, the Lord pronounced this sentence against him: "It is the word of the Lord: as surely as I saw yesterday the blood of Naboth and the blood of his sons, I will requite you on this plot of land." Pick him up, therefore, and throw him into the plot and so fulfil the word of the Lord.'

# THE DEATH OF JEZEBEL
## 2 Kings 9:30–37

Then Jehu came to Jezreel. When Jezebel heard what had happened she painted her eyes and adorned her hair, and she stood looking down from a window. As Jehu entered the gate, she said, 'Is it peace, you Zimri, you murderer of your master?' He looked up at the window and said, 'Who is on my side? Who?' Two or three eunuchs looked out to him, and he said, 'Throw her down.' They threw her down, and some of her blood splashed on to the wall and the horses, which trampled her underfoot. Jehu went in and ate and drank. 'See to this accursed woman,' he said, 'and bury her; for she is a king's daughter.' But when they went to bury her they found nothing of her but the skull, the feet, and the palms of her hands. When they went back and told him, Jehu said, 'It is the word of the Lord which his servant Elijah the Tishbite spoke, when he said, "In the plot of ground at Jezreel the dogs will devour the flesh of Jezebel, and Jezebel's corpse will lie like dung on the ground in the plot at Jezreel so that no one will be able to say: This is Jezebel."'

# THE DESTRUCTION OF THE HOUSE OF AHAB
## 2 Kings 10:1–17

There were seventy sons of Ahab left in Samaria. Jehu therefore sent a letter to Samaria, addressed to the rulers of the city, the elders, and the guardians of Ahab's sons, in which he wrote: 'You have in your care your master's family as well as his chariots and horses, fortified cities, and weapons; therefore, whenever this letter reaches you, choose the best and the most suitable of your master's sons, set him on his father's throne, and fight for your master's house.' They were panic-stricken and said, 'If two kings could not stand against him, what hope is there that we can?' Therefore the comptroller of the household and the governor of the city, with the elders and the children's guardians, sent this message to Jehu: 'We are your servants.

Whatever you tell us we shall do; but we shall not make anyone king. Do as you think fit.'

So in a second letter to them Jehu wrote: 'If you are on my side and will obey my orders, then bring the heads of your master's sons to me at Jezreel by this time tomorrow.' The royal princes, seventy in all, were with the nobles of the city who had charge of their upbringing. When the letter arrived, they took the royal princes and killed all seventy; they piled their heads in baskets and sent the heads to Jehu in Jezreel. When the messenger came to him and reported that they had brought the heads of the royal princes, he ordered them to be piled in two heaps and left till morning at the entrance to the city gate.

In the morning Jehu went out, and standing there said to all the people, 'You are fair-minded judges. I conspired against my master and killed him, but who put all these to death? Be sure then that every word which the Lord has spoken against the house of Ahab will be fulfilled, and that the Lord has now done what he promised through his servant Elijah.' So Jehu put to death all who were left of the house of Ahab in Jezreel, as well as all Ahab's nobles, his close friends, and priests, until he had left not one survivor.

Then he set out for Samaria, and on the way there, when he had reached a shepherds' shelter, he came upon the kinsmen of King Ahaziah of Judah and demanded to know who they were. 'We are kinsmen of Ahaziah,' they replied, 'and we have come down to pay our respects to the families of the king and of the queen mother.' 'Take them alive,' he said. They were taken alive, all forty-two of them, then slain, and flung into a pit that was there; he did not leave a single survivor.

When he had left that place, he found Jehonadab son of Rechab coming to meet him. Jehu greeted him and said, 'Are you with me wholeheartedly, as I am with you?' 'I am,' replied Jehonadab. 'Then if you are,' said Jehu, 'give me your hand,' and he did so. Jehu had him come up into his chariot. 'Come with me,' he said, 'and you will see my zeal for the Lord.' So he took him with him in his chariot. When he came to Samaria, he put to death all of Ahab's house who were left there and so blotted it out, in fulfilment of the word which the Lord had spoken to Elijah.

# THE DESTRUCTION OF THE PROPHETS OF BAAL
## 2 Kings 10:18–30, 35–36

Jehu called all the people together and said to them, 'Ahab served the Baal a little; Jehu will serve him much. Now summon all the prophets of Baal, all his ministers and priests; not one must be missing. For I am holding a great sacrifice to Baal, and no one who is missing from it shall live.' In this way Jehu outwitted the ministers of Baal in order to destroy them. Jehu gave the order, 'Proclaim a sacred ceremony for Baal.' This was done, and Jehu himself sent word throughout Israel. All the ministers of Baal came; there was not a man left who did not come, and when they went into the temple of Baal, it was filled from end to end. Jehu said to the person who had charge of the wardrobe, 'Bring out robes for all the ministers of Baal'; and he brought them out. Then Jehu and Jehonadab son of Rechab went into the temple of Baal and said to the ministers, 'Look carefully and make sure that there are no servants of the Lord here with you, but only the ministers of Baal.' Then they went in to offer sacrifices and whole-offerings.

Jehu had stationed eighty of his men outside and warned them, 'I shall hold you responsible for these men, and if anyone of you lets one of them escape he will pay for it with his own life.' When he had finished offering the whole-offering, Jehu ordered the guards and officers to go in and cut them all down, and let not one of them escape. They were slain without quarter, and the guard and the officers threw them out. Then going into the keep of the temple of Baal, they brought out the sacred pole from the temple and burnt it; they overthrew the sacred pillar of the Baal and pulled down the temple itself and made a privy of it – as it is today. Thus Jehu stamped out the worship of Baal in Israel. He did not however abandon the sins of Jeroboam son of Nebat who led Israel into sin: he maintained the worship of the golden calves of Bethel and Dan.

The Lord said to Jehu, 'You have done well in carrying out what is right in my eyes, and you have done to the house of Ahab all that it was in my mind to do. Therefore your sons to the fourth generation will occupy the throne of Israel.' Jehu rested with his forefathers and was buried in Samaria. His son Jehoahaz succeeded him. Jehu had reigned over Israel in Samaria for twenty-eight years.

## JEHOAHAZ
2 Kings 13:1–7

Jehoahaz son of Jehu became king over Israel in Samaria and he reigned for seventeen years. He did what was wrong in the eyes of the Lord and continued the sinful practices of Jeroboam son of Nebat who led Israel into sin, and did not give them up. This roused the anger of the Lord against Israel, and he made them subject for some years to King Hazael of Aram and Ben-hadad his son. When Jehoahaz sought to placate the Lord, the Lord heard his prayer, for he saw how the king of Aram oppressed Israel. The Lord appointed a deliverer for Israel, and they escaped from the power of Aram and settled down again in their own homes. But they did not give up the sinful practices of the house of Jeroboam who led Israel into sin, but continued in them; the goddess Asherah remained in Samaria. Hazael had left Jehoahaz no armed force except fifty horsemen, ten chariots, and ten thousand infantry; all the rest the king of Aram had destroyed and made like dust under foot.

## JEHOASH
2 Kings 13:10–11, 13

Jehoash son of Jehoahaz became king over Israel in Samaria and reigned for sixteen years. He did what was wrong in the eyes of the Lord; he did not give up any of the sinful practices of Jeroboam son of Nebat who led Israel into sin, but continued in them... Jehoash rested with his forefathers and was buried in Samaria with the kings of Israel. Jeroboam ascended the throne.

## THE DEATH OF ELISHA
2 Kings 13:14–21

When Elisha fell ill and lay on his deathbed, King Jehoash of Israel went down to him and, weeping over him, said, 'My father! My father! The chariots and horsemen of Israel!' Elisha said, 'Take a bow and arrows,' and he did so. 'Put your hand to the bow,' said the prophet.

He did so, and Elisha laid his hands on those of the king. Then he said, 'Open the window towards the east'; he opened it and Elisha told him to shoot, and he did so. Then the prophet said, 'An arrow for the Lord's victory, an arrow for victory over Aram! You will utterly defeat Aram at Aphek.' He went on, 'Now take up your arrows.' When he did so, Elisha said, 'Strike the ground with them.' He struck three times and stopped. The man of God was angry with him and said, 'You should have struck five or six times; then you would have defeated Aram utterly; as it is, you will strike Aram three times and no more.' Elisha died and was buried.

Year after year Moabite raiders used to invade the land. Once some men were burying a dead man when they caught sight of the raiders, and they threw the body into the grave of Elisha and made off. When the body touched the prophet's bones, the man came to life and rose to his feet.

## JEROBOAM II
### 2 Kings 14:23–27

Jeroboam son of Jehoash, king of Israel, became king in Samaria and reigned for forty-one years. He did what was wrong in the eyes of the Lord; he did not give up the sinful practices of Jeroboam son of Nebat who led Israel into sin. He re-established the frontiers of Israel from Lebo-hamath to the sea of the Arabah, in fulfilment of the word of the Lord the God of Israel spoken by his servant the prophet Jonah son of Amittai, from Gath-hepher. For the Lord had seen how bitterly Israel had suffered; no one was safe, whether under the protection of his family or not, and Israel was left defenceless. But the Lord had made no threat to blot out the name of Israel under heaven, and he saved them through Jeroboam son of Jehoash.

## ZECHARIAH
### 2 Kings 15:8–10, 12

Zechariah son of Jeroboam became king over Israel in Samaria and reigned for six months. He did what was wrong in the eyes of the

Lord, as his forefathers had done; he did not give up the sinful practices of Jeroboam son of Nebat who led Israel into sin. Shallum son of Jabesh formed a conspiracy against him, attacked and killed him in Ibleam, and usurped the throne... Thus the word of the Lord spoken to Jehu was fulfilled: 'Your sons to the fourth generation will occupy the throne of Israel.'

## SHALLUM
### 2 Kings 15:13–14

Shallum son of Jabesh became king... and he reigned for one full month in Samaria. Menahem son of Gadi came up from Tirzah to Samaria, attacked Shallum son of Jabesh there, killed him, and usurped the throne.

## MENAHEM
### 2 Kings 15:16–20

Then Menahem, starting out from Tirzah, destroyed Tappuah and everything in it and ravaged its territory; he ravaged it because it had not opened its gates to him, and he ripped open every pregnant woman there.

...Menahem son of Gadi became king over Israel and he reigned in Samaria for ten years. He did what was wrong in the eyes of the Lord; he did not give up the sinful practices of Jeroboam son of Nebat who led Israel into sin. In Menahem's time King Pul of Assyria invaded the country, and Menahem gave him a thousand talents of silver to obtain his help in strengthening his hold on the kingdom. Menahem laid a levy on all the men of wealth in Israel; each had to give the king of Assyria fifty silver shekels, and he withdrew without occupying the country.

## PEKAHIAH
### 2 Kings 15:23–25

Pekahiah son of Menahem became king over Israel in Samaria and reigned for two years. He did what was wrong in the eyes of the Lord; he did not give up the sinful practices of Jeroboam son of Nebat who led Israel into sin. Pekah son of Remaliah, his lieutenant, formed a conspiracy against him and, with the help of fifty Gileadites, attacked and killed him in the citadel of the royal palace in Samaria, and usurped the throne.

## PEKAH
### 2 Kings 15:27–30

Pekah son of Remaliah became king over Israel in Samaria and reigned for twenty years. He did what was wrong in the eyes of the Lord; he did not give up the sinful practices of Jeroboam son of Nebat who led Israel into sin. In the days of King Pekah of Israel, King Tiglath-pileser of Assyria came and seized Iyyon, Abel-beth-maacah, Janoah, Kedesh, Hazor, Gilead, and Galilee, with all the land of Naphtali, and deported the people to Assyria. Then Hoshea son of Elah formed a conspiracy against Pekah son of Remaliah, attacked and killed him, and usurped the throne in the twentieth year of Jotham son of Uzziah.

## HOSHEA
### 2 Kings 17:1–5

Hoshea son of Elah became king over Israel and he reigned in Samaria for nine years. He did what was wrong in the eyes of the Lord, but not as previous kings of Israel had done. King Shalmaneser of Assyria marched up against Hoshea, who had been tributary to him, but when the king of Assyria discovered that Hoshea was being disloyal to him, sending envoys to the king of Egypt at So, and withholding the annual tribute which he had been paying, the king of Assyria seized and imprisoned him. He overran the whole country and, reaching Samaria, besieged it for three years.

## THE END OF THE KINGDOM OF ISRAEL
### 2 Kings 17:6–23

In the ninth year of Hoshea [the king of Assyria] captured Samaria and deported its people to Assyria, and settled them in Halah and on the

Habor, the river of Gozan, and in the towns of Media. All this came about because the Israelites had sinned against the Lord their God who brought them up from Egypt, from the despotic rule of Pharaoh king of Egypt; they paid homage to other gods and observed the laws and customs of the nations whom the Lord had dispossessed before them, and uttered blasphemies against the Lord their God; they built shrines for themselves in all their settlements, from watch-tower to fortified city; they set up for themselves sacred pillars and sacred poles on every high hill and under every spreading tree, and burnt offerings at all the shrines there, as the nations did whom the Lord had displaced before them. By this wickedness of theirs they provoked the Lord's anger. They worshipped idols, a thing which the Lord had forbidden them to do.

Still the Lord solemnly charged Israel and Judah by every prophet and seer, saying, 'Give up your evil ways; keep my commandments and statutes given in all the law which I enjoined on your forefathers and delivered to you through my servants the prophets.' They would not listen, however, but were as stubborn and rebellious as their forefathers had been, for they too refused to put their trust in the Lord their God. They rejected his statutes and the covenant which he had made with their forefathers and the solemn warnings which he had given to them. Following worthless idols they became worthless themselves and imitated the nations round about them, which the Lord had forbidden them to do. Forsaking every commandment of the Lord their God, they made themselves images, two calves of cast metal, and also a sacred pole. They prostrated themselves to all the host of heaven and worshipped Baal; they made their sons and daughters pass through the fire. They practised augury and divination; they sold themselves to do what was wrong in the eyes of the Lord and so provoked his anger.

Thus it was that the Lord was incensed against Israel and banished them from his presence; only the tribe of Judah was left. Even Judah did not keep the commandments of the Lord their God but followed the practices adopted by Israel; so the Lord rejected all the descendants of Israel and punished them and gave them over to plunderers and finally flung them out from his presence. When he tore Israel from the house of David, they made Jeroboam son of Nebat king, and he seduced Israel from their allegiance to the Lord and led them into grave sin. The Israelites persisted in all the sins that Jeroboam had committed and did not give them up, until finally the Lord banished the Israelites from his presence, as he had threatened through all his servants the prophets, and they were deported from their own land to exile in Assyria; and there they are to this day.

## THE ORIGIN OF THE SAMARITANS
### 2 Kings 17:24–41

Then the king of Assyria brought people from Babylon, Cuthah, Avva, Hamath, and Sepharvaim, and settled them in the towns of Samaria in place of the Israelites; so they occupied Samaria and lived in its towns. In the early years of their settlement they did not pay homage to the Lord, so the Lord sent lions among them to prey on them. The king of Assyria was told that the deported peoples whom he had settled in the towns of Samaria did not know the established usage of the God of the country, and that he had sent lions among them which were preying on them because they did not know this. The king, therefore, gave orders that one of the priests taken captive from Samaria should be sent back to live there and teach the people the usage of the God of the country. So one of the deported priests came and lived at Bethel, and taught them how to worship the Lord.

But each of the nations went on making its own god. They set them up in niches at the shrines which the Samaritans had made, each nation in its own settlements. Succoth-benoth was worshipped by the men of Babylon, Nergal by the men of Cuth, Ashima by the men of Hamath, Nibhaz and Tartak by the Avvites; and the Sepharvites burnt their children as offerings to Adrammelech and Anammelech, the gods of Sepharvaim. While still paying homage to the Lord, they appointed all sorts of people to act as priests of the shrines and they resorted to them there. They paid homage to the Lord, while at the same time they served their own gods, according to the custom of the nations from which they had been carried into exile.

They keep up these old practices to this day; they do not pay homage to the Lord, for they do not keep his statutes and his judgments, the law and commandment, which he enjoined on the descendants of Jacob whom he named Israel. When the Lord made a covenant with them, he gave them this commandment: 'Do not pay homage to other gods or bow down to them or serve them or sacrifice to them, but pay homage to the Lord who brought you up from Egypt with great power and with outstretched arm; to him alone you are to bow down, to him alone you are to offer sacrifice. You must faithfully keep the statutes, the judgments, the law, and the commandments which he wrote for you; you must not pay homage to other gods. Do not forget the covenant which I made with you; do not pay homage to other gods. But to the Lord your God you are to pay homage; it is he who will preserve you from all your enemies.' However, they would not listen but continued their former practices. While these nations paid homage to the Lord they continued to serve their images, and their children and their children's children have maintained the practice of their forefathers to this day.

# Part Five

# The Kings of Judah

## REHOBOAM
### 2 Chronicles 11:1–5, 12–17, 12:1–16

When Rehoboam reached Jerusalem, he mustered the tribes of Judah and Benjamin, a hundred and eighty thousand chosen warriors, to fight against Israel and recover his kingdom. But this word of the Lord came to Shemaiah the man of God: 'Say to Rehoboam son of Solomon, king of Judah, and to all the Israelites in Judah and Benjamin, This is the word of the Lord: You are not to go up to make war on your kinsmen. Return to your homes, for this is my doing.' They listened to the word of the Lord and abandoned their campaign against Jeroboam.

Rehoboam resided in Jerusalem and built up the defences of certain towns in Judah... Also he stored shields and spears in each of them, and made them very strong. Thus he retained possession of Judah and Benjamin.

The priests and the Levites throughout the whole of Israel resorted to Rehoboam from all their territories; for the Levites had left all their common land and their own property and had gone to Judah and Jerusalem, because Jeroboam and his successors rejected their services as priests of the Lord, and he appointed his own priests for the shrines, for the demons, and for the calves which he had made. Out of all the tribes of Israel, those who were resolved to seek the Lord the God of Israel followed the Levites to Jerusalem to sacrifice to the Lord the God of their fathers. They strengthened the kingdom of Judah and for three years made Rehoboam son of Solomon secure, because he followed the example of David and Solomon during that time...

When Rehoboam's kingdom was firmly established and he grew powerful, he along with all Israel forsook the law of the Lord. In the fifth year of Rehoboam's reign, because of this disloyalty to the Lord, King Shishak of Egypt attacked Jerusalem with twelve hundred chariots and sixty thousand horsemen; he also brought with him from Egypt an innumerable following of Libyans, Sukkites, and Cushites. He captured the fortified towns of Judah and reached Jerusalem. Then Shemaiah the prophet came to Rehoboam and the leading men of Judah, who had collected together at Jerusalem in the face of the advance of Shishak, and said, 'This is the word of the Lord: You have abandoned me; therefore I now abandon you to Shishak.' The princes of Israel and the king submitted and said, 'The Lord is just.' When the Lord saw that they had submitted, there came from him this word to Shemaiah: 'Because they have submitted I shall not destroy them; I shall grant them some measure of relief: my wrath will not be poured out on Jerusalem by means of Shishak, but they will become his servants; then they will know the difference between serving me and serving the rulers of other countries.' King Shishak of Egypt in his attack on Jerusalem carried away the treasures of the house of the Lord and of the king's palace, and seized everything, including the gold shields made for Solomon. King Rehoboam replaced them with bronze shields and entrusted them to the officers of the escort who guarded the entrance of the palace. Whenever the king entered the house of the Lord, the escort entered, carrying the shields; afterwards they returned them to the guardroom. Because Rehoboam submitted, the Lord's wrath was averted from him, and he was not utterly destroyed; Judah enjoyed prosperity.

King Rehoboam increased his power in Jerusalem. He was forty-one years old when he came to the throne, and he reigned for seventeen years in Jerusalem, the city which the Lord had chosen out of all the tribes of Israel as the place to receive his name. Rehoboam's mother was an Ammonite woman called Naamah. He did what was wrong; he did not make a practice of seeking guidance of the Lord. The events of Rehoboam's reign, from first to last, are recorded in the histories of Shemaiah the prophet and Iddo the seer. There was continual fighting between Rehoboam and Jeroboam. Rehoboam rested with his forefathers and was buried in the city of David. His son Abijah succeeded him.

# ABIJAH
## 2 Chronicles 13:1–18

In the eighteenth year of King Jeroboam's reign Abijah became king of Judah. He reigned in Jerusalem for three years; his mother was Maacah daughter of Uriel of Gibeah.

When war broke out between Abijah and Jeroboam, Abijah drew up his army of four hundred thousand picked troops in order of battle, while Jeroboam formed up against him with eight hundred thousand picked troops. Abijah stood up on the slopes of Mount Zemaraim in the hill-country of Ephraim and called out, 'Jeroboam and all Israel, hear me: Do you not know that the Lord the God of Israel gave the kingship over Israel to David and his descendants for ever by a covenant of salt? Yet Jeroboam son of Nebat, a servant of Solomon son of David, rose in rebellion against his lord, and certain worthless scoundrels gathered round him, who stubbornly opposed Solomon's son Rehoboam when he was young and inexperienced, and he was no match for them.

'Now you propose to match yourselves against the kingdom of the Lord as ruled by David's sons, you with your mob of supporters and the golden calves which Jeroboam has made to be your gods. Have you not dismissed from office the Aaronites, priests of the Lord, and the Levites, and followed the practice of other lands in appointing your own priests? If any man comes for ordination with an offering of a young bull and seven rams, you accept him as a priest to a god who is no god.

'But as for us, the Lord is our God and we have not forsaken him. We have Aaronites as priests ministering to the Lord with the Levites, duly discharging their office. Morning and evening, these burn whole-offerings and fragrant incense to the Lord and offer the Bread of the Presence arranged in rows on a table ritually clean; they also kindle the lamps on the gold lampstand every evening. Thus we do indeed keep the charge of the Lord our God, whereas you have forsaken him. God is with us at our head, and his priests stand there with trumpets to signal the battle cry against you. Men of Israel, do not fight the Lord the God of your forefathers; you will have no success.'

Jeroboam sent a detachment of his troops to go round and lay an ambush in the rear, so that his main body faced Judah while the ambush lay behind them. The men of Judah turned to find that they were engaged front and rear. They cried to the Lord for help; the priests sounded their trumpets, and the men of Judah raised their battle cry; and when they shouted, God put Jeroboam and all Israel to rout before Abijah and Judah. The Israelites fled before the men of Judah, and God delivered them into their power. Abijah and his men defeated them with very heavy losses: five hundred thousand picked men of Israel fell in the battle. On that occasion the Israelites had to submit; Judah prevailed because they relied on the Lord the God of their forefathers.

## ASA

2 Chronicles 14:1–5, 16:1–7, 9–14

Abijah rested with his forefathers and was buried in the city of David. His son Asa succeeded him, and in his time the land had peace for ten years.

Asa did what was good and right in the eyes of the Lord his God. He suppressed the foreign altars and the shrines, smashed the sacred pillars and hacked down the sacred poles, and ordered Judah to seek guidance of the Lord the God of their forefathers and to keep the law and the commandments. In all the towns he suppressed the shrines and the incense-altars, and the kingdom was at peace under him…

In the thirty-sixth year of the reign of Asa, King Baasha of Israel invaded Judah and fortified Ramah to prevent anyone leaving or entering the kingdom of Asa of Judah. Asa brought out silver and gold from the treasuries of the house of the Lord and the king's palace, and sent them to Ben-hadad king of Aram, whose capital was Damascus, with this request: 'Let there be an alliance between us, as there was between our fathers. Herewith I send you silver and gold; break off your alliance with King Baasha of Israel, so that he may abandon his campaign against me.' Ben-hadad listened with approval to King Asa; he ordered his army commanders to move against the towns of Israel, and they attacked Iyyon, Dan, Abel-mayim, and all the store-cities of Naphtali. When Baasha heard of it, he discontinued the fortifying of Ramah and stopped all work on it. Then King Asa took with him all the men of Judah and they removed the stones of Ramah and the timbers with which Baasha had fortified it, and he used them to fortify Geba and Mizpah.

At that time the seer Hanani came to King Asa of Judah and said to him, 'Because you relied on the king of Aram and not on the Lord your God, the army of the king of Israel has escaped... The eyes of the Lord range through the whole world, to bring aid and comfort to those whose hearts are loyal to him. You have acted foolishly in this affair; you will have wars from now on.' Asa was vexed with the seer and had him put in the stocks; for those words had made the king very indignant. At the same time he treated some of the people with great brutality.

The events of Asa's reign, from beginning to end, are recorded in the annals of the kings of Judah and Israel. In the thirty-ninth year of his reign Asa became gravely affected with disease in his feet; he did not seek guidance of the Lord but resorted to physicians. He rested with his forefathers, in the forty-first year of his reign, and was buried in the tomb which he had bought for himself in the city of David, being laid on a bier which had been heaped with all kinds of spices skilfully compounded; and a great fire was kindled in his honour.

## JEHOSHAPHAT
### 2 Chronicles 17:1–6, 20:31

Asa was succeeded by his son Jehoshaphat, who strengthened his position against Israel, posting troops in all the fortified towns of Judah and stationing garrisons throughout Judah and in the towns of Ephraim which his father Asa had captured. The Lord was with Jehoshaphat, for he followed the example his father had set in his early years and did not resort to the baalim; he sought guidance of the God of his father and obeyed his commandments and did not follow the practices of Israel. The Lord established the kingdom under his control; all Judah brought him gifts, and his wealth and fame became very great. He took pride in the service of the Lord; he again suppressed the shrines and the sacred poles in Judah...

Thus Jehoshaphat reigned over Judah. He was thirty-five years old when he came to the throne, and he reigned in Jerusalem for twenty-five years; his mother was Azubah daughter of Shilhi.

# JORAM

2 Chronicles 21:1, 4, 6–7, 20

Jehoshaphat rested with his forefathers and was buried with them in the city of David. He was succeeded by his son Joram...

When Joram was firmly established on his father's throne, he put to the sword all his brothers, as well as some of the leading figures in Israel... He followed the practices of the kings of Israel as the house of Ahab had done, for he had married Ahab's daughter; he did what was wrong in the eyes of the Lord. Yet for the sake of the covenant which he had made with David, the Lord was unwilling to destroy the house of David, as he had promised to give him and his descendants a lamp for all time...

Joram was thirty-two years old when he became king, and he reigned in Jerusalem for eight years. His passing went unsung, and he was buried in the city of David, but not in the burial-place of the kings.

# AHAZIAH

2 Chronicles 22:1–9

Ahaziah son of Joram became king of Judah. He was twenty-two years old when he came to the throne, and he reigned in Jerusalem for one year; his mother was Athaliah granddaughter of Omri. He too followed the practices of the house of Ahab, for his mother was his counsellor in wickedness. He did what was wrong in the eyes of the Lord like the house of Ahab, for they had been his counsellors after his father's death, to his undoing. He followed their counsel also in the alliance he made with Jehoram son of Ahab king of Israel, to fight against King Hazael of Aram at Ramoth-gilead. But Jehoram was wounded by the Arameans, and retired to Jezreel to recover from the wounds inflicted on him at Ramoth in battle with King Hazael.

Because of Jehoram's injury Ahaziah son of Joram king of Judah went down to Jezreel to visit him. It was God's will that the visit of Ahaziah to Jehoram should be the occasion of his downfall. During the visit he went out with Jehoram to meet Jehu son of Nimshi, whom the Lord had anointed to bring the house of Ahab to an end. So it came about that Jehu, who was then at variance with the house of Ahab, found the officers of Judah and the kinsmen of Ahaziah who were his attendants, and killed them. He then searched out Ahaziah himself, and his men captured him in Samaria, where he had gone into hiding. They brought him to Jehu and put him to death; they gave him burial, for they said, 'He was descended from Jehoshaphat who sought the guidance of the Lord with his whole heart.' There was no one left of the house of Ahaziah strong enough to rule.

## QUEEN ATHALIAH
### 2 Chronicles 22:10 – 23:21

As soon as Athaliah mother of Ahaziah saw that her son was dead, she set out to get rid of the whole royal line of the house of Judah. But Jehosheba the daughter of King Joram took Ahaziah's son Joash and stole him away from among the princes who were being murdered; she put him and his nurse in a bedchamber. Thus Jehosheba daughter of King Joram and wife of Jehoiada the priest, because she was Ahaziah's sister, hid Joash from Athaliah so that she did not put him to death. He remained concealed with them in the house of God for six years, while Athaliah ruled the country.

In the seventh year Jehoiada felt himself strong enough to make an agreement with Azariah son of Jeroham, Ishmael son of Jehohanan, Azariah son of Obed, Maaseiah son of Adaiah, and Elishaphat son of Zichri, all captains of units of a hundred. They went throughout Judah and gathered to Jerusalem the Levites from all the cities of Judah and the heads of clans in Israel, and they came to Jerusalem. The whole assembly made a compact with the king in the house of God, and Jehoiada said to them, 'Here is the king's son! He will be king, as the

Lord promised that David's descendants should be. This is what you must do: one third of you, priests and Levites, as you come on duty on the sabbath, are to be on guard at the threshold gates, another third are to be in the royal palace, and another third are to be at the Foundation Gate, while all the people will be in the courts of the house of the Lord. No one must enter the house of the Lord except the priests and the attendant Levites; they may enter, for they are holy, but all the people must continue to keep the Lord's charge. The Levites must mount guard round the king, each man holding his weapons, and anyone who tries to enter the house is to be put to death. They are to stay with the king wherever he goes.'

The Levites and all Judah carried out the orders of Jehoiada the priest to the letter: each captain took his men, both those who came on duty on the sabbath and those who went off, for Jehoiada the priest had not released the outgoing divisions. Jehoiada the priest handed out to the captains King David's spears, shields, and bucklers, which were kept in the house of God. He stationed all the troops round the king, each man holding his weapon, from corner to corner of the house to north and south. Then they brought out the king's son, put the crown on his head, handed him the testimony, and proclaimed him king. When Jehoiada and his sons anointed him, a shout went up: 'Long live the king!'

When Athaliah heard the noise made by the people as they ran and cheered the king, she came into the house of the Lord where the people were, and found the king standing by the pillar at the entrance, amidst outbursts of song and fanfares of trumpets in his honour; all the populace were rejoicing and blowing trumpets, and singers with musical instruments were leading the celebrations. Athaliah tore her clothes and cried, 'Treason! Treason!' Jehoiada the priest gave orders to the captains in command of the troops: 'Bring her outside the precincts and put to the sword anyone in attendance on her'; for the priest said, 'Do not kill her in the house of the Lord.' They took her and brought her to the royal palace and there at the passage to the Horse Gate they put her to death.

Jehoiada made a covenant between the Lord on one side and the whole people and the king on the other, that they should be the Lord's people. The people all went to the temple of Baal and pulled it down; they smashed its altars and images, and they slew Mattan the priest of Baal before the altars.

Jehoiada committed the supervision of the house of the Lord to the charge of the priests and the Levites whom David had allocated to the house of the Lord, to offer whole-offerings to the Lord as prescribed in the law of Moses, with the singing and rejoicing as handed down from David. He stationed the door-keepers at the gates of the house of the Lord, to prevent anyone entering who was in any way unclean. Then he took the captains of units of a hundred, the nobles, and the governors of the people, and all the people of the land, and they escorted the king from the house of the Lord through the Upper Gate to the palace, and seated him on the royal throne. The whole people rejoiced and the city had quiet. That is how Athaliah was put to the sword.

# JOASH
## 2 Chronicles 24:1–27

Joash was seven years old when he became king, and he reigned in Jerusalem for forty years; his mother was Zibiah from Beersheba. He did what was right in the eyes of the Lord as long as Jehoiada the priest was alive. Jehoiada chose him two wives, and he had a family of sons and daughters.

Some time afterwards, Joash decided to renovate the house of the Lord. He assembled the priests and Levites and said to them, 'Go through the cities and towns of Judah and collect without delay the annual tax from all the Israelites for the restoration of the house of your God.' But the Levites did not act quickly. The king summoned Jehoiada the chief priest and asked him, 'Why have you not required the Levites to bring in from Judah and Jerusalem the tax imposed by Moses the servant of the Lord and by the assembly of Israel for the Tent of the Testimony?' For the wicked Athaliah and her adherents had broken into the house of God and had even devoted all its holy things to the service of the baalim.

The king ordered a chest to be made and placed outside the gate of the house of the Lord; and proclamation was made throughout

Judah and Jerusalem that the people should bring to the Lord the tax imposed on Israel in the wilderness by Moses the servant of God. All the leaders and the people gladly brought their taxes and dropped them into the chest until it was full. Whenever the chest was brought by the Levites to the king's officers and they saw that it was well filled, the king's secretary and the chief priest's officer would come to empty it, after which it was returned to its place. This they did daily, and a large sum of money was collected. The king and Jehoiada handed it over to those responsible for carrying out the work in the house of the Lord, and they hired masons and carpenters to do the renovation, as well as craftsmen in iron and copper to restore the house. The workmen got on with their task and the work progressed under their hands; they restored the house of God according to its original design and strengthened it. When they had finished, they brought what was left of the money to the king and Jehoiada, and it was made into vessels for the house of the Lord, both for service and for sacrificing, saucers and other articles of gold and silver. During Jehoiada's lifetime whole-offerings were offered regularly in the house of the Lord.

Jehoiada, now old and weighed down with years, died at the age of a hundred and thirty and was buried with the kings in the city of David, because he had done good in Israel in the service of God and of his house.

After the death of Jehoiada the leading men of Judah came and made obeisance to the king. He listened to them, and they forsook the house of the Lord the God of their forefathers and worshipped sacred poles and idols. For this wickedness Judah and Jerusalem suffered. The Lord sent prophets to bring them back to himself, prophets who denounced them but were not heeded. Then the spirit of God took possession of Zechariah son of Jehoiada the priest. Taking his stance looking down on the people he declared, 'This is the word of God: Why do you disobey the commands of the Lord and court disaster? Because you have forsaken the Lord, he has forsaken you.' But they made common cause against him, and on orders from the king they stoned him to death in the court of the house of the Lord. King Joash, forgetful of the loyalty of Zechariah's father Jehoiada, killed his son. As he was dying he said, 'May the Lord see this and exact the penalty.'

At the turn of the year a force of Arameans advanced against

Joash; they invaded Judah and Jerusalem and massacred all the officers of the army, so that it ceased to exist, and they sent all their spoil to the king of Damascus.

Although the Arameans had invaded with a small force, the Lord delivered a very great army into their power, because the people had forsaken the Lord the God of their forefathers; and Joash suffered just punishment.

When the Arameans had withdrawn, leaving the king severely wounded, his servants conspired against him to avenge the death of the son of Jehoiada the priest, and they murdered him on his bed. Thus he died and was buried in the city of David, but not in the burial-place of the kings. The conspirators were Zabad son of Shimeath an Ammonite woman and Jehozabad son of Shimrith a Moabite woman. His children, the many oracles about him, and his reconstruction of the house of God are all on record in the discourse given in the annals of the kings. His son Amaziah succeeded him.

## AMAZIAH
### 2 Chronicles 25:1–5, 11–12, 14–17, 21–28

Amaziah was twenty-five years old when he came to the throne, and he reigned in Jerusalem for twenty-nine years; his mother was Jehoaddan from Jerusalem. He did what was right in the eyes of the Lord, yet not wholeheartedly. As soon as the royal power was firmly in his grasp, he put to death those of his servants who had murdered the king his father; but he spared their children, in obedience to the Lord's command written in the law of Moses: 'Parents are not to be put to death for their children, nor children for their parents; each one may be put to death only for his own sin.'

Amaziah assembled the men of Judah and drew them up by families, and Benjamin as well as all Judah, under officers over units of a thousand and a hundred. He mustered those of twenty years old and upwards and found their number to be three hundred thousand, all picked troops ready for service, able to handle spear and shield...

Amaziah led his men with resolution to the valley of Salt and there killed ten thousand men of Seir. The men of Judah captured another ten thousand men alive, brought them to the top of a cliff, and hurled them over so that they were all dashed to pieces...

After Amaziah had returned from the defeat of the Edomites, he brought the gods of the people of Seir and, setting them up as his own gods, worshipped them and burnt sacrifices to them. The Lord was angry with Amaziah for this and sent a prophet who said to him, 'Why have you resorted to gods who could not save their own people from you?' While he was speaking, the king said to him, 'Have we appointed you counsellor to the king? Stop! Why risk your life?' The prophet did stop, but first he said, 'I know that God has determined to destroy you because you do this and do not listen to my counsel.'

King Amaziah of Judah, after consultation, sent envoys to Jehoash son of Jehoahaz son of Jehu, king of Israel, to propose a confrontation... So King Jehoash of Israel marched out, and he and King Amaziah of Judah clashed at Beth-shemesh in Judah. The men of Judah were routed by Israel and fled to their homes. King Jehoash of Israel captured Amaziah king of Judah, son of Joash, son of Jehoahaz, at Beth-shemesh. He brought him to Jerusalem, where he broke down the city wall from the Ephraim Gate to the Corner Gate, a distance of four hundred cubits. He took all the gold and silver and all the vessels found in the house of God, in the care of Obed-edom, and the treasures of the palace, as well as hostages, and then returned to Samaria.

Amaziah son of Joash, king of Judah, outlived Jehoash son of Jehoahaz, king of Israel, by fifteen years. The other events of Amaziah's reign, from first to last, are recorded in the annals of the kings of Judah and Israel. From the time when he turned away from the Lord, a conspiracy was formed against him in Jerusalem, and he fled to Lachish; the conspirators sent after him to Lachish and put him to death there. His body was conveyed on horseback to Jerusalem, and there he was buried with his forefathers in the city of David.

## UZZIAH
### 2 Chronicles 26:1–5, 15–21

The people of Judah, acting together, took Uzziah, now sixteen years old, and made him king in succession to his father Amaziah. It was he who built Eloth and restored it to Judah after the king rested with his forefathers.

Uzziah was sixteen years old when he came to the throne, and he reigned in Jerusalem for fifty-two years; his mother was Jecoliah from Jerusalem. He did what was right in the eyes of the Lord, as Amaziah his father had done. He set himself to seek the guidance of God in the days of Zechariah, who instructed him in the fear of God; as long as he sought guidance from the Lord, God caused him to prosper...

In Jerusalem he had machines designed by engineers for use on towers and battlements to discharge arrows and large stones. His fame spread far and wide, for he was so wonderfully gifted that he became very powerful.

But when he grew powerful his pride became great and led to his own undoing: he offended against the Lord his God by entering the temple of the Lord to burn incense on the incense-altar. Azariah the priest and eighty others of the Lord's priests, courageous men, went in after King Uzziah, confronted him, and said, 'It is not for you, Uzziah, to burn incense to the Lord, but for the Aaronite priests who have been consecrated for that office. Leave the sanctuary; for you have offended, and that will certainly bring you no honour from the Lord God.' The king, who had a censer in his hand ready to burn incense, was enraged; but while he was raging at the priests, leprosy broke out on his forehead in the presence of the priests, there in the house of the Lord, beside the altar of incense. When Azariah the chief priest and the other priests looked towards him, they saw that his forehead was leprous. They hurried him out of the temple, and indeed he himself hastened to leave, because the Lord had struck him with the disease. King Uzziah remained a leper till the day of his death; he lived in his palace as a leper, relieved of all duties and excluded from the house of the Lord, while his son Jotham was comptroller of the household and regent over the country.

## JOTHAM
2 Chronicles 27:1–2, 8–9

Jotham was twenty-five years old when he came to the throne, and he reigned in Jerusalem for sixteen years; his mother was Jerushah daughter of Zadok. He did what was right in the eyes of the Lord, as his father Uzziah had done, but unlike him he did not enter the temple of the Lord; the people, however, continued their corrupt practices...

He was twenty-five years old when he came to the throne, and he reigned in Jerusalem for sixteen years. He rested with his forefathers and was buried in the city of David. His son Ahaz succeeded him.

## AHAZ
### 2 Chronicles 28:1–6, 16–25

Ahaz was twenty years old when he came to the throne, and he reigned in Jerusalem for sixteen years. He did not do what was right in the eyes of the Lord like his forefather David, but followed in the footsteps of the kings of Israel, and cast metal images for the baalim. He also burnt sacrifices in the valley of Ben-hinnom; he even burnt his sons in the fire according to the abominable practice of the nations whom the Lord had dispossessed in favour of the Israelites. He sacrificed and burned offerings at the shrines and on the hilltops and under every spreading tree.

The Lord his God let Ahaz suffer at the hands of the king of Aram: the Arameans defeated him, took many captives, and brought them to Damascus. He was also made to suffer at the hands of the king of Israel, who inflicted a severe defeat on him. This was Pekah son of Remaliah, who killed in one day a hundred and twenty thousand men of Judah, seasoned troops, for they had forsaken the Lord the God of their forefathers...

At that time King Ahaz sent to the king of Assyria for help. The Edomites had invaded again and defeated Judah and carried away prisoners, while the Philistines had raided towns of the Shephelah and of the Negeb of Judah; they had captured and occupied Beth-shemesh, Aijalon, and Gederoth, as well as Soco, Timnah, and Gimzo with their villages. The Lord had reduced Judah to submission because of Ahaz king of Judah; for his actions in Judah had been unbridled and he had been grossly unfaithful to the Lord. Then King Tiglath-pileser of Assyria came to him and, far from assisting him, pressed him hard. Ahaz stripped the house of the Lord, the king's palace, and the houses of his officers, and gave the plunder to the king of Assyria; but all to no purpose.

This king, Ahaz, when hard pressed, became more and more unfaithful to the Lord; he sacrificed to the gods of Damascus who had defeated him, for he said, 'The gods of the kings of Aram helped them; I shall sacrifice to them so that they may help me.' But in fact they caused his downfall and that of all Israel. Then Ahaz gathered together the vessels of the house of God and broke them up, and shut up the doors of the house of the Lord; he made himself altars at every corner in Jerusalem, and at every town of Judah he made shrines to burn sacrifices to other gods and provoked the anger of the Lord the God of his forefathers.

## HEZEKIAH
### 2 Kings 18:1–6

In the third year of Hoshea son of Elah, king of Israel, Hezekiah son of King Ahaz of Judah became king. He was twenty-five years old when he came to the throne, and he reigned in Jerusalem for twenty-nine years; his mother was Abi daughter of Zechariah. He did what was right in the eyes of the Lord, as his ancestor David had done. It was he who suppressed the shrines, smashed the sacred pillars, cut down every sacred pole, and broke up the bronze serpent that Moses had made, for up to that time the Israelites had been in the habit of burning sacrifices to it; they called it Nehushtan. He put his trust in the Lord the God of Israel; there was nobody like him among all the kings of Judah who succeeded him or among those who had gone before him. He remained loyal to the Lord and did not fail in his allegiance to him, and he kept the commandments which the Lord had given to Moses.

## SENNACHERIB INVADES JUDAH
### 2 Kings 18:13 – 19:37

In the fourteenth year of King Hezekiah's reign, King Sennacherib of Assyria attacked and captured all the fortified towns of Judah.

Hezekiah sent a message to the king of Assyria at Lachish: 'I have done wrong; withdraw from me, and I shall pay any penalty you impose upon me.' The king of Assyria laid on Hezekiah king of Judah a penalty of three hundred talents of silver and thirty talents of gold; and Hezekiah gave him all the silver found in the house of the Lord and in the treasuries of the palace. At that time Hezekiah stripped of their gold the doors of the temple of the Lord and the door-frames which he himself had plated, and gave it to the king of Assyria.

From Lachish the king of Assyria sent the commander-in-chief, the chief eunuch, and the chief officer with a strong force to King Hezekiah at Jerusalem. They marched up and when they reached Jerusalem they halted by the conduit of the Upper Pool on the causeway leading to the Fuller's Field. When they called for the king, the comptroller of the household, Eliakim son of Hilkiah, came out to them with Shebna, the adjutant-general, and Joah son of Asaph, the secretary of state.

The chief officer said to them, 'Tell Hezekiah that this is the message of the Great King, the king of Assyria: "What ground have you for this confidence of yours? Do you think words can take the place of skill and military strength? On whom then do you rely for support in your rebellion against me? On Egypt? Egypt is a splintered cane that will run into a man's hand and pierce it if he leans on it. That is what Pharaoh king of Egypt proves to all who rely on him. And if you tell me that you are relying on the Lord your God, is he not the god whose shrines and altars Hezekiah has suppressed, telling Judah and Jerusalem they must worship at this altar in Jerusalem?"

'Now, make a deal with my master the king of Assyria: I shall give you two thousand horses if you can find riders for them. How then can you reject the authority of even the least of my master's servants and rely on Egypt for chariots and horsemen? Do you think that I have come to attack this place and destroy it without the consent of the Lord? No; the Lord himself said to me, "Go up and destroy this land."'

Eliakim son of Hilkiah, Shebna, and Joah said to the chief officer, 'Please speak to us in Aramaic, for we understand it; do not speak Hebrew to us within earshot of the people on the city wall.' The chief officer answered, 'Is it to your master and to you that my master has sent me to say this? Is it not to the people sitting on the wall who, like you, will have to eat their own dung and drink their own urine?'

Then he stood and shouted in Hebrew, 'Hear the message of the Great King, the king of Assyria! These are the king's words: "Do not be taken in by Hezekiah. He is powerless to save you from me. Do not let him persuade you to rely on the Lord, and tell you that the Lord will surely save you and that this city will never be surrendered to the king of Assyria." Do not listen to Hezekiah, for this is what the king of Assyria says: "Make your peace with me, and surrender. Then every one of you will eat the fruit of his own vine and of his own fig tree, and drink the water of his own cistern, until I come and take you to a land like your own, a land of grain and new wine, of bread and vineyards, of olives, fine oil, and honey – life for you all, instead of death. Do not listen to Hezekiah; he will only mislead you by telling you that the Lord will save you. Did any god of the nations save his land from the king of Assyria's power? Where are the gods of Hamath and Arpad? Where are the gods of Sepharvaim, Hena, and Ivvah? Where are the gods of Samaria? Did they save Samaria from me? Among all the gods of the nations is there one who saved his land from me? So how is the Lord to save Jerusalem?"'

The people remained silent and said not a word in reply, for the king had given orders that no one was to answer him. Eliakim son of Hilkiah, comptroller of the household, Shebna the adjutant-general, and Joah son of Asaph, secretary of state, came to Hezekiah with their clothes torn and reported the words of the chief officer.

When King Hezekiah heard their report, he tore his clothes, put on sackcloth, and went into the house of the Lord. He sent Eliakim comptroller of the household, Shebna the adjutant-general, and the senior priests, all wearing sackcloth, to the prophet Isaiah son of Amoz, to give him this message from the king: 'Today is a day of trouble for us, a day of reproof and contumely. We are like a woman who has no strength to bring to birth the child she is carrying. It may be that the Lord your God will give heed to all the words of the chief officer whom his master the king of Assyria sent to taunt the living God, and will confute the words which the Lord your God heard. Offer a prayer for those who still survive.'

When King Hezekiah's servants came to Isaiah, they were given this answer for their master: 'Here is the word of the Lord: Do not be alarmed at what you heard when the Assyrian king's minions blasphemed me. I shall sap his morale till at a mere rumour he will withdraw to his own country; and there I shall make him fall by the sword.'

Meanwhile the chief officer went back, and having heard that the king of Assyria had moved camp from Lachish, he found him attacking Libnah. But when the king learnt that King Tirhakah of Cush was on the way to engage him in battle, he sent messengers again to King Hezekiah of Judah to say to him, 'How can you be deluded by your God on whom you rely when he promises that Jerusalem will not fall into the hands of the king of Assyria? You yourself must have heard what the kings of Assyria have done to all countries: they utterly destroyed them. Can you then hope to escape? Did their gods save the nations which my predecessors wiped out: Gozan, Harran, Rezeph, and the people of Eden living in Telassar? Where are the kings of Hamath, of Arpad, and of Lahir, Sepharvaim, Hena, and Ivvah?'

Hezekiah received the letter from the messengers and, having read it, he went up to the house of the Lord and spread it out before the Lord with this prayer: 'Lord God of Israel, enthroned on the cherubim, you alone are God of all the kingdoms of the world; you made heaven and earth. Incline your ear, Lord, and listen; open your eyes, Lord, and see; hear the words that Sennacherib has sent to taunt the living God. Lord, it is true that the kings of Assyria have laid waste the nations and their lands and have consigned their gods to the flames. They destroyed them, because they were no gods but the work of men's hands, mere wood and stone. Now, Lord our God, save us from his power, so that all the kingdoms of the earth may know that you alone, Lord, are God.'

Isaiah son of Amoz sent Hezekiah the following message: 'This is the word of the Lord the God of Israel: I have heard your prayer to me concerning King Sennacherib of Assyria, and this is the word which the Lord has spoken against him:

The virgin daughter of Zion disdains you,
she laughs you to scorn;
the daughter of Jerusalem tosses her head as you retreat.

Whom have you taunted and blasphemed?
Against whom did you raise an outcry,
casting haughty glances at the Holy One of Israel?
You sent your messengers to taunt the Lord, and said:
"I have mounted my chariot and performed mighty deeds;
I have ascended the mountain heights,
gone to the remote recesses of Lebanon.
I have felled its tallest cedars,
the finest of its pines;
I have reached its farthest corners,
the most luxuriant forest.
I have dug wells
and drunk the waters of a foreign land,
and with the sole of my foot I have dried up
all the streams of Egypt."

'Have you not heard?
Long ago I did it all.
In days gone by I planned it
and now I have brought it about,
till your fortified cities have crashed
into heaps of rubble.
Their inhabitants, shorn of strength,
disheartened and put to shame,
were but as plants in the field, frail as green herbs,
as grass on the rooftops blasted by the east wind.
I know your rising up and your sitting down,
your going out and your coming in.
The frenzy of your rage against me
and your arrogance have come to my ears.
I shall put a ring in your nose
and a bridle in your mouth,
and I shall take you back
by the way on which you came.

'This will be the sign for you: this year you will eat the leavings of the grain and in the second year what is self-sown; but in the third year you will sow and reap, plant vineyards and eat their fruit. The survivors left in Judah will strike fresh root below ground and yield fruit above ground, for a remnant will come out of Jerusalem and survivors from Mount Zion. The zeal of the Lord will perform this.

'Therefore, this is the word of the Lord about the king of Assyria:

> He will not enter this city
> or shoot an arrow there,
> he will not advance against it with shield
> or cast up a siege-ramp against it.
> By the way he came he will go back;
> he will not enter this city.
> This is the word of the Lord.
> I shall shield this city to deliver it
> for my own sake and for the sake of my servant David.'

That night the angel of the Lord went out and struck down a hundred and eighty-five thousand in the Assyrian camp; when morning dawned, there they all lay dead. King Sennacherib of Assyria broke camp and marched away; he went back to Nineveh and remained there. One day, while he was worshipping in the temple of his god Nisroch, Adrammelech and Sharezer his sons assassinated him and made their escape to the land of Ararat. His son Esarhaddon succeeded him.


## HEZEKIAH'S FINAL YEARS
### 2 Kings 20

At this time Hezekiah became mortally ill, and the prophet Isaiah son of Amoz came to him with this message from the Lord: 'Give your last instructions to your household, for you are dying; you will not recover.' Hezekiah turned his face to the wall and offered this prayer to the Lord: 'Lord, remember how I have lived before you, faithful and loyal in your service, doing always what was pleasing to you.' And he wept bitterly. But before Isaiah had left the citadel, the word of the Lord came to him: 'Go back and say to Hezekiah, the prince of my people: This is the word of the Lord the God of your father David: I have heard your prayer and seen your tears; I shall heal you, and on the third day you will go up to the house of the Lord. I shall add fifteen years to your life and deliver you and this city from the king of Assyria. I shall protect this city for my own sake and for the sake of my servant David.'

Isaiah told them to prepare a fig-plaster; when it was made and applied to the inflammation, Hezekiah recovered. He asked Isaiah what proof there was that the Lord would cure him and that he would go up to the house of the Lord on the third day. Isaiah replied, 'This will be your proof from the Lord that he will do what he has promised; will the shadow go forward ten steps or back ten steps?' Hezekiah answered, 'It is an easy thing for the shadow to move forward ten steps; rather let it go back ten steps.' Isaiah the prophet called to the Lord, and he made the shadow go back ten steps where it had advanced down the stairway of Ahaz.

At that time the king of Babylon, Merodach-baladan son of Baladan, sent envoys with a gift to Hezekiah, for he heard that he had been ill. Hezekiah welcomed them and showed them all his treasury, the silver and gold, the spices and fragrant oil, his armoury, and everything to be found among his treasures; there was nothing in his palace or in his whole realm that Hezekiah did not show them.

The prophet Isaiah came to King Hezekiah and asked, 'What did these men say? Where did they come from?' 'They came from a distant country,' Hezekiah answered, 'from Babylon.' 'What did they see in your palace?' Isaiah demanded. 'They saw everything,' was the reply; 'there was nothing among my treasures that I did not show them.' Isaiah said to Hezekiah, 'Hear the word of the Lord: The time is coming, says the Lord, when everything in your palace, and all that your forefathers have amassed till the present day, will be carried away to Babylon; not a thing will be left. And some of your sons, your own offspring, will be taken from you to serve as eunuchs in the palace of the king of Babylon.' Hezekiah answered, 'The word of the Lord which you have spoken is good,' for he was thinking to himself that peace and security would last out his lifetime.

The other events of Hezekiah's reign, his exploits, and how he made the pool and the conduit and brought water into the city, are recorded in the annals of the kings of Judah. Hezekiah rested with his forefathers, and his son Manasseh succeeded him.

## MANASSEH
### 2 Kings 21:1–16

Manasseh was twelve years old when he came to the throne, and he reigned in Jerusalem for fifty-five years; his mother was Hephzibah. He did what was wrong in the eyes of the Lord, in following the abominable practices of the nations which the Lord had dispossessed in favour of the Israelites. He rebuilt the shrines which his father Hezekiah had destroyed, he erected altars to the Baal, made a sacred pole as Ahab king of Israel had done, and prostrated himself before all the host of heaven and served them. He built altars in the house of the Lord, that house of which the Lord had said, 'I shall set my name in Jerusalem.' He built altars for all the host of heaven in the two courts of the house of the Lord; he made his son pass through the fire, he practised soothsaying and divination, and dealt with ghosts and spirits. He did much wrong in the eyes of the Lord and provoked his anger. He made an image of the goddess Asherah and set it up in the house of which the Lord had said to David and Solomon his son, 'In this house and Jerusalem, which I chose out of all the tribes of Israel, I shall establish my name for all time. I shall not again make Israel outcasts from the land which I gave to their forefathers, if only they are careful to observe all my commands and all the law that my servant Moses gave them.' But they did not obey, and Manasseh led them astray into wickedness far worse than that of the nations which the Lord had exterminated in favour of the Israelites.

The Lord spoke through his servants the prophets: 'Because King Manasseh of Judah has done these abominable things, outdoing the Amorites before him in wickedness, and because he has led Judah into sin with his idols, this is the word of the Lord the God of Israel: I am about to bring such disaster on Jerusalem and Judah that it will ring in the ears of all who hear of it. I shall use against Jerusalem the measuring line used against Samaria and the plummet used against the house of Ahab. I shall wipe Jerusalem as one wipes a plate and turns it upside down. I shall cast off what is left of my people, my own possession, and hand them over to their enemies. They will be plundered, a prey to all their enemies, for they have done what is wrong in my eyes and have provoked my anger from the day their forefathers left Egypt up to the present day. This Manasseh shed so much innocent blood that he filled Jerusalem with it from end to end, not to mention the sin into which he led Judah by doing what is wrong in my eyes.'

## AMON
### 2 Kings 21:19–24

Amon was twenty-two years old when he came to the throne, and he reigned in Jerusalem for two years; his mother was Meshullemeth daughter of Haruz from Jotbah. He did what was wrong in the eyes of the Lord as his father Manasseh had done. Following in his father's footsteps he served the idols that his father had served and prostrated himself before them. He forsook the Lord the God of his forefathers and did not conform to the Lord's ways. Amon's courtiers conspired against him and assassinated him in the palace; but the people of the land killed all the conspirators and made his son Josiah king in his place.

## JOSIAH
### 2 Kings 22

Josiah was eight years old when he came to the throne, and he reigned in Jerusalem for thirty-one years; his mother was Jedidah daughter of Adaiah of Bozkath. He did what was right in the eyes of the Lord, following in the footsteps of his forefather David and deviating neither to the right nor to the left.

In the eighteenth year of his reign, Josiah sent Shaphan son of Azaliah, son of Meshullam, the adjutant-general, to the house of the Lord. 'Go to the high priest Hilkiah,' he said, 'and tell him to melt down the silver that has been brought into the house of the Lord, which those on duty at the entrance have received from the people; tell him to hand it over to those supervising in the house of the Lord, to pay the workmen who are carrying out repairs in it, the carpenters, builders, and masons, and to purchase timber and hewn stones for its repair. They are not to be asked to account for the money that has been given them; they are acting on trust.'

The high priest Hilkiah told Shaphan the adjutant-general that he had discovered the scroll of the law in the house of the Lord, and he gave it to him to read. When Shaphan came to report to the king that his servants had melted down the silver in the house of the Lord and handed it over to those supervising there, he told the king of the scroll the high priest Hilkiah had given him, and he read it in the king's presence. When the king heard what was written in the book of the law, he tore his clothes. He ordered the priest Hilkiah, Ahikam son of Shaphan, Akbor son of Micaiah, Shaphan the adjutant-general, and Asaiah the king's attendant to go and seek guidance of the Lord for himself, for the people, and for all Judah, about the contents of this book that had been discovered. 'Great must be the wrath of the Lord', he said, 'that has been kindled against us, because our forefathers did not obey the commands in this scroll and do all that is laid on us.'

Hilkiah the priest, Ahikam, Akbor, Shaphan, and Asaiah went to Huldah the prophetess, wife of Shallum son of Tikvah, son of Harhas, the keeper of the wardrobe, and consulted her at her home in the Second Quarter of Jerusalem. 'This is the word of the Lord the God of Israel,' she answered: 'Tell the man who sent you to me, that this is what the Lord says: I am about to bring disaster on this place and its inhabitants as foretold in the scroll which the king of Judah has read, because they have forsaken me and burnt sacrifices to other gods, provoking my anger with all the idols they have made with their own hands; for this my wrath is kindled against this place and will not be quenched. Tell the king of Judah who sent you to seek guidance of the Lord that this is what the Lord the God of Israel says: You have listened to my words and shown a willing heart and humbled yourself before the Lord when you heard me say that this place and its inhabitants would become objects of loathing and scorn, and have torn your clothes and wept before me. Because of this, I for my part have listened to you. This is the word of the Lord. Therefore I shall gather you to your forefathers, and you will be gathered to your grave in peace; you will not live to see all the disaster which I am bringing on this place.' They brought back this answer to the king.

# JOSIAH'S REFORMS
## 2 Kings 23:1–30

At the king's summons all the elders of Judah and Jerusalem were assembled, and he went up to the house of the Lord, taking with him all the men of Judah, the inhabitants of Jerusalem, the priests, and the prophets, the entire population, high and low. There he read out to them the whole scroll of the covenant which had been discovered in the house of the Lord. Then, standing by the pillar, the king entered into a covenant before the Lord to obey him and keep his commandments, his testimonies, and his statutes, with all his heart and soul, and so carry out the terms of the covenant written in the scroll. All the people pledged themselves to the covenant.

The king ordered the high priest Hilkiah, the deputy high priest, and those on duty at the entrance to remove from the house of the Lord all the objects made for Baal, for Asherah, and for all the host of heaven, and he burnt these outside Jerusalem on the slope by the Kidron, and carried the ashes to Bethel. He suppressed the heathen priests whom the kings of Judah had appointed to burn sacrifices at the shrines in the towns of Judah and in the neighbourhood of Jerusalem, as well as those who burnt sacrifices to Baal, to the sun and moon, to the planets and all the host of heaven. He took the Asherah from the house of the Lord to the wadi of the Kidron outside Jerusalem, burnt it there, and pounded it to dust, which was then scattered over the common burial-ground. He also pulled down the quarters of the male prostitutes attached to the house of the Lord, where the women wove vestments in honour of Asherah.

The king brought in all the priests from the towns of Judah and desecrated the shrines where they had burnt sacrifices, from Geba to Beersheba, and dismantled the shrines of the demons in front of the gate of Joshua, the city governor, which is to the left of the city gate.

These priests, however, never came up to the altar of the Lord in Jerusalem but used to eat unleavened bread with the priests of their clan. He desecrated Topheth in the valley of Ben-hinnom, so that no one might make his son or daughter pass through the fire for Molech. He did away with the horses that the kings of Judah had set up in honour of the sun at the entrance to the house of the Lord, beside the room of the eunuch Nathan-melech in the colonnade, and he burnt the chariots of the sun. He demolished the altars made by the kings of Judah on the roof by the upper chamber of Ahaz and the altars made by Manasseh in the two courts of the house of the Lord; he pounded them to dust and threw it into the wadi of the Kidron. Also, on the east of Jerusalem, to the south of the mount of Olives, the king desecrated the shrines which Solomon the king of Israel had built for Ashtoreth the loathsome goddess of the Sidonians, and for Kemosh the loathsome god of Moab, and for Milcom the abominable god of the Ammonites; he smashed the sacred pillars and cut down the sacred poles and filled the places where they had stood with human bones.

At Bethel he dismantled the altar by the shrine made by Jeroboam son of Nebat who led Israel into sin, together with the shrine itself; he broke its stones in pieces, crushed them to dust, and burnt the sacred pole. When Josiah saw the graves which were there on the hill, he sent and had the bones taken from them, and he burnt them on the altar to desecrate it, thus fulfilling the word of the Lord announced by the man of God when Jeroboam stood by the altar at the feast. When Josiah saw the grave of the man of God who had foretold these things, he asked, 'What is that monument I see?' The people of the town answered, 'It is the grave of the man of God who came from Judah and foretold all that you have done to the altar at Bethel.' 'Leave it alone,' he said; 'let no one disturb his bones.' So they spared his bones along with those of the prophet who came from Samaria. Josiah also suppressed all the temples at the shrines in the towns of Samaria, which the kings of Israel had set up and thereby provoked the Lord's anger, and he did to them what he had done at Bethel. He slaughtered on the altars all the priests of the shrines who were there, and he burnt human bones on them. Then he went back to Jerusalem.

The king ordered all the people to keep the Passover to the Lord their God, as this scroll of the covenant prescribed; no Passover like it had been kept either when the judges were ruling Israel or during the times of the kings of Israel and of Judah, until in the eighteenth year of Josiah's reign this Passover was kept to the Lord in Jerusalem.

Further, Josiah got rid of all who called up ghosts and spirits, and of all household gods and idols and all the loathsome objects to be seen in the land of Judah and in Jerusalem, so that he might fulfil the requirements of the law written in the scroll which the priest Hilkiah had discovered in the house of the Lord. No king before him had turned to the Lord as he did, with all his heart and soul and strength, following the whole law of Moses; nor did any king like him appear again.

Yet the Lord did not abate his fierce anger; it still burned against Judah because of all the provocation which Manasseh had given him. 'Judah also I shall banish from my presence', he declared, 'as I banished Israel; and I shall reject this city of Jerusalem which once I chose, and the house where I promised that my name should be.'

The other events and acts of Josiah's reign are recorded in the annals of the kings of Judah. It was in his reign that Pharaoh Necho king of Egypt set out for the river Euphrates to help the king of Assyria. King Josiah went to meet him; and when they met at Megiddo, Pharaoh Necho slew him. His attendants conveyed his body in a chariot from Megiddo to Jerusalem and buried him in his own burial-place. Then the people of the land took Josiah's son Jehoahaz and anointed him king in place of his father.

## JEHOAHAZ
### 2 Kings 23:31–35

Jehoahaz was twenty-three years old when he came to the throne, and he reigned in Jerusalem for three months; his mother was Hamital daughter of Jeremiah from Libnah. He did what was wrong in the eyes of the Lord, as his forefathers had done. Pharaoh Necho removed him from the throne in Jerusalem, and imposed on the land an indemnity of a hundred talents of silver and one talent of gold. He made Josiah's son Eliakim king in place of his father and changed his name to Jehoiakim. He carried Jehoahaz away to Egypt, where he died. Jehoiakim handed over the silver and gold to Pharaoh, taxing the country to meet Pharaoh's demands; he exacted it from the people, from every man according to his assessment, so that he could pay Pharaoh Necho.

## JEHOIAKIM
### 2 Kings 23:36 – 24:7

Jehoiakim was twenty-five years old when he came to the throne, and he reigned in Jerusalem for eleven years; his mother was Zebidah daughter of Pedaiah of Rumah. He did what was wrong in the eyes of the Lord as his forefathers had done. During his reign an attack was launched by King Nebuchadnezzar of Babylon, and Jehoiakim became his vassal; three years later, however, he broke with him and revolted. The Lord sent against him raiding parties of Chaldaeans, Arameans, Moabites, and Ammonites, letting them range through Judah and ravage it, as the Lord had foretold through his servants the prophets. All this happened to Judah in fulfilment of the Lord's purpose, to banish them from his presence because of all the sin Manasseh had committed and because of the innocent blood he had shed; he had flooded Jerusalem with innocent blood, and the Lord would not forgive him. The other events and acts of Jehoiakim's reign are recorded in the annals of the kings of Judah. He rested with his forefathers, and his son Jehoiachin succeeded him. The Egyptian king did not leave his own land again, because the king of Babylon had stripped him of all he possessed from the wadi of Egypt to the river Euphrates.

## JEHOIACHIN
### 2 Kings 24:8–17

Jehoiachin was eighteen years old when he came to the throne, and he reigned in Jerusalem for three months; his mother was Nehushta daughter of Elnathan from Jerusalem. He did what was wrong in the eyes of the Lord, as his father had done.

At that time the troops of King Nebuchadnezzar of Babylon advanced on Jerusalem and the city came under siege. Nebuchadnezzar arrived while his troops were besieging it, and King Jehoiachin of Judah, along with his mother, his courtiers, his officers, and his eunuchs surrendered to the king of Babylon. The king of Babylon, now in the eighth year of his reign, made him a prisoner; and, as the Lord had foretold, he carried off all the treasures of the house of the Lord and of the palace and broke up all the vessels of gold which King Solomon of Israel had made for the temple of the Lord. He took into exile the people of Jerusalem, the officers and all the fighting men, ten thousand in number, together with all the craftsmen and smiths; only the poorest class of the people was left. He deported Jehoiachin to Babylon; he also took into exile from Jerusalem to Babylon the king's mother and his wives, his eunuchs, and the foremost men of the land. He took also all the people of substance, seven thousand in number, and a thousand craftsmen and smiths, all of them able-bodied men and skilled armourers. He made Mattaniah, uncle of Jehoiachin, king in his place and changed his name to Zedekiah.

# ZEDEKIAH
## 2 Kings 24:18 – 25:2

Zedekiah was twenty-one years old when he came to the throne, and he reigned in Jerusalem for eleven years; his mother was Hamital daughter of Jeremiah from Libnah. He did what was wrong in the eyes of the Lord, as Jehoiakim had done. Jerusalem and Judah so angered the Lord that in the end he banished them from his sight.

Zedekiah rebelled against the king of Babylon. In the ninth year of his reign, on the tenth day of the tenth month, King Nebuchadnezzar of Babylon advanced with his whole army against Jerusalem, invested it, and erected siege-towers against it on every side; the siege lasted till the eleventh year of King Zedekiah.

# THE FALL OF JERUSALEM
2 Kings 25:3–21

In the fourth month of that year, on the ninth day of the month, when famine was severe in the city and there was no food for the people, the city capitulated. When King Zedekiah of Judah saw this, he and all his armed escort left the city and, fleeing by night through the gate called Between the Two Walls, near the king's garden, they made their escape towards the Arabah, although the Chaldaeans were surrounding the city. The Chaldaean army pursued the king and overtook him in the lowlands of Jericho. His men all forsook him and scattered, and the king was captured and, having been brought before the king of Babylon at Riblah, he was put on trial and sentenced. Zedekiah's sons were slain before his eyes; then his eyes were put out, and he was brought to Babylon bound in bronze fetters.

In the fifth month, on the seventh day of the month, in the nineteenth year of King Nebuchadnezzar of Babylon, Nebuzaradan, captain of the king of Babylon's bodyguard, came to Jerusalem. He set fire to the house of the Lord and the royal palace, indeed all the houses in the city; every notable's house was burnt down. The whole Chaldaean force which was with the captain of the guard razed to the ground the walls on every side of Jerusalem. Nebuzaradan captain of the guard deported the people who were left in the city, those who had deserted to the king of Babylon, and any remaining artisans. He left only the poorest class of the people, to be vine-dressers and labourers.

The Chaldaeans broke up the bronze pillars in the house of the Lord, the trolleys, and the bronze Sea, and took the metal to Babylon. They took also the pots, shovels, snuffers, saucers, and all the bronze vessels used in the service of the temple. The captain of the guard took away the precious metal, whether gold or silver, of which the firepans and the tossing-bowls were made. The bronze of the two pillars, the one Sea, and the trolleys, which Solomon had made for the house of the Lord, was beyond weighing. One pillar was eighteen cubits high and its capital was bronze; the capital was three cubits high, and a decoration of network and pomegranates ran all round it, wholly of bronze. The other pillar, with its network, was exactly like it.

The captain of the guard took Seraiah the chief priest, Zephaniah the deputy chief priest, and the three on duty at the entrance; he took also from the city a eunuch who was in charge of the fighting men, five of those with right of access to the king who were still in the city, the adjutant-general whose duty was to muster the people for war, and sixty men of the people who were still there. These Nebuzaradan captain of the guard brought to the king of Babylon at Riblah. There, in the land of Hamath, the king had them flogged and put to death. So Judah went into exile from her own land.

## Part Six

# The Return from Exile

## THE DECREE OF CYRUS
### Ezra 1:1–5

In the first year of King Cyrus of Persia the Lord, to fulfil his word spoken through Jeremiah, inspired the king to issue throughout his kingdom the following proclamation, which he also put in writing:

> The decree of King Cyrus of Persia.
>
> The Lord the God of the heavens has given me all the kingdoms of the earth, and he himself has charged me to build him a house at Jerusalem in Judah. Whoever among you belongs to his people, may his God be with him; and let him go up to Jerusalem in Judah, and build the house of the Lord the God of Israel, the God who is in Jerusalem. Let every Jew left among us, wherever he is settled throughout the country, be helped by his neighbours with silver and gold, goods and livestock, in addition to the voluntary offerings for the house of God in Jerusalem.

Thereupon the heads of families of Judah and Benjamin came forward, along with the priests and the Levites, all whom God had moved to go up and rebuild the house of the Lord in Jerusalem.

## THE REBUILDING OF THE TEMPLE
### Ezra 2:68 – 3:3, 8 – 4:5, 4:24–5:17

On their arrival at the house of the Lord in Jerusalem, certain of the heads of families offered to rebuild the house of God on its original site. According to their ability they gave to the treasury for the fabric a total of sixty-one thousand drachmas of gold, five thousand minas of silver, and one hundred priestly vestments.

The priests, the Levites, and some of the people stayed in Jerusalem and the neighbourhood; the singers, the door-keepers and the temple servitors, and all the rest of the Israelites, lived in their own towns.

When the seventh month came, the Israelites now being settled in their towns, the people came together with one accord to Jerusalem, and Jeshua son of Jozadak along with his fellow-priests, and Zerubbabel son of Shealtiel, with his colleagues, set to work to build the altar of the God of Israel, in order to offer on it whole-offerings as prescribed in the law of Moses, the man of God. They put the altar in place first, because they lived in fear of the foreign population; and they offered on it whole-offerings to the Lord, both morning and evening offerings...

In the second month of the second year, after they came to the house of God in Jerusalem, Zerubbabel son of Shealtiel and Jeshua son of Jozadak began the work. They were aided by all their fellow-Israelites, the priests and the Levites and all who had returned to Jerusalem from captivity. Levites who were aged twenty years and upwards were appointed to supervise the work of the house of the Lord. Jeshua, with his sons and his kinsmen Kadmiel, Binnui, and Hodaviah, together assumed control of those doing the work on the house of God.

When the builders had laid the foundation of the temple of the Lord, the priests in their robes took their places with their trumpets, and the Levites, the sons of Asaph, with cymbals, to praise the Lord in the manner prescribed by King David of Israel. They chanted praises and thanksgiving to the Lord, singing, 'It is good to give thanks to the Lord, for his love towards Israel endures for ever.' The whole people raised a great shout of praise to the Lord because the foundation of the Lord's house had been laid. Many of the priests and Levites and heads of families, who were old enough to have seen the former house, wept and wailed aloud when they saw the foundation of this house laid, while many others shouted for joy at the tops of their voices. The people could not distinguish the sound of the shout of joy from that of the weeping and wailing, so great was the shout which the people were raising, and the sound could be heard a long way off.

When those who were hostile to Judah and Benjamin heard that the returned exiles were building a temple to the Lord the God of Israel, they approached Zerubbabel and Jeshua and the heads of families. 'Let us build with you,' they said, 'for like you we seek your God, and have sacrificed to him ever since the days of King Esarhaddon of Assyria who brought us here.' But Zerubbabel and Jeshua and the rest of the heads of the Israelite families replied, 'It is not for you to share in building the house for our God; we alone are to build it for the Lord the God of Israel, as his majesty King Cyrus of Persia commanded us.'

Then the people of the land caused the Jews to lose heart and made them afraid to continue building; and, in order to thwart the purpose of the Jews, those people bribed officials at court to act against them. This continued throughout the lifetime of King Cyrus of Persia and into the reign of King Darius...

From then onwards the work on the house of God in Jerusalem ceased; it remained at a standstill till the second year of the reign of King Darius of Persia.

The prophets Haggai and Zechariah son of Iddo prophesied to the Jews in Judah and Jerusalem, rebuking them in the name of the God of Israel. Then Zerubbabel son of Shealtiel and Jeshua son of Jozadak, with the prophets of God at their side to help them, began at once to rebuild the house of God in Jerusalem. Immediately Tattenai, governor of the province of Beyond-Euphrates, Shethar-bozenai, and their colleagues came to them and asked, 'Who has given you authority to rebuild this house and complete its furnishings?' They also asked for the names of the men engaged in the building. But the elders of the Jews were under God's watchful eye, and they were not prevented from continuing the work, until such time as a report should reach Darius and an official reply should be received.

Here follows a copy of the letter to King Darius sent by Tattenai, governor of the province of Beyond-Euphrates, Shethar-bozenai, and his colleagues, the inspectors in the province of Beyond-Euphrates. This is the written report that they sent:

To King Darius.
    All greetings.
    Be it known to your majesty that we went to the province of Judah and found the house of the great God being rebuilt, with massive stones and beams set in the walls. The work was being done energetically and was

making rapid headway under the direction of the elders. We then enquired of them by whose authority they were building this house and completing the furnishings. We also asked them for their names, so that we might provide for your information a list of those in charge. Their reply was as follows: 'We are servants of the God of heaven and earth, and we are rebuilding the house first erected many years ago; it was built and completed by a great king of Israel. But because our forefathers provoked the anger of the God of heaven, he delivered them into the power of the Chaldaean, King Nebuchadnezzar of Babylon. The house was demolished and the people carried away captive to Babylon.

'But King Cyrus of Babylon in the first year of his reign issued a decree that this house of God should be rebuilt. He brought out from the temple in Babylon the gold and silver vessels of the house of God, which Nebuchadnezzar had taken from the temple in Jerusalem and put in the temple in Babylon, and he delivered them to a man named Sheshbazzar, whom he had appointed governor. He said to him, "Take these vessels; go and restore them to the temple in Jerusalem, and let the house of God be rebuilt on its original site." Then this Sheshbazzar came and laid the foundations of the house of God in Jerusalem; and from that time until now the rebuilding has continued, and is still not completed.'

Now, therefore, if it please your majesty, let search be made in the royal treasury in Babylon, to discover whether a decree was issued by King Cyrus for the rebuilding of the house of God in Jerusalem, and let the king convey to us his wishes in the matter.

## THE DECREE OF DARIUS
### Ezra 6:1–14

King Darius ordered search to be made in the archives where treasures were deposited in Babylon, and there was found in Ecbatana, in the royal residence in the province of Media, a scroll on which was written the following memorandum:

> In the first year of his reign King Cyrus issued this decree concerning the house of God in Jerusalem: Let the house be rebuilt as a place where sacrifices are offered and fire-offerings brought. Its height is to be sixty cubits and its breadth sixty cubits, with three courses of massive stones to one course of timber, the cost to be defrayed from the royal treasury. Also the gold and silver vessels of the house of God, which Nebuchadnezzar carried away from the temple in Jerusalem and brought to Babylon, are to be returned; they are all to be taken back to the temple in Jerusalem, and restored each to its place in the house of God.

Then King Darius issued this instruction:

> Now, Tattenai, governor of the province of Beyond-Euphrates, Shethar-bozenai, and your colleagues, the inspectors in the province of Beyond-Euphrates, you are to keep away from the place, and to leave the governor of the Jews and their elders free to rebuild this house of God; let them rebuild it on its original site. I also issue an order prescribing what you are to do for these elders of the Jews, so that the said house of God may be rebuilt. Their expenses are to be defrayed in full from the royal funds accruing from the taxes of the province of Beyond-Euphrates, so that the work may not be brought to a standstill.
>
> Let there be provided for them daily without fail whatever they need, young bulls, rams, and lambs as whole-offerings for the God of heaven, and wheat, salt, wine, and oil, as the priests in Jerusalem require, so that they may offer soothing sacrifices to the God of heaven, and pray for the life of the king and his sons.
>
> Furthermore, I decree that whoever tampers with this edict will have a beam torn out of his house, and he will be fastened erect to it and flogged; in addition, his house is to be razed to the ground. May the God who made that

place a dwelling for his name overthrow any king or people that presumes to tamper with this edict or to destroy this house of God in Jerusalem.

I Darius have decreed it; let it be strictly obeyed.

Then Tattenai, governor of the province of Beyond-Euphrates, Shethar-bozenai, and their colleagues carried out to the letter the instructions which King Darius had sent them, and the elders of the Jews went on with the rebuilding. Good progress was made with the sacred works, as the result of the prophecies of Haggai and Zechariah son of Iddo, and they finished the rebuilding as commanded by the God of Israel and according to the decrees of Cyrus and Darius and King Artaxerxes of Persia.


# THE REDEDICATION OF THE TEMPLE
Ezra 6:15–22

The house was completed on the third day of the month of Adar, in the sixth year of the reign of King Darius.

Then the Israelites, priests, Levites, and all the other exiles who had returned, celebrated the rededication of this house of God with great rejoicing. At its rededication they offered one hundred bulls, two hundred rams, and four hundred lambs, and as a purification-offering for all Israel twelve he-goats, corresponding to the number of the tribes of Israel. They re-established the priests in their groups and the Levites in their divisions for the service of God in Jerusalem, as prescribed in the book of Moses.

On the fourteenth day of the first month the returned exiles observed the Passover. The priests and the Levites, one and all, had purified themselves; all of them were ritually clean, and they killed the Passover lamb for all the exiles who had returned, for their fellow-priests, and for themselves. It was eaten by the Israelites who had returned from exile and by all who had held aloof from the peoples of the land and their uncleanness, and had sought the Lord the God of Israel. They observed the pilgrim-feast of Unleavened Bread for seven days with rejoicing; for the Lord had given them cause for joy by changing the disposition of the Assyrian king towards them, so that he supported them in the work of the house of God, the God of Israel.

## EZRA THE SCRIBE
### Ezra 7:1, 6–17, 25–28, 8:15–25, 31 – 9:4

It was after these events, in the reign of King Artaxerxes of Persia, that Ezra... had come up from Babylon; he was a scribe, expert in the law of Moses which the Lord the God of Israel had given them. The king granted him everything he requested, for the favour of the Lord his God was with him. He was accompanied to Jerusalem by some Israelites, priests, Levites, temple singers, door-keepers, and temple servitors in the seventh year of King Artaxerxes. They reached Jerusalem in the fifth month, in the seventh year of the king.

On the first day of the first month Ezra fixed the day for departure from Babylon, and on the first day of the fifth month he arrived at Jerusalem; the favour of God was with him, for he had devoted himself to the study and observance of the law of the Lord and to teaching statute and ordinance in Israel.

This is a copy of the letter which King Artaxerxes had given to Ezra the priest and scribe, a scribe versed in questions concerning the commandments and the statutes of the Lord laid upon Israel:

Artaxerxes, King of Kings, to Ezra the priest and scribe learned in the law of the God of heaven.

This is my decision. I hereby issue a decree that any of the people of Israel or of its priests or Levites in my kingdom who volunteer to go to Jerusalem may go with you. You are sent by the king and his seven counsellors to consider the situation in Judah and Jerusalem with regard to the law of your God with which you are entrusted. You are also to convey the silver and gold which the king and his counsellors have freely offered to the God of Israel whose dwelling is in Jerusalem, together with any silver and gold that you may find throughout the province of Babylon, and the voluntary offerings of the people and of the priests which they freely offer for the house of their God in Jerusalem. In pursuance of this decree you are to expend the money solely on the purchase of bulls, rams, and lambs, and the proper grain-offerings and drink-offerings, to be offered on the altar in the house of your God in Jerusalem...

You, Ezra, in accordance with the wisdom of your God with which you are entrusted, are to appoint arbitrators and judges to administer justice for all your people in the province of Beyond-Euphrates, all who acknowledge the laws of your God, and you with them are to instruct those who do not know those laws. Whoever will not obey the law of your God and the law of the king, let judgment be rigorously executed on him, be it death, banishment, confiscation of property, or imprisonment.

Then Ezra the scribe said, 'Blessed is the Lord the God of our fathers who has put such a thing as this into the king's mind, to glorify the house of the Lord in Jerusalem, and has made the king and his counsellors and all his high officers well disposed towards me!'

Encouraged by the help of the Lord my God, I gathered leading men out of Israel to go up with me...

I assembled them by the river which flows towards Ahava, and we encamped there for three days. I checked the people and the priests, and finding no one there who was a Levite, I sent to Eliezer, Ariel, Shemaiah, Elnathan, Jarib, Elnathan, Nathan, Zechariah, and Meshullam, prominent men, and Joiarib and Elnathan, men of discretion, and instructed them to go to Iddo, the head of the settlement at Casiphia; and I gave them a message for him and his colleagues, the temple servitors there, asking that there should be sent to us men to serve in the house of our God. Under the providence of God they sent us Sherebiah, a man of discretion, of the line of Mahli son of Levi, son of Israel, together with his sons and kinsmen, eighteen men in all; also Hashabiah, together with Isaiah of the line of Merari, his kinsmen and their sons, twenty men; besides two hundred and twenty temple servitors, an order instituted by David and his officers to assist the Levites. These were all indicated by name.

I proclaimed a fast there by the river Ahava, so that we might mortify ourselves before our God and ask him for a straightforward journey for ourselves, our dependants, and all our possessions. I was ashamed to apply to the king for an escort of infantry and cavalry to protect us against enemies on the way, for we had told him that the might of our God would ensure a successful outcome for all those who looked to him; but his fierce anger is on all who forsake him. So we fasted and asked our God for a safe journey, and he answered our prayer.

Then I set apart twelve of the chiefs of the priests, together with Sherebiah and Hashabiah and ten of their kinsmen. I weighed out for them the silver and gold and the vessels, the contribution for the house of our God presented by the king, his counsellors and officers, and by all the Israelites there present, as their contribution to the house of our God...

On the twelfth day of the first month we struck camp at the river Ahava and set out for Jerusalem. Under the protection of our God, who saved us from enemy attack and ambush on the way, we reached Jerusalem and rested there for three days. On the fourth day the silver and gold and vessels were weighed and handed over in the house of our God into the charge of Meremoth son of Uriah the priest, with whom was Eleazar son of Phinehas; present with them were the Levites Jozabad son of Jeshua and Noadiah son of Binnui. Everything was counted and weighed and every weight recorded then and there.

Those who had returned from captivity offered as whole-offerings to the God of Israel twelve bulls for all Israel, ninety-six rams, and seventy-seven lambs, with twelve he-goats as a purification-offering; all these were offered as a whole-offering to the Lord. They also delivered the king's commission to the royal satraps and governors in the province of Beyond-Euphrates; and these gave support to the people and the house of God.

Once this business had been concluded, the leaders came to me and said, 'The people of Israel, including even priests and Levites, have not kept themselves apart from the alien population and from the abominable practices of the Canaanites, Hittites, Perizzites, Jebusites, Ammonites, Moabites, Egyptians, and Amorites. They have taken women of these nations as wives for themselves and their sons, so that the holy race has become mixed with the alien population; and the leaders and magistrates have been the chief offenders.'

At this news I tore my robe and mantle; I plucked tufts from my beard and the hair of my head and sat appalled. All who went in fear of the words of the God of Israel gathered round me because of the offence of these exiles; and I sat appalled until the evening sacrifice.

## EZRA'S PRAYER OF INTERCESSION
### Ezra 9:5–15

Then, at the evening sacrifice, with my robe and mantle torn, I rose from my self-abasement and, kneeling down, held out my hands in prayer to the Lord my God.

'I am humiliated, my God,' I said, 'I am ashamed, my God, to lift my face to you. Our sins tower above us, and our guilt is so great that it reaches high heaven. From the days of our forefathers down to this present day our guilt has been great. Because of our iniquities we and our kings and priests have been given into the power of foreign rulers to be killed, taken captive, pillaged, and humiliated to this very day. But now, for a brief moment, the Lord our God has been gracious to us, leaving us some survivors and giving us a foothold in his holy place; our God has brought light to our eyes again and given us some chance to renew our lives in our slavery. For slaves we are; nevertheless, our God has not forsaken us in our slavery, but has secured for us the favour of the kings of Persia: they have provided us with the means of renewal, so that we may repair the house of our God and rebuild its ruins, thereby giving us a wall of defence for Judah and Jerusalem.

'Now, our God, in the face of this, what are we to say? For we have neglected your commandments, given us through your servants the prophets. You said: "The land which you are going to occupy is a land defiled with the pollution of its heathen population and their abominable practices; they have filled it with their impure ways from end to end. Now therefore do not marry your daughters to their sons or take their daughters for your sons; nor must you ever seek their welfare or prosperity. Only thus will you be strong and enjoy the good things of the land, and hand it on as an everlasting possession to your descendants." After all that has come upon us through our evil deeds and great guilt – although you, our God, have punished us less than our iniquities deserved and have allowed us to survive as now we do – shall we once again disobey your commands and intermarry with peoples who indulge in such abominable practices? Would you not be so angry with us as to destroy us till no remnant, no survivor was left? Lord God of Israel, you are just; for we today are a remnant that has survived. In all our guilt we are here before you; because of it we can no longer stand in your presence.'

## THE MEN OF JUDAH
## RENOUNCE THEIR FOREIGN WIVES
### Ezra 10:1–17

While Ezra was praying and making confession, prostrate in tears before the house of God, there gathered round him a vast throng of Israelites, men, women, and children, and there was widespread lamentation among the crowd. Shecaniah son of Jehiel, one of the family of Elam, spoke up and said to Ezra, 'We have broken faith with our God in taking foreign wives from the peoples of the land. But in spite of this, there is still hope for Israel. Let us now pledge ourselves to our God to get rid of all such wives with their children, according to your counsel, my lord, and the counsel of those who go in fear of the command of our God; and let the law take its course. Rise up, the matter is in your hands; and we are with you. Take strong action!' Ezra got up and put the chiefs of the priests, the Levites, and all the Israelites on oath to act in this way, and they took the oath. Ezra then left the forecourt of the house of God and went to the room of Jehohanan grandson of Eliashib. He stayed there, eating no bread and drinking no water, for he was still mourning for the unfaithfulness of the returned exiles.

A proclamation was issued throughout Judah and Jerusalem directing all the returned exiles to assemble at Jerusalem. If any failed to arrive within three days, as decided by the chief officers and the elders, they were to have all their property confiscated and would themselves be excluded from the community that had come from exile. Three days later, on the twentieth day of the ninth month, all the men of Judah and Benjamin had assembled in Jerusalem, where they all sat in the open space before the house of God, full of apprehension and shivering in the heavy rain. Ezra the priest stood up and addressed them: 'You have broken faith in marrying foreign women,' he said 'and have added to Israel's guilt. Now, make confession to the Lord the God of your fathers; do his will, cut yourselves off from the peoples of the land and from your foreign wives.'

The whole company assented loudly, saying, 'We shall do as you say! But', they added, 'our numbers are great; it is the rainy season and we cannot stay out in the open. Besides, this is not the work of one or two days only, for the offence is rife amongst us. Let our leading men act for the whole assembly, and let all those who have married foreign wives present themselves at stated times, accompanied by the elders and judges for each town, until our God's fierce anger at what has been done is averted from us.' Only Jonathan son of Asahel and Jahzeiah son of Tikvah, supported by Meshullam and Shabbethai the Levite, opposed this.

The returned exiles duly put this into effect, and Ezra the priest selected, each by name, certain men, heads of households representing their families. They met in session to investigate the matter on the first day of the tenth month, and by the first day of the first month the enquiry into all the marriages with foreign women was brought to a conclusion.

## NEHEMIAH THE KING'S CUPBEARER
### Nehemiah 1:1 – 2:8

The narrative of Nehemiah son of Hacaliah.

In the month of Kislev in the twentieth year, when I was in Susa the capital city, it happened that one of my brothers, Hanani, arrived with some other Judaeans. I asked them about Jerusalem and about the Jews, the families still remaining of those who survived the captivity. They told me that those who had survived the captivity and still lived in the province were facing dire trouble and derision; the wall of Jerusalem was broken down and its gates had been destroyed by fire.

When I heard this news, I sat and wept, mourning for several days, fasting and praying before the God of heaven. This was my prayer: 'Lord God of heaven, great and terrible God faithfully keeping covenant with those who love him and observe his commandments, let your ear be attentive and your eyes open to my humble prayer, which now day and night I make in your presence on behalf of your servants, the people of Israel. I confess the sins which we Israelites have committed against you, and of which my father's house and I are also guilty. We have acted very wrongly towards you and have not observed the commandments, statutes, and rules which you enjoined on your servant Moses.

'Remember what you impressed on him when you said: "If you are unfaithful, I shall scatter you among the nations; but if you return to me and observe my commandments and fulfil them, I shall gather those of you who have been scattered to the far corners of the world and bring you to the place I have chosen as a dwelling for my name."

'They are your servants and people, whom you have redeemed with your great might and your strong hand. Lord, let your ear be attentive to my humble prayer, and to the prayer of your servants who delight to revere your name. Grant me success this day, and put it into this man's heart to show me kindness.' I was then cupbearer to the king.

One day, in the month of Nisan, in the twentieth year of King Artaxerxes, when his wine was ready, I took it and handed it to the king, and as I stood before him my face revealed my unhappiness. The king asked, 'Why do you look so unhappy? You are not ill; it can be nothing but a feeling of unhappiness.' I was very much afraid, but I answered, 'May the king live for ever! But how can I help looking unhappy when the city where my forefathers are buried lies in ruins with its gates burnt down?' 'What then do you want?' asked the king. With a prayer to the God of heaven, I answered, 'If it please your majesty, and if I enjoy your favour, I beg you to send me to Judah, to the city where my forefathers are buried, so that I may rebuild it.' The king, with the queen consort sitting beside him, asked me, 'How long will the journey last, and when will you return?' When I told him how long I should be, the king approved the request and let me go.

I then said to him, 'If it please your majesty, let letters be given me for the governors in the province of Beyond-Euphrates, with orders to grant me safe passage until I reach Judah. Let me have also a letter for Asaph, the keeper of your royal forests, instructing him to supply me with timber to make beams for the gates of the citadel, which adjoins the temple, and for the city wall, and for the temple which is the object of my journey.' The king granted my requests, for the gracious hand of my God was upon me.

## THE REBUILDING OF THE CITY WALL
### Nehemiah 2:9–18, 4:1–23

I came in due course to the governors in the province of Beyond-Euphrates and presented the king's letters to them; the king had given me an escort of army officers with cavalry. But when Sanballat the Horonite and the slave Tobiah, an Ammonite, heard this, they were greatly displeased that someone should have come to promote the interests of the Israelites.

When I arrived in Jerusalem, I waited three days. Then I set out by night, taking a few men with me, but without telling anyone what my God was prompting me to do for Jerusalem. Taking no beast with me except the one on which I myself rode, I went out by night through the Valley Gate towards the Dragon Spring and the Dung Gate; and I inspected the places where the walls of Jerusalem had been broken down, and its gates, which had been destroyed by fire. Then I passed on to the Fountain Gate and the King's Pool; but there was no room for me to ride through. I went up the valley by night and inspected the city wall; then I re-entered the city through the Valley Gate. So I arrived back without the magistrates knowing where I had been or what I was doing, for I had not yet told the Jews, neither the priests, the nobles, the magistrates, nor any of those who would be responsible for the work.

Then I said to them, 'You see what trouble we are in: Jerusalem lies in ruins, its gates destroyed by fire. Come, let us rebuild the wall of Jerusalem and suffer derision no more.' I told them also how the gracious hand of my God had been upon me and also what the king had said to me. They replied, 'Let us start the rebuilding,' and they set about the work vigorously and to good purpose...

The news that we were rebuilding the wall roused the indignation of Sanballat, and angrily he jeered at the Jews, saying in front of his companions and of the garrison in Samaria, 'What do these feeble Jews think they are doing? Do they mean to reconstruct the place? Do they hope to offer sacrifice and finish the work in a day? Can they make stones again out of heaps of rubble, and burnt rubble at that?' Tobiah the Ammonite, who was beside him, said, 'Whatever it is they are building, if a fox climbs up their stone walls, it will break them down.'

Hear, our God, how we are treated with contempt. Make their derision recoil on their own heads; let them become objects of contempt in a land of captivity. Do not condone their guilt or let their sin be struck off the record, for they have openly provoked the builders.

We built up the wall until it was continuous all round up to half its height; and the people worked with a will. But when Sanballat and Tobiah, and the Arabs and Ammonites and Ashdodites, heard that the new work on the walls of Jerusalem had made progress and that the closing up of the breaches had gone ahead, they were furious, and all banded together to launch an attack on Jerusalem and create confusion. So we prayed to our God, and posted a guard against them day and night.

In Judah it was said:

'The labourers' strength has failed,
and there is too much rubble;
by ourselves we shall never be able
to rebuild the wall.'

Our adversaries said, 'Before they know it or see anything, we shall be upon them, killing them and putting an end to the work.' When the Jews living nearby came into the city, they warned us a dozen times that our adversaries would gather from every place where they lived to attack us, and that they would station themselves on the lowest levels below the wall, on patches of open ground. Accordingly I posted my people by families, armed with swords, spears, and bows. Then having surveyed the position I addressed the nobles, the magistrates, and the rest of the people. 'Do not be afraid of them,' I said. 'Remember the Lord, great and terrible, and fight for your brothers, your sons and daughters, your wives and your homes.' When our enemies heard that everything was known to us, and that God had frustrated their plans, we all returned to the wall, each to his task.

From that day forward half the men under me were engaged in the actual building, while the other half stood by holding their spears, shields, and bows, and wearing coats of mail; and officers supervised all the people of Judah who were engaged on the wall. The porters carrying the loads held their load with one hand and a weapon with the other. The builders had their swords attached to their belts as they built. The trumpeter stayed beside me, and I said to the nobles, the magistrates, and all the people: 'The work is great and extends over much ground, and we are widely separated on the wall, each man at some distance from his neighbour. Wherever you hear the trumpet sound, rally to us there, and our God will fight for us.' So with half the men holding spears we continued the work from daybreak until the stars came out. At the same time I had said to the people, 'Let every man and his servant remain all night inside Jerusalem, to act as a guard for us by night and a working party by day.' Neither I nor my kinsmen nor the men under me nor my bodyguard ever took off our clothes; each one kept his right hand on his spear.

## NEHEMIAH SPEAKS OUT FOR THE POOR
### Nehemiah 5:1–13

There came a time when the common people, both men and women, raised a great outcry against their fellow-Jews. Some complained that they had to give their sons and daughters as pledges for food to eat to keep themselves alive; others that they were mortgaging their fields, vineyards, and homes to buy grain during the famine; still others that they were borrowing money on their fields and vineyards to pay the king's tax. 'But', they said, 'our bodily needs are the same as other people's, our children are as good as theirs; yet here we are, forcing our sons and daughters into slavery. Some of our daughters are already enslaved, and there is nothing we can do, because our fields and vineyards now belong to others.'

When I heard their outcry and the story they told, I was greatly incensed, but I controlled my feelings and reasoned with the nobles and the magistrates. I said to them, 'You are holding your fellow-Jews as pledges for debt.' I rebuked them severely and said, 'As far as we have been able, we have bought back our fellow-Jews who had been sold to foreigners; but you are now selling your own fellow-countrymen, and they will have to be bought back by us!' They were silent and had not a word to say.

I went on, 'What you are doing is wrong. You ought to live so much in the fear of our God that you are above reproach in the eyes of the nations who are our enemies. Speaking for myself, I and my kinsmen and the men under me are advancing them money and grain. Let us give up this taking of pledges for debt. This very day give them back their fields and vineyards, their olive groves and houses, as well as the income in money, in grain, new wine, and oil.' 'We shall give them back', they promised, 'and exact nothing more. We shall do as you say.' Then after summoning the priests I put the offenders on oath to do as they had promised. Also I shook out the fold of my robe and said, 'So may God shake out from house and property every man who fails to keep this promise. May he be shaken out like this and emptied!' All the assembled people said 'Amen' and praised the Lord; and they did as they had promised.

## THE TREACHERY OF SANBALLAT AND TOBIAH
### Nehemiah 6:1–16

When it was reported to Sanballat, Tobiah, Geshem the Arab, and the rest of our enemies that I had rebuilt the wall and not a single gap remained in it – although I had not yet set up the gates in the gateways – Sanballat and Geshem sent me an invitation to come and confer with them at Hakkephirim in the plain of Ono; their intention was to do me some harm. So I sent messengers to them with this reply: 'I have important work on my hands at the moment and am unable to come down. Why should the work be brought to a standstill while I leave it and come down to you?' Four times they sent me a similar invitation, and each time I gave them the same answer. On a fifth occasion Sanballat made a similar approach, but this time his servant came with an open letter. It ran as follows: 'It is reported among the nations, and Gashmu confirms it, that you and the Jews are plotting rebellion, and that is why you are building the wall; it is further reported that you yourself want to be king, and have even appointed prophets to make this proclamation concerning you in Jerusalem: "Judah has a king!" Such matters will certainly get to the king's notice; so come at once and let us talk them over.' I sent this reply: 'No such thing as you allege has taken place; your imagination has invented the whole story.' They were all trying to intimidate us, in the hope that we should then relax our efforts and that the work would never be completed. Strengthen me for the work, was my prayer.

One day I went to the house of Shemaiah son of Delaiah, son of Mehetabel, for he was confined to his house. He said,

'Let us meet in the house of God,
within the sanctuary,
and let us shut the doors,
for they are coming to kill you,
and they will come to do it by night.'

But I said, 'Should a man like me run away? Can a man like me go into the sanctuary to save his life? I will not go.' Then it dawned on me: God had not sent him. His prophecy aimed at harming me, and Tobiah and Sanballat had bribed him to utter it. He had been bribed to frighten me into compliance and into committing sin; then they could give me a bad name and discredit me.

God, remember Tobiah and Sanballat for what they have done, and also the prophetess Noadiah and all the other prophets who tried to intimidate me!

On the twenty-fifth day of the month of Elul the wall was finished; it had taken fifty-two days. When all our enemies heard of it, and all the surrounding nations saw it, they thought it a very wonderful achievement, and recognized it was by the help of our God that this work had been accomplished.

## EZRA READS THE BOOK OF THE LAW TO THE PEOPLE
Nehemiah 7:73 – 8:18

When the seventh month came, and the Israelites were now settled in their towns, all the people assembled with one accord in the broad space in front of the Water Gate, and requested Ezra the scribe to bring the book of the law of Moses, which the Lord had enjoined upon Israel. On the first day of the seventh month, Ezra the priest brought the law before the whole assembly, both men and women, and all who were capable of understanding what they heard. From early morning till noon he read aloud from it, facing the square in front of the Water Gate, in the presence of the men and the women, and those who could understand; the people all listened attentively to the book of the law.

Ezra the scribe stood on a wooden platform which had been made for this purpose; beside him stood Mattithiah, Shema, Anaiah, Uriah, Hilkiah, and Maaseiah on his right hand, and on his left Pedaiah, Mishael, Malchiah, Hashum, Hashbaddanah, Zechariah, and Meshullam. Then Ezra opened the book in the sight of all the people, for he was standing above them; and when he opened it, they all stood. Ezra blessed the Lord, the great God, and all the people raised their hands and responded, 'Amen, Amen'; then they bowed their heads and prostrated themselves before the Lord. Jeshua, Bani, Sherebiah, Jamin, Akkub, Shabbethai, Hodiah, Maaseiah, Kelita, Azariah, Jozabad, Hanan, and Pelaiah, the Levites, expounded the law to the people while the people remained in their places. They read from the book of the law of God clearly, made its sense plain, and gave instruction in what was read.

Then Nehemiah the governor and Ezra the priest and scribe, and the Levites who instructed the people, said to them all, 'This day is holy to the Lord your God; do not mourn or weep'; for the people had all been weeping while they listened to the words of the law. 'Go now,' he continued, 'feast yourselves on rich food and sweet drinks, and send a share to all who cannot provide for themselves, for the day is holy to our Lord. Let there be no sadness, for joy in the Lord is your strength.' The Levites calmed the people, saying, 'Be quiet, for this day is holy; let there be no sadness.' So all the people went away to eat and to drink, to send shares to others, and to celebrate the day with great rejoicing, because they had understood what had been explained to them.

On the second day the heads of families of the whole people, with the priests and the Levites, assembled before Ezra the scribe to study the law. They found written in the law that the Lord had given commandment through Moses that the Israelites were to live in booths during the feast of the seventh month; they should issue this proclamation throughout all their towns and in Jerusalem: 'Go out to the hills and fetch branches of olive and wild olive, myrtle and palm, and other leafy boughs, to make booths as prescribed.' So the people went and fetched branches and made booths for themselves, each on his own roof, and in their courtyards and in the precincts of the house of God, and in the square at the Water Gate and the square at the Ephraim Gate. The whole community of those who had returned from the captivity made booths and lived in them, a thing that the Israelites had not done from the days of Joshua son of Nun until that day; and there was very great rejoicing. The book of the law of God was read day by day, from the first day to the last. They kept the feast for seven days, and on the eighth day there was a closing ceremony, according to the rule.

## THE PEOPLE CONFESS THEIR SINS
### Nehemiah 9:1–38, 10:28–29

On the twenty-fourth day of this month the Israelites, clothed in sackcloth and with dust on their heads, assembled for a fast. Those who were of Israelite descent separated themselves from all who were foreigners; they stood and confessed their sins and the iniquities of their forefathers. Then, while they stood up where they were, the book of the law of the Lord their God was read for one quarter of the day, and another quarter of the day they spent in confession and in worshipping the Lord their God. On the steps assigned to the Levites

stood Jeshua, Bani, Kadmiel, Shebaniah, Bunni, Sherebiah, Bani, and
Kenani, and they cried aloud to the Lord their God. Then the Levites,
Jeshua, Kadmiel, Bani, Hashabniah, Sherebiah, Hodiah, Shebaniah,
and Pethahiah, said, 'Stand up and bless the Lord your God in these
words: From everlasting to everlasting may your glorious name be
blessed and exalted above all blessing and praise.

'You alone are the Lord;
you created the heavens,
the highest heavens with all their host,
the earth and all that is on it,
the seas and all that is in them.
You give life to them all,
and the heavenly host worships you.

'You are the Lord,
the God who chose Abram,
who brought him from Ur of the Chaldees
and named him Abraham.
Finding him faithful you made a covenant with him
to give to his descendants
the land of the Canaanites,
Hittites, Amorites, and Perizzites,
Jebusites, and Girgashites;
you fulfilled your promise,
for you are just.

'You saw the misery of our forefathers in Egypt
and heard their cry at the Red Sea.
You worked signs and portents against Pharaoh,
against all his courtiers and the people of his land,
for you knew how arrogantly
they treated our forefathers;
and you won for yourself renown
that lives to this day.
You divided asunder the sea before them,
and they passed through on dry ground;
but their pursuers you flung into the depths,
like a stone flung into turbulent waters.

By a pillar of cloud you guided them in the daytime,
and at night by a pillar of fire
to light the road they were to travel.
You came down on Mount Sinai
and spoke to them from heaven;
you gave them right judgments and true laws,
statutes and commandments which were good.
You made known to them your holy sabbath,
and through Moses your servant
you gave them commandments, statutes, and laws.
You gave them bread from heaven to stay their hunger
and brought water out from a rock to quench their thirst.
You bade them enter and take possession of the land
which you had solemnly sworn to give them.

'But they, our forefathers, were arrogant;
stubbornly they flouted your commandments.
They refused to listen,
forgetful of the miracles you had accomplished among them.
In their stubbornness they appointed a leader
to bring them back to slavery in Egypt.
But you are a forgiving God,
gracious and compassionate,
long-suffering and ever constant,
and you did not abandon them.

'Even when they made for themselves
the metal image of a bull-calf
and said, "This is your god
who brought you up from Egypt,"
and were guilty of gross blasphemies,
you in your great compassion
did not abandon them in the wilderness.
The pillar of cloud never failed
to guide them on their journey by day,
nor did the pillar of fire fail by night
to light the road they were to travel.
You gave your good spirit to instruct them;

you did not withhold your manna,
and you gave them water for their thirst.
During forty years you sustained them;
in the wilderness they lacked nothing,
their clothes did not wear out,
and their feet were not swollen.

'You gave them kings and their people as spoils of war.
They took possession
of the land of King Sihon of Heshbon
and the land of King Og of Bashan.
You made their descendants numerous,
countless as the stars in the sky,
and brought them into the land
you had promised their forefathers
they would enter and possess.
When their descendants came into the land
to take possession of it,
you subdued the Canaanite inhabitants before them,
giving kings and peoples into their hands
to do with them as they pleased.
They captured fortified towns and fertile land,
taking possession of houses
filled with all good things,
of rock-hewn cisterns, vineyards, olive groves,
and fruit trees in abundance.
They ate and were satisfied and grew fat;
they found delight in your great goodness.

'In growing defiance, they rebelled
and turned their backs on your law.
They killed your prophets,
who with warnings admonished them
to bring them again to you;
they were guilty of great blasphemies.
You handed them over to enemies to be oppressed.
But when they, under oppression, appealed to you,
from heaven you heard them

and in your great compassion sent saviours
to save them from their enemies.
After some respite
again they did what was wrong in your eyes,
and you abandoned them to their enemies,
who held them in subjection.
Yet once more they appealed to you,
and time after time you heard them from heaven
and in your compassion saved them.
To bring them back to your law
you solemnly warned them,
but arrogantly they flouted your commandments,
sinning against the ordinances
which bring life to those who keep them.
Stubbornly they turned aside;
in their obstinacy they would not obey.
For many years you were patient
and your spirit admonished them through the prophets.
Still they would not listen,
and so you handed them over
to the peoples of other countries.
Nevertheless in your great compassion
you did not make an end of them or forsake them;
for you are a gracious and compassionate God.

'Now, great and mighty and terrible God,
faithfully keeping covenant, our God,
do not regard as a small thing the hardships
that have befallen us, our kings and princes,
our priests, our prophets, our forefathers,
and all your people from the time of the kings of Assyria
up to the present day.
In all that has come upon us
you have been just,
for you have kept faith
while we have done wrong.
Our kings, our princes, our priests, and our forefathers

did not keep your law;
they paid no heed to your commandments
and the warnings you gave them.
Even in their own kingdom,
while they were enjoying
the great prosperity you gave them,
and the broad, fertile land you bestowed on them,
they did not serve you or renounce their evil ways.

'Today we are slaves,
slaves here in the land
which you gave to our forefathers
so that they might eat its fruits
and enjoy its good things.
All its produce now goes to the kings
whom you have set over us
because of our sins.
They have power over our bodies,
and they do as they please with our livestock:
we are in dire distress.

'Because of all this we make a binding declaration in writing, and our princes, our Levites, and our priests witness the sealing...

'The rest of the people, the priests, the Levites, the door-keepers, the singers, the temple servitors, with their wives, their sons, and their daughters, all who are capable of understanding, all who for the sake of the law of God have kept themselves apart from the foreign population, join with the leading brethren, when the oath is put to them, in swearing to obey God's law given by Moses the servant of God, and to observe and fulfil all the commandments of the Lord our Lord, his rules and his statutes.'

## THE DEDICATION OF THE CITY WALL
### Nehemiah 12:27–31, 37–43

At the dedication of the wall of Jerusalem the Levites, wherever they had settled, were sought out and brought to the city to celebrate the dedication with rejoicing, with thanksgiving and song, to the accompaniment of cymbals, harps, and lyres. The Levites, the singers, were assembled from the district round Jerusalem and from the hamlets of the Netophathites, also from Beth-gilgal and the region of Geba and Beth-azmoth; for the singers had built themselves hamlets in the neighbourhood of Jerusalem. When the priests and the Levites had purified themselves, they purified the people, the gates, and the wall.

Then I assembled the leading men of Judah on the city wall, and appointed two large choirs to give thanks. One went in procession to the right, going along the wall to the Dung Gate… they went past the Fountain Gate and thence straight forward by the steps up to the City of David, by the ascent to the city wall, past the house of David, and on to the Water Gate on the east.

The other thanksgiving choir went to the left, and I followed it with half the leading men of the people, continuing along the wall, past the Tower of the Ovens to the Broad Wall, and past the Ephraim Gate, and over the Jeshanah Gate, and over the Fish Gate, taking in the Tower of Hananel and the Tower of the Hundred, as far as the Sheep Gate; and they halted at the Guardhouse Gate.

Then the two thanksgiving choirs took their place in the house of God, and I and half the magistrates with me; and the priests Eliakim, Maaseiah, Miniamin, Micaiah, Elioenai, Zechariah, and Hananiah, with trumpets; Maaseiah, Shemaiah, Eleazar, Uzzi, Jehohanan, Malchiah, Elam, and Ezer. The singers, led by Izrahiah, raised their voices. A great sacrifice was celebrated that day, and they all rejoiced because God had given them great cause for rejoicing; the women and children rejoiced with them. And the rejoicing in Jerusalem was heard a long way off.

# Part Seven

# The Story of Jonah

## JONAH FLEES FROM THE LORD
### Jonah 1:1 – 2:10

The word of the Lord came to Jonah son of Amittai: 'Go to the great city of Nineveh; go and denounce it, for I am confronted by its wickedness.' But to escape from the Lord Jonah set out for Tarshish. He went down to Joppa, where he found a ship bound for Tarshish. He paid the fare and went on board to travel with it to Tarshish out of the reach of the Lord.

The Lord let loose a hurricane on the sea, which rose so high that the ship threatened to break up in the storm. The sailors were terror-stricken; everyone cried out to his own god for help, and they threw things overboard to lighten the ship. Meanwhile Jonah, who had gone below deck, was lying there fast asleep. When the captain came upon him he said, 'What, fast asleep? Get up and call to your god! Perhaps he will spare a thought for us, and we shall not perish.'

The sailors said among themselves, 'Let us cast lots to find who is to blame for our misfortune.' They cast lots, and when Jonah was singled out they wanted to be told how he was to blame. They questioned him: 'What is your business? Where do you come from? Which is your country? What is your nationality?' 'I am a Hebrew,' he answered, 'and I worship the Lord the God of heaven, who made both sea and dry land.' At this the sailors were even more afraid. 'What is this you have done?' they said, because they knew he was trying to escape from the Lord, for he had told them. 'What must we do with you to make the sea calm for us?' they asked; for it was getting worse. 'Pick me up and throw me overboard,' he replied; 'then the sea will go down. I know it is my fault that this great storm has struck you.' Though the crew rowed hard to put back to land it was no use, for the sea was running higher and higher. At last they called to the

Lord, 'Do not let us perish, Lord, for this man's life; do not hold us responsible for the death of an innocent man, for all this, Lord, is what you yourself have brought about.' Then they took Jonah and threw him overboard, and the raging of the sea subsided. Seized by a great fear of the Lord, the men offered a sacrifice and made vows to him.

The Lord ordained that a great fish should swallow Jonah, and he remained in its belly for three days and three nights. From the fish's belly Jonah offered this prayer to the Lord his God:

'In my distress I called to the Lord,
and he answered me;
from deep within Sheol I cried for help,
and you heard my voice.
You cast me into the depths,
into the heart of the ocean,
and the flood closed around me;
all your surging waves swept over me.
I thought I was banished from your sight
and should never again look towards your holy temple.

'The water about me rose to my neck,
for the deep was closing over me;
seaweed twined about my head
at the roots of the mountains;
I was sinking into a world
whose bars would hold me fast for ever.
But you brought me up, Lord my God,
alive from the pit.
As my senses failed I remembered the Lord,
and my prayer reached you in your holy temple.

'Those who cling to false gods
may abandon their loyalty,
but I with hymns of praise
shall offer sacrifice to you;
what I have vowed I shall fulfil.
Victory is the Lord's!'

The Lord commanded the fish, and it spewed Jonah out on the dry land.

# JONAH AND THE NINEVITES
## Jonah 3:1 – 4:11

A second time the word of the Lord came to Jonah: 'Go to the great city of Nineveh; go and denounce it in the words I give you.' Jonah obeyed and went at once to Nineveh. It was a vast city, three days' journey across, and Jonah began by going a day's journey into it. Then he proclaimed: 'In forty days Nineveh will be overthrown!'

The people of Nineveh took to heart this warning from God; they declared a public fast, and high and low alike put on sackcloth. When the news reached the king of Nineveh he rose from his throne, laid aside his robes of state, covered himself with sackcloth, and sat in ashes. He had this proclamation made in Nineveh: 'By decree of the king and his nobles, neither man nor beast is to touch any food; neither herd nor flock may eat or drink. Every person and every animal is to be covered with sackcloth. Let all pray with fervour to God, and let them abandon their wicked ways and the injustice they practise. It may be that God will relent and turn from his fierce anger: and so we shall not perish.' When God saw what they did and how they gave up their wicked ways, he relented and did not inflict on them the punishment he had threatened.

This greatly displeased Jonah. In anger he prayed to the Lord: 'It is just as I feared, Lord, when I was still in my own country, and it was to forestall this that I tried to escape to Tarshish. I knew that you are a gracious and compassionate God, long-suffering, ever constant, always ready to relent and not inflict punishment. Now take away my life, Lord: I should be better dead than alive.' 'Are you right to be angry?' said the Lord.

Jonah went out and sat down to the east of Nineveh, where he made himself a shelter and sat in its shade, waiting to see what would happen in the city. The Lord God ordained that a climbing gourd should grow up above Jonah's head to throw its shade over him and relieve his discomfort, and he was very glad of it. But at dawn the next day God ordained that a worm should attack the gourd, and it withered; and when the sun came up God ordained that a scorching wind should blow from the east. The sun beat down on Jonah's head till he grew faint, and he prayed for death; 'I should be better dead than alive,' he said. At this God asked, 'Are you right to be angry over the gourd?' 'Yes,' Jonah replied, 'mortally angry!' But the Lord said, 'You are sorry about the gourd, though you did not have the trouble of growing it, a plant which came up one night and died the next. And should not I be sorry about the great city of Nineveh, with its hundred and twenty thousand people who cannot tell their right hand from their left, as well as cattle without number?'

# Part Eight

# The Story of Daniel

## DANIEL IN BABYLON
### Daniel 1:1–21

In the third year of the reign of King Jehoiakim of Judah, Nebuchadnezzar, the Babylonian king, came and laid siege to Jerusalem. The Lord handed King Jehoiakim over to him, together with all that was left of the vessels from the house of God; and he carried them off to the land of Shinar, to the temple of his god, where he placed the vessels in the temple treasury.

The king ordered Ashpenaz, his chief eunuch, to bring into the palace some of the Israelite exiles, members of their royal house and of the nobility. They were to be young men free from physical defect, handsome in appearance, at home in all branches of knowledge, well-informed, intelligent, and so fitted for service in the royal court; and he was to instruct them in the writings and language of the Chaldaeans. The king assigned them a daily allowance of fine food and wine from the royal table, and their training was to last for three years; at the end of that time they would enter his service. Among them were certain Jews: Daniel, Hananiah, Mishael, and Azariah. To them the master of the eunuchs gave new names: Daniel he called Belteshazzar, Hananiah Shadrach, Mishael Meshach, and Azariah Abed-nego.

Daniel determined not to become contaminated with the food and wine from the royal table, and begged the master of the eunuchs to excuse him from touching it. God caused the master to look on Daniel with kindness and goodwill, and to Daniel's request he replied, 'I am afraid of my lord the king: he has assigned you food and drink, and if he were to see you and your companions looking miserable compared with the other young men of your own age, my head would be forfeit.' Then Daniel said to the attendant whom the master of the eunuchs had put in charge of Hananiah, Mishael, Azariah, and himself, 'Submit us to this test for ten days: give us only vegetables to eat and water to drink; then compare our appearance with that of the young men who have lived on the king's food, and be guided in your treatment of us by what you see for yourself.' He agreed to the proposal and submitted them to this test. At the end of the ten days they looked healthier and better nourished than any of the young men who had lived on the food from the king. So the attendant took away the food assigned to them and the wine they were to drink, and gave them vegetables only.

To all four of these young men God gave knowledge, understanding of books, and learning of every kind, and Daniel had a gift for interpreting visions and dreams of every kind. At the time appointed by the king for introducing the young men to court, the master of the eunuchs brought them into the presence of Nebuchadnezzar. The king talked with them all, but found none of them to compare with Daniel, Hananiah, Mishael, and Azariah; so they entered the royal service. Whenever the king consulted them on any matter calling for insight and judgment, he found them ten times superior to all the magicians and exorcists in his whole kingdom.

Daniel remained there until the accession of King Cyrus.

## NEBUCHADNEZZAR'S DREAM
Daniel 2:1–49

In the second year of his reign Nebuchadnezzar was troubled by dreams he had, so much so that he could not sleep. He gave orders for the magicians, exorcists, sorcerers, and Chaldaeans to be summoned to expound to him what he had been dreaming. When they presented themselves before the king, he said to them, 'I have had a dream, and my mind has been troubled to know what the dream was.' The Chaldaeans, speaking in Aramaic, said, 'Long live the king! Relate the dream to us, your servants, and we shall give you the interpretation.' The king answered, 'This is my firm decision: if you do not make both dream and interpretation known to me, you will be hacked limb from limb and your houses will be reduced to rubble.

But if you tell me the dream and its interpretation, you will be richly rewarded by me and loaded with honours. Tell me, then, the dream and its interpretation.' They said again, 'Let the king relate the dream to his servants, and we shall tell him the interpretation.' The king rejoined, 'It is clear to me that you are trying to gain time, because you see that I have come to this firm decision: if you do not make the dream known to me, there is but one verdict for you, and one only. What is more, you have conspired to tell me mischievous lies to my face in the hope that with time things may alter. Relate the dream to me, therefore, and then I shall know that you can give me its interpretation.' The Chaldaeans answered, 'No one on earth can tell your majesty what you wish to know. No king, however great and powerful, has ever made such a demand of a magician, exorcist, or Chaldaean. What your majesty asks is too hard; none but the gods can tell you, and they dwell remote from mortals.' At this the king became furious, and in great rage he ordered all the wise men of Babylon to be put to death. A decree was issued for the execution of the wise men, and search was made for Daniel and his companions.

As Arioch, captain of the royal bodyguard, set out to execute the wise men of Babylon, Daniel made a discreet and tactful approach to him. He said, 'May I ask you, sir, as the king's representative, why his majesty has issued so peremptory a decree?' Arioch explained the matter, and Daniel went to the king and begged to be allowed a certain time by which he would give the king the interpretation. He then went home and made the matter known to Hananiah, Mishael, and Azariah, his companions, saying they should implore the God of heaven to disclose this secret in his mercy, so that they should not be put to death along with the rest of the wise men of Babylon. The secret was then revealed to Daniel in a vision by night, and he blessed the God of heaven in these words:

'Blessed be God's name from age to age,
    for to him belong wisdom and power.
He changes seasons and times;
    he deposes kings and sets up kings;
he gives wisdom to the wise
    and knowledge to those who have discernment;

he reveals deep mysteries;
he knows what lies in darkness;
with him light has its dwelling.
God of my fathers, to you I give thanks and praise,
for you have given me wisdom and power.
Now you have made known to me what we asked;
you have given us the answer for the king.'

Daniel therefore went to Arioch, whom the king had charged with the execution of the wise men of Babylon. He approached him and said, 'Do not put the wise men to death; bring me before the king and I shall tell him the interpretation of his dream.' Greatly agitated, Arioch brought Daniel before the king. 'I have found among the Jewish exiles', he said, 'a man who will make known to your majesty the interpretation of your dream.' The king asked Daniel (who was also called Belteshazzar), 'Are you able to make known to me what I saw in my dream and to interpret it?' Daniel answered: 'No wise man, exorcist, magician, or diviner can tell your majesty the secret about which you ask. But there is in heaven a God who reveals secrets, and he has made known to King Nebuchadnezzar what is to be at the end of this age. This is the dream and these are the visions that came into your head: the thoughts that came to you, your majesty, as you lay on your bed, concerned the future, and he who reveals secrets has made known to you what is to be. This secret has been revealed to me, not because I am wiser than anyone alive, but in order that your majesty may know the interpretation and understand the thoughts which have entered your mind.

'As you watched, there appeared to your majesty a great image. Huge and dazzling, it stood before you, fearsome to behold. The head of the image was of fine gold, its chest and arms of silver, its belly and thighs of bronze, its legs of iron, its feet part iron and part clay. While you watched, you saw a stone hewn from a mountain by no human hand; it struck the image on its feet of iron and clay and shattered them. Then the iron, the clay, the bronze, the silver, and the gold were all shattered into fragments, and as if they were chaff from a summer threshing-floor the wind swept them away until no trace of them remained. But the stone which struck the image grew and became a huge mountain and filled the whole earth.

'That was the dream; now we shall relate to your majesty its interpretation. Your majesty, the king of kings, to whom the God of heaven has given the kingdom with its power, its might, and its honour, in whose hands he has placed mankind wherever they live, the wild animals, and the birds of the air, granting you sovereignty over them all: you yourself are that head of gold. After you there will arise another kingdom, inferior to yours, then a third kingdom, of bronze, which will have sovereignty over the whole world. There will be a fourth kingdom, strong as iron; just as iron shatters and breaks all things, it will shatter and crush all the others. As in your vision the feet and toes were part potter's clay and part iron, so it will be a divided kingdom, and just as you saw iron mixed with clay from the ground, so it will have in it something of the strength of iron. The toes being part iron and part clay means that the kingdom will be partly strong and partly brittle. As in your vision the iron was mixed with the clay, so there will be a mixing of families by intermarriage, but such alliances will not be stable: iron does not mix with clay. In the times of those kings the God of heaven will establish a kingdom which will never be destroyed, nor will it ever pass to another people; it will shatter all these kingdoms and make an end of them, while it will itself endure for ever. This is the meaning of your vision of the stone being hewn from a mountain by no human hand, and then shattering the iron, the bronze, the clay, the silver, and the gold. A mighty God has made known to your majesty what is to be hereafter. The dream and its interpretation are true and trustworthy.'

At this King Nebuchadnezzar prostrated himself and did homage to Daniel, and he gave orders that there should be presented to him a tribute of grain and soothing offerings. 'Truly,' he said, 'your God is indeed God of gods and Lord over kings, and a revealer of secrets, since you have been able to reveal this secret.' The king then promoted Daniel to high position and bestowed on him many rich gifts. He gave him authority over the whole province of Babylon and put him in charge of all Babylon's wise men. At Daniel's request the king appointed Shadrach, Meshach, and Abed-nego to administer the province of Babylon, while Daniel himself remained at court.

# THE FIERY FURNACE
Daniel 3:1–30

King Nebuchadnezzar made a gold image, ninety feet high and nine feet broad, and had it set up on the plain of Dura in the province of Babylon. The king then summoned the satraps, prefects, governors, counsellors, treasurers, judges, magistrates, and all the provincial officials to assemble and attend the dedication of the image he had set up. The satraps, prefects, governors, counsellors, treasurers, judges, magistrates, and all governors of provinces assembled for the dedication of the image King Nebuchadnezzar had set up, and they took their places in front of the image. A herald proclaimed in a loud voice, 'Peoples and nations of every language, you are commanded, when you hear the sound of horn, pipe, zither, triangle, dulcimer, a full consort of music, to prostrate yourselves and worship the gold image which King Nebuchadnezzar has set up. Whosoever does not prostrate himself and worship will be thrown forthwith into a blazing furnace.' Accordingly, no sooner did the sound of horn, pipe, zither, triangle, dulcimer, a full consort of music, reach them than all the peoples and nations of every language prostrated themselves and worshipped the gold image set up by King Nebuchadnezzar.

Some Chaldaeans seized the opportunity to approach the king with a malicious accusation against the Jews. They said, 'Long live the king! Your majesty has issued a decree that everyone who hears the sound of horn, pipe, zither, triangle, dulcimer, a full consort of music, must fall down and worship the gold image; and whoever does not do so will be thrown into a blazing furnace. There are certain Jews whom you have put in charge of the administration of the province of Babylon. These men, Shadrach, Meshach, and Abed-nego, have disregarded your royal command; they do not serve your gods, nor do they worship the gold image you set up.' In furious rage Nebuchadnezzar ordered Shadrach, Meshach, and Abed-nego to be fetched, and when they were brought into his presence, he asked them, 'Is it true, Shadrach, Meshach, and Abed-nego, that you do not serve my gods or worship the gold image which I have set up? Now if you are ready to prostrate yourselves as soon as you hear the sound of horn, pipe, zither, triangle, dulcimer, a full consort of music, and to worship the image that I have made, well and good. But if you do not worship it, you will be thrown forthwith into the blazing furnace; and what god is there that can deliver you from my power?' Their reply to the king was: 'Your majesty, we have no need to answer you on this matter. If there is a god who is able to save us from the blazing furnace, it is our God whom we serve; he will deliver us from your majesty's power. But if not, be it known to your majesty that we shall neither serve your gods nor worship the gold image you have set up.'

At this Nebuchadnezzar was furious with them, and his face became distorted with anger. He ordered that the furnace should be heated to seven times its usual heat, and commanded some of the strongest men in his army to bind Shadrach, Meshach, and Abed-nego and throw them into the blazing furnace. Then, just as they were, in trousers, shirts, headdresses, and their other clothes, they were bound and thrown into the furnace. Because the king's order was peremptory and the furnace exceedingly hot, those who were carrying the three men were killed by the flames; and Shadrach, Meshach, and Abed-nego fell bound into the blazing furnace.

Then King Nebuchadnezzar, greatly agitated, sprang to his feet, saying to his courtiers, 'Was it not three men whom we threw bound into the fire?' They answered, 'Yes, certainly, your majesty.' 'Yet', he insisted, 'I can see four men walking about in the fire, free and unharmed; and the fourth looks like a god.' Nebuchadnezzar approached the furnace door and called, 'Shadrach, Meshach, and Abed-nego, servants of the Most High God, come out!' When Shadrach, Meshach, and Abed-nego emerged from the fire, the satraps, prefects, governors, and the king's courtiers gathered round them and saw how the fire had had no power to harm their bodies. The hair of their heads had not been singed, their trousers were untouched, and no smell of fire lingered about them.

Nebuchadnezzar declared: 'Blessed be the God of Shadrach, Meshach, and Abed-nego! He has sent his angel to save his servants who, trusting in him, disobeyed the royal command; they were willing to submit themselves to the fire rather than to serve or worship any god other than their own God. I therefore issue this decree: anyone, whatever his people, nation, or language, if he speaks blasphemy against the God of Shadrach, Meshach, and Abed-nego, is to be hacked limb from limb and his house is to be reduced to rubble; for there is no other god who can save in such a manner.' Then the king advanced the fortunes of Shadrach, Meshach, and Abed-nego in the province of Babylon.

## NEBUCHADNEZZAR'S MADNESS
### Daniel 4

King Nebuchadnezzar to all peoples and nations of every language throughout the whole world: May your prosperity increase! It is my pleasure to recount the signs and wonders which the Most High God has worked for me:

> How great are his signs,
> how mighty his wonders!
> His kingdom is an everlasting kingdom,
> his sovereignty endures through all generations.

I, Nebuchadnezzar, was living contentedly at home in the luxury of my palace, but as I lay on my bed, I had a dream which filled me with fear, and the fantasies and visions which came into my head caused me dismay. I issued an order summoning to my presence all the wise men of Babylon to make known to me the interpretation of the dream. When the magicians, exorcists, Chaldaeans, and diviners came in, I related my dream to them, but they were unable to interpret it for me. Finally there came before me Daniel, who is called Belteshazzar after the name of my god, a man in whom resides the spirit of the holy gods. To him also I related the dream: 'Belteshazzar, chief of the magicians, you have in you, as I know, the spirit of the holy gods, and no secret baffles you; listen to what I saw in my dream, and tell me its interpretation.

'This is the vision which came to me while I lay on my bed:

> As I was looking,
> there appeared a very lofty tree at the centre of the earth;
> the tree grew great and became strong;
> its top reached to the sky,

and it was visible to earth's farthest bounds.
Its foliage was beautiful
and its fruit abundant,
and it yielded food for all.
Beneath it the wild beasts found shelter,
the birds lodged in the branches,
and from it all living creatures fed.

'This is what I saw in the vision which came to me while I lay on my bed:

There appeared a watcher,
a holy one coming down from heaven.
In a mighty voice he cried,
"Hew down the tree, lop off the branches,
strip away its foliage and scatter the fruit;
let the wild beasts flee from beneath it
and the birds from its branches;
but leave the stump with its roots in the ground.

So, bound with iron and bronze among the lush grass,
let him be drenched with the dew of heaven
and share the lot of the beasts in their pasture –
his mind will cease to be human,
and he will be given the mind of a beast.
Seven times will pass over him.
The issue has been determined by the watchers
and the sentence pronounced by the holy ones.

Thereby the living will know that the Most High is sovereign in the kingdom of men: he gives the kingdom to whom he wills, and may appoint over it the lowliest of mankind."

'This is the dream which I, King Nebuchadnezzar, dreamt; now, Belteshazzar, tell me its interpretation, for, though not one of the wise men in all my kingdom is able to make its meaning known to me, you can do it, because in you is the spirit of the holy gods.'

Daniel, who was called Belteshazzar, was dumbfounded for a moment, dismayed by his thoughts; but the king said, 'Do not let the dream and its interpretation dismay you.' Belteshazzar answered, 'My lord, if only the dream applied to those who hate you and its interpretation to your enemies! The tree which you saw grow great and become strong, reaching with its top to the sky and visible to earth's farthest bounds, its foliage beautiful and its fruit abundant, a tree which yielded food for all, beneath which the wild beasts dwelt and in whose branches the birds lodged: that tree, your majesty, is you. You have become great and strong; your power has grown and reaches the sky; your sovereignty extends to the ends of the earth. Also, your majesty, you saw a watcher, a holy one, coming down from heaven and saying, "Hew down the tree and destroy it, but leave the stump with its roots in the ground. So, bound with iron and bronze among the lush grass, let him be drenched with the dew of heaven and share the lot of the beasts until seven times pass over him."

'This is the interpretation, your majesty: it is a decree of the Most High which affects my lord the king. You will be banished from human society; you will be made to live with the wild beasts; like oxen you will feed on grass, and you will be drenched with the dew of heaven. Seven times will pass over you until you have acknowledged that the Most High is sovereign over the realm of humanity and gives it to whom he wills. As the command was given to leave the stump of the tree with its roots, by this you may know that from the time you acknowledge the sovereignty of Heaven your rule will endure. Your majesty, be advised by me: let charitable deeds replace your sins, generosity to the poor your wrongdoing. It may be that you will long enjoy contentment.'

All this befell King Nebuchadnezzar. At the end of twelve months the king was walking on the roof of the royal palace at Babylon, and he exclaimed, 'Is not this Babylon the great which I have built as a royal residence by my mighty power and for the honour of my own majesty?' The words were still on his lips, when there came a voice from heaven: 'To you, King Nebuchadnezzar, the word is spoken: the kingdom has passed from you. You are banished from human society; you are to live with the wild beasts and feed on grass like oxen. Seven times will pass over you until you have acknowledged that the Most High is sovereign over the realm of humanity and gives it to whom he will.' At that very moment this judgment came upon Nebuchadnezzar: he was banished from human society to eat grass like oxen, and his body was drenched with the dew of heaven, until his hair became shaggy like an eagle and his nails grew like birds' claws.

At the end of the appointed time, I, Nebuchadnezzar, looked up towards heaven and I was restored to my right mind. I blessed the Most High, praising and glorifying the Ever-living One:

> His sovereignty is everlasting
> and his kingdom endures through all generations.
> All who dwell on earth count for nothing;
> he does as he pleases with the host of heaven
> and with those who dwell on earth.
> No one can oppose his power
> or question what he does.

At that very time I was restored to my right mind and, for the glory of my kingdom, my majesty and royal splendour returned to me. My courtiers and my nobles sought audience of me, and I was re-established in my kingdom and my power was greatly increased. Now I, Nebuchadnezzar, praise and exalt and glorify the King of heaven; for all his acts are right and his ways are just, and he can bring low those whose conduct is arrogant.

## THE WRITING ON THE WALL
### Daniel 5

King Belshazzar gave a grand banquet for a thousand of his nobles and he was drinking wine in their presence. Under the influence of the wine, Belshazzar gave orders for the vessels of gold and silver which his father Nebuchadnezzar had taken from the temple at Jerusalem to be fetched, so that he and his nobles, along with his concubines and courtesans, might drink from them. So those vessels belonging to the house of God, the temple at Jerusalem, were brought, and the king, the nobles, and the concubines and courtesans drank from them. They drank their wine and they praised their gods of gold, silver, bronze, iron, wood, and stone.

Suddenly there appeared the fingers of a human hand writing on the plaster of the palace wall opposite the lamp, and the king saw the palm of the hand as it wrote. At this the king turned pale; dismay filled his mind, the strength went from his legs, and his knees knocked together. He called in a loud voice for the exorcists, Chaldaeans, and diviners to be brought in; then, addressing Babylon's wise men, he said, 'Whoever reads this writing and tells me its interpretation shall be robed in purple and have a gold chain hung round his neck, and he shall rank third in the kingdom.' All the king's wise men came, but they could neither read the writing nor make known to the king its interpretation. Then his deep dismay drove all colour from King Belshazzar's cheeks, and his nobles were in a state of confusion.

Drawn by what the king and his nobles were saying, the queen entered the banqueting hall: 'Long live the king!' she said. 'Why this dismay, and why do you look so pale? There is a man in your kingdom who has the spirit of the holy gods in him; he was known in your father's time to possess clear insight and godlike wisdom, so that King Nebuchadnezzar, your father, appointed him chief of the magicians, exorcists, Chaldaeans, and diviners. This Daniel, whom the king named Belteshazzar, is known to have exceptional ability, with knowledge and insight, and the gift of interpreting dreams, explaining riddles, and unravelling problems; let him be summoned now and he will give the interpretation.'

Daniel was then brought into the royal presence, and the king addressed him: 'So you are Daniel, one of the Jewish exiles whom my royal father brought from Judah. I am informed that the spirit of the gods resides in you and that you are known as a man of clear insight and exceptional wisdom. The wise men, the exorcists, have just been brought before me to read this writing and make known its interpretation to me, but they have been unable to give its meaning. I am told that you are able to furnish interpretations and unravel problems. Now, if you can read the writing and make known the interpretation, you shall be robed in purple and have a gold chain hung round your neck, and you shall rank third in the kingdom.' Daniel replied, 'Your majesty, I do not look for gifts from you; give your rewards to another. Nevertheless I shall read your majesty the writing and make known to you its interpretation.

'My lord king, the Most High God gave a kingdom with power, glory, and majesty to your father Nebuchadnezzar; and, because of the power he bestowed on him, all peoples and nations of every language trembled with fear before him. He put to death whom he would and spared whom he would, he promoted them at will and at will abased them. But, when he became haughty and stubborn and presumptuous, he was deposed from his royal throne and stripped of his glory. He was banished from human society, and his mind became like that of an animal; he had to live with the wild asses and to feed on grass like oxen, and his body was drenched with the dew of heaven, until he came to acknowledge that the Most High God is sovereign over the realm of humanity and appoints over it whom he will. But although you knew all this, you, his son Belshazzar, did not humble your heart. You have set yourself up against the Lord of heaven; his temple vessels have been fetched for you and your nobles, your concubines and courtesans to drink from them. You have praised gods fashioned from silver, gold, bronze, iron, wood, and stone, which cannot see or hear or know, and you have not given glory to God, from whom comes your every breath, and in whose charge are all your ways. That is why he sent the hand and why it wrote this inscription.

'The words inscribed were: "Mene mene tekel u-pharsin." Their interpretation is this: mene, God has numbered the days of your kingdom and brought it to an end; tekel, you have been weighed in the balance and found wanting; u-pharsin, your kingdom has been divided and given to the Medes and Persians.' Then at Belshazzar's command Daniel was robed in purple and a gold chain was hung round his neck, and proclamation was made that he should rank third in the kingdom.

That very night Belshazzar king of the Chaldaeans was slain, and Darius the Mede took the kingdom, being then about sixty-two years old.

## DANIEL AND THE LIONS
### Daniel 6

It pleased Darius to appoint a hundred and twenty satraps to be in charge throughout his kingdom, and over them three chief ministers, to whom the satraps were to submit their reports so that the king's interests might not suffer; of these three ministers, Daniel was one. Daniel outshone the other ministers and the satraps because of his exceptional ability, and it was the king's intention to appoint him over the whole kingdom. Then the ministers and satraps began to look round for some pretext to attack Daniel's administration of the kingdom, but they failed to find any malpractice on his part, for he was faithful to his trust. Since they could discover neither negligence nor malpractice, they said, 'We shall not find any ground for bringing a charge against this Daniel unless it is connected with his religion.' These ministers and satraps, having watched for an opportunity to approach the king, said to him, 'Long live King Darius! We, the ministers of the kingdom, prefects, satraps, courtiers, and governors, have taken counsel and all are agreed that the king should issue a decree and bring into force a binding edict to the effect that whoever presents a petition to any god or human being other than the king during the next thirty days is to be thrown into the lion-pit. Now let your majesty issue the edict and have it put in writing so that it becomes unalterable, for the law of the Medes and Persians may never be revoked.' Accordingly the edict was signed by King Darius.

When Daniel learnt that this decree had been issued, he went into his house. It had in the roof-chamber windows open towards Jerusalem; and there he knelt down three times a day and offered prayers and praises to his God as was his custom. His enemies, on the watch for an opportunity to catch him, found Daniel at his prayers making supplication to his God. They then went into the king's presence and reminded him of the edict. 'Your majesty,' they said, 'have you not issued an edict that any person who, within the next thirty days, presents a petition to any god or human being other than your majesty is to be thrown into the lion-pit?' The king answered, 'The matter has been determined in accordance with the law of the Medes and Persians, which may not be revoked.' So they said to the king, 'Daniel, one of the Jewish exiles, has disregarded both your majesty and the edict, and is making petition to his God three times a day.' When the king heard this, he was greatly distressed; he tried to think of a way to save Daniel, and continued his efforts till sunset. The men watched for an opportunity to approach the king, and said to him, 'Your majesty must know that by the law of the Medes and Persians no edict or decree issued by the king may be altered.' Then the king gave the order for Daniel to be brought and thrown into the lion-pit; but he said to Daniel, 'Your God whom you serve at all times, may he save you.' A stone was brought and put over the mouth of the pit, and the king sealed it with his signet and with the signets of his nobles, so that no attempt could be made to rescue Daniel.

The king went to his palace and spent the night fasting; no woman was brought to him, and sleep eluded him. He was greatly agitated and, at the first light of dawn, he rose and went to the lion-pit. When he came near he called anxiously, 'Daniel, servant of the living God, has your God whom you serve continually been able to save you from the lions?' Daniel answered, 'Long live the king! My God sent his angel to shut the lions' mouths and they have not injured me; he judged me innocent, and moreover I had done your majesty no injury.' The king was overjoyed and gave orders that Daniel should be taken up out of the pit. When this was done no trace of injury was found on him, because he had put his faith in his God. By order of the king those who out of malice had accused Daniel were brought and flung into the lion-pit along with their children and their wives, and before they reached the bottom the lions were upon them and devoured them, bones and all.

King Darius wrote to all peoples and nations of every language throughout the whole world: 'May your prosperity increase! I have issued a decree that in all my royal domains everyone is to fear and reverence the God of Daniel,

for he is the living God, the everlasting,
whose kingly power will never be destroyed;
whose sovereignty will have no end –
a saviour, a deliverer, a worker of signs and wonders
in heaven and on earth,
who has delivered Daniel from the power of the lions.'

Prosperity attended Daniel during the reigns of Darius and Cyrus the Persian.

# Part Nine

# The Story of Esther

## QUEEN VASHTI IS DEPOSED
### Esther 1

The events here related happened in the days of Ahasuerus, that Ahasuerus who ruled from India to Ethiopia, a hundred and twenty-seven provinces, at the time when he was settled on the royal throne in Susa, the capital city. In the third year of his reign he gave a banquet for all his officers and his courtiers; the Persians and Medes in full force, along with his nobles and provincial rulers, were in attendance. He put on display for many days, a hundred and eighty in all, the dazzling wealth of his kingdom and the pomp and splendour of his realm. At the end of that time the king gave a banquet for all the people present in Susa the capital city, both high and low; it lasted for seven days and was held in the garden court of the royal pavilion. There were white curtains and violet hangings fastened to silver rings by cords of fine linen with purple thread; the pillars were of marble, and gold and silver couches were placed on a mosaic pavement of malachite, marble, mother-of-pearl, and turquoise. Wine was served in golden goblets, each of a different design: the king's wine flowed in royal style, and the drinking was according to no fixed rule, for the king had laid down that all the palace stewards should respect the wishes of each guest. Queen Vashti too gave a banquet for the women inside the royal palace of King Ahasuerus.

On the seventh day, when he was merry with wine, the king ordered Mehuman, Biztha, Harbona, Bigtha, Abagtha, Zethar, and Carcas, the seven eunuchs who were in attendance on the king's person, to bring Queen Vashti into his presence wearing her royal diadem, in order to display her beauty to the people and to the officers; for she was indeed a beautiful woman. But when the royal command was conveyed to her by the eunuchs, Queen Vashti refused to come. This greatly incensed the king, and his wrath flared up. He conferred with wise men versed in precedents, for it was his custom to consult all who were expert in law and usage. Those closest to the king were Carshena, Shethar, Admatha, Tarshish, Meres, Marsena, and Memucan, the seven vicegerents of Persia and Media; they had access to the king and occupied the premier positions in the kingdom. 'What', he asked, 'does the law require to be done with Queen Vashti for disobeying my royal command conveyed to her by the eunuchs?'

In the presence of the king and the vicegerents, Memucan declared: 'Queen Vashti has done wrong, not to the king alone, but also to all the officers and to all the peoples in every province of King Ahasuerus. The queen's conduct will come to the ears of all women and embolden them to treat their husbands with disrespect; they will say, "King Ahasuerus ordered Queen Vashti to be brought before him, but she would not come!" The great ladies of Persia and Media, who have heard what the queen has said, will quote this day to all the king's officers, and there will be no end to the disrespect and discord!

'If it please your majesty, let a royal decree be issued by you, and let it be inscribed among the laws of the Persians and Medes, never to be revoked, that Vashti shall not again appear before King Ahasuerus; and let your majesty give her place as queen to another who is more worthy of it than she. When the edict made by the king is proclaimed throughout the length and breadth of the kingdom, all women, high and low alike, will give honour to their husbands.'

The advice pleased the king and the vicegerents, and the king did as Memucan had proposed. Dispatches were sent to all the king's provinces, to every province in its own script and to every people in their own language, in order that each man, whatever language he spoke, should be master in his own house.

## ESTHER BECOMES QUEEN
### Esther 2

Some time later, when the anger of King Ahasuerus had died down, he called Vashti to mind, remembering what she had done and what had been decreed against her. The king's attendants said: 'Let there be sought out for your majesty beautiful young virgins; let your majesty appoint commissioners in every province of your kingdom to assemble all these beautiful young virgins and bring them to the women's quarters in the capital Susa. Have them placed under the care of Hegai, the king's eunuch who has charge of the women, and let him provide the cosmetics they need. The girl who is most acceptable to the king shall become queen in place of Vashti.' The advice pleased the king, and he acted on it.

In Susa the capital there lived a Jew named Mordecai son of Jair, son of Shimei, son of Kish, a Benjamite; he had been taken into exile from Jerusalem among those whom King Nebuchadnezzar of Babylon had carried away with King Jeconiah of Judah. He had a foster-child Hadassah, that is, Esther, his uncle's daughter, who had neither father nor mother. She was a beautiful and charming girl, and after the death of her parents, Mordecai had adopted her as his own daughter.

When the king's order and decree were proclaimed and many girls were brought to Susa the capital to be committed to the care of Hegai, who had charge of the women, Esther too was taken to the palace to be entrusted to him. He found her pleasing, and she received his special favour: he promptly supplied her with her cosmetics and her allowance of food, and also with seven specially chosen maids from the king's palace. She and her maids were marked out for favourable treatment in the women's quarters.

Esther had not disclosed her race or family, because Mordecai had forbidden her to do so. Every day Mordecai would walk past the forecourt of the women's quarters to learn how Esther fared and what was happening to her.

The full period of preparation before a girl went to King Ahasuerus was twelve months: six months' treatment with oil of myrrh, and six months' with perfumes and cosmetics. At the end of this each girl's turn came, and, when she went from the women's quarters to the king's palace, she was allowed to take with her whatever she asked. She would enter the palace in the evening and return in the morning to another part of the women's quarters, to be under the care of Shaashgaz, the king's eunuch in charge of the concubines. She would not go again to the king unless he expressed a wish for her and she was summoned by name.

When the turn came for Esther, the girl Mordecai had adopted, the daughter of his uncle Abihail, to go in to the king, she asked for nothing to take with her except what was advised by Hegai, the king's eunuch in charge of the women. Esther charmed all who saw her, and when she was brought to King Ahasuerus in the royal palace, in the tenth month, the month of Tebeth, in the seventh year of his reign, the king loved her more than any of his other women. He treated her with greater favour and kindness than all the rest of the virgins, and placed a royal diadem on her head, making her queen in place of Vashti. Then in Esther's honour the king gave a great banquet, to which were invited all his officers and courtiers. He also proclaimed a holiday throughout his provinces and distributed gifts worthy of a king.

Mordecai was in attendance in the court. On his instructions Esther had not disclosed her family or her race, obeying Mordecai in this as she used to do when she was his ward. One day when Mordecai was at court, two of the king's eunuchs, Bigthan and Teresh, keepers of the threshold who were disaffected, were plotting to assassinate King Ahasuerus. This became known to Mordecai, who told Queen Esther; and she, on behalf of Mordecai, informed the king. The matter was investigated and, the report being confirmed, the two men were hanged on the gallows. All this was recorded in the court chronicle in the king's presence.

## HAMAN PLOTS TO DESTROY THE JEWS
### Esther 3:1–15

It was after those events that King Ahasuerus promoted Haman son of Hammedatha the Agagite, advancing him and giving him precedence above all his fellow-officers. Everyone in attendance on the king at court bowed down and did obeisance to Haman, for so the king had commanded; but Mordecai would not bow or do obeisance. The courtiers said to him, 'Why do you flout his majesty's command?' They challenged him day after day, and when he refused to listen they informed Haman, in order to discover if

Mordecai's conduct would be tolerated, for he had told them that he was a Jew. Haman was furious when he saw that Mordecai was not bowing down or doing obeisance to him; but having learnt who Mordecai's people were, he scorned to lay hands on him alone; he looked for a way to exterminate not only Mordecai but all the Jews throughout the whole kingdom.

In the twelfth year of King Ahasuerus, in the first month, Nisan, they cast lots – Pur as it is called – in the presence of Haman, taking the days and months one by one, and the lot fell on the thirteenth day of the twelfth month, the month of Adar.

Haman said to King Ahasuerus: 'Dispersed in scattered groups among the peoples throughout the provinces of your realm, there is a certain people whose laws are different from those of every other people. They do not observe the king's laws, and it does not befit your majesty to tolerate them. If it please your majesty, let an order be drawn up for their destruction; and I shall hand over to your majesty's officials the sum of ten thousand talents of silver, to be deposited in the royal treasury.' The king drew off the signet ring from his finger and gave it to Haman son of Hammedatha the Agagite, the enemy of the Jews. 'Keep the money,' he said, 'and deal with the people as you think best.'

On the thirteenth day of the first month the king's secretaries were summoned and, in accordance with Haman's instructions, a writ was issued to the king's satraps and the governors of every province, and to the rulers over each separate people. It was drawn up in the name of King Ahasuerus and sealed with the king's signet, and transcribed for each province in its own script and for each people in their own language. Dispatches were sent by courier to all the king's provinces with orders to destroy, slay, and exterminate all Jews, young and old, women and children, in one day, the thirteenth day of the twelfth month, the month of Adar; their goods were to be treated as spoil. A copy of the writ was to be issued as a decree in every province and to be publicly displayed to all the peoples, so that they might be ready for that day. At the king's command the couriers set off post-haste, and the decree was issued in Susa the capital city. The king and Haman sat down to carouse, but in the city of Susa confusion reigned.

# ESTHER AND MORDECAI WIN THE KING'S FAVOUR
## Esther 4:1–6:14

When Mordecai learnt of all that had been done, he tore his clothes and put on sackcloth and ashes. He went out through the city, lamenting loudly and bitterly, until he came right in front of the palace gate; no one wearing sackcloth was allowed to pass through that gate. In every province reached by the royal command and decree there was great mourning among the Jews, with fasting and weeping and beating of the breast; most of them lay down on beds of sackcloth and ashes. When Queen Esther's maids and eunuchs came in and told her, she was greatly distraught. She sent clothes for Mordecai to wear instead of his sackcloth; but he would not accept them.

Esther then summoned Hathach, one of the king's eunuchs appointed to wait on her, and ordered him to find out from Mordecai what was the trouble and the reason for it. Hathach went out to Mordecai in the city square opposite the palace, and Mordecai told him all that had happened to him and how much money Haman had offered to pay into the royal treasury for the destruction of the Jews. He also gave him a copy of the writ for their extermination, which had been issued in Susa, so that he might show it to Esther and tell her about it, directing her to go to the king to implore his favour and intercede for her people. When Hathach came in and informed Esther of what Mordecai had said, she told him to take back this message: 'All the courtiers and the people in the king's provinces know that if any person, man or woman, enters the royal presence in the inner court without being summoned, there is but one law: that person shall be put to death, unless the king extends to him the gold sceptre; only then may he live. What is more, I have not been summoned to the king for the last thirty days.'

When Mordecai was told what Esther had said, he sent this reply, 'Do not imagine, Esther, that, because you are in the royal palace, you alone of all the Jews will escape. If you remain silent at such a time as this, relief and deliverance for the Jews will appear from another quarter; but you and your father's family will perish. And who knows whether it is not for a time like this that you have become queen?' Esther sent this answer back to Mordecai: 'Go and assemble all the Jews that are in Susa, and fast on my behalf; for three days, night and day, take neither food nor drink, and I also will fast with my maids. After that, in defiance of the law, I shall go to the king; if I perish, I perish.' Mordecai then went away and did exactly as Esther had bidden him.

On the third day Esther arrayed herself in her royal robes and stood in the inner court, facing the palace itself; the king was seated on his royal throne in the palace, opposite the entrance. When he caught sight of Queen Esther standing in the court, he extended to her the gold sceptre he held, for she had obtained his favour. Esther approached and touched the tip of the sceptre. The king said to her, 'What is it, Queen Esther? Whatever you request, up to half my kingdom, it shall be granted you.' 'If it please your majesty,' she answered, 'will you come today, my lord, and Haman with you, to a banquet I have prepared for you?' The king gave orders for Haman to be brought with all speed to meet Esther's wishes; and the king and Haman went to the banquet she had prepared.

Over the wine the king said to Esther, 'Whatever you ask will be given you; whatever you request, up to half my kingdom, will be granted.' Esther replied, 'What I ask and request is this: If I have found favour with your majesty, and if it please you, my lord, to give me what I ask and to grant my request, will your majesty and Haman come again tomorrow to the banquet that I shall prepare for you both? Tomorrow I shall do as your majesty says.'

Haman left the royal presence that day overjoyed and in the best of spirits, but as soon as he saw Mordecai in the king's court and observed that he did not rise or defer to him, he was furious; yet he kept control of himself. When he arrived home, he sent for his friends and for Zeresh his wife and held forth to them about the splendour of his wealth and his many sons, and how the king had promoted him and advanced him above the other officers and courtiers. 'Nor is that all,' Haman went on; 'Queen Esther had no one but myself come with the king to the banquet which she had prepared; and I am invited by her again tomorrow with the king. Yet all this gives me no satisfaction so long as I see that Jew Mordecai in attendance at the king's court.' His wife Zeresh and all his friends said to him, 'Have a gallows set up, seventy-five feet high, and in the morning propose to the king that

Mordecai be hanged on it. Then you can go with the king to the banquet and enjoy yourself.' This advice seemed good to Haman, and he set up the gallows.

That night sleep eluded the king, so he ordered the chronicle of memorable events to be brought, and it was read to him. There it was found recorded how Mordecai had furnished information about Bigthana and Teresh, the two royal eunuchs among the keepers of the threshold who had plotted to assassinate King Ahasuerus. When the king asked what honour or dignity had been conferred on Mordecai for this, his attendants said, 'Nothing has been done for him.' 'Who is in the court?' said the king. As Haman had just then entered the outer court of the palace to propose to the king that Mordecai should be hanged on the gallows he had prepared for him, the king's attendants replied, 'Haman is standing there in the court.' 'Let him enter!' commanded the king. When he came in, the king asked him, 'What should be done for the man whom the king wishes to honour?' Haman thought to himself, 'Whom, other than myself, would the king wish to honour?' So he answered, 'For the man whom the king wishes to honour, let there be brought a royal robe which the king himself has worn, and a horse on which the king rides, with a royal diadem on its head. Let the robe and the horse be handed over to one of the king's noble officers, and let him invest the man whom the king wishes to honour and lead him mounted on the horse through the city square, proclaiming as he goes: "This is what is done for the man whom the king wishes to honour."' The king said to Haman, 'Take the robe and the horse at once, as you have said, and do this for Mordecai the Jew who is present at court. Let nothing be omitted of all you have proposed.' Haman took the robe and the horse, invested Mordecai, and led him on horseback through the city square, proclaiming before him: 'This is what is done for the man whom the king wishes to honour.'

Mordecai then returned to court, while Haman in grief hurried off home with his head veiled. When he told his wife Zeresh and all his friends everything that had happened to him, the response he got from his advisers and Zeresh was: 'If you have begun to fall before Mordecai, and he is a Jew, you cannot get the better of him; your downfall before him is certain.'

While they were still talking with him, the king's eunuchs arrived and Haman was hurried off to the banquet Esther had prepared.

## ESTHER SAVES HER PEOPLE
Esther 7:1–9:19

So the king and Haman went to Queen Esther's banquet, and again on that second day over the wine the king said, 'Whatever you ask will be given you, Queen Esther. Whatever you request, up to half my kingdom, it will be granted.' She answered, 'If I have found favour with your majesty, and if it please you, my lord, what I ask is that my own life and the lives of my people be spared. For we have been sold, I and my people, to be destroyed, slain, and exterminated. If it had been a matter of selling us, men and women alike, into slavery, I should have kept silence; for then our plight would not have been such as to injure the king's interests.' King Ahasuerus demanded, 'Who is he, and where is he, who has dared to do such a thing?' 'A ruthless enemy,' she answered, 'this wicked Haman!' Haman stood aghast before the king and queen. In a rage the king rose from the banquet and went into the garden of the pavilion, while Haman remained where he was to plead for his life with Queen Esther; for he saw that in the king's mind his fate was determined. When the king returned from the pavilion garden to the banqueting hall, Haman had flung himself on the couch where Esther was reclining. The king exclaimed, 'Will he even assault the queen in the palace before my very eyes?' The words had no sooner left the king's lips than Haman's face was covered. Harbona, one of the eunuchs in attendance on the king, said, 'There is a gallows seventy-five feet high standing at Haman's house; he had it erected for Mordecai, whose evidence once saved your majesty.' 'Let Haman be hanged on it!' said the king. So they hanged Haman on the gallows he had prepared for Mordecai. Then the king's anger subsided.

That same day King Ahasuerus gave Queen Esther the property of Haman, the enemy of the Jews, and Mordecai came into the king's presence, for Esther had revealed his relationship to her. The king drew off his signet ring, which he had taken back from Haman, and gave it to Mordecai. Esther put Mordecai in charge of Haman's property.

Once again Esther addressed the king, falling at his feet and imploring him with tears to thwart the wickedness of Haman the Agagite and frustrate his plot against the Jews. The king extended his gold sceptre towards her, and she rose and stood before him. 'May it please your majesty,' Esther said; 'if I have found favour with you, and if what I propose seems right to your majesty and I have won your approval, let a writ be issued to recall the dispatches which Haman son of Hammedatha the Agagite wrote in pursuance of his plan to destroy the Jews in all the royal provinces. For how can I bear to witness the disaster which threatens my people? How can I bear to witness the destruction of my kindred?' King Ahasuerus said to Queen Esther and to Mordecai the Jew, 'I have given Haman's property to Esther, and he has been hanged on the gallows because he threatened the lives of the Jews. Now you may issue a writ in my name concerning the Jews, in whatever terms you think fit, and seal it with the royal signet; no order written in the name of the king and sealed with the royal signet can be rescinded.'

On the twenty-third day of the third month, the month of Sivan, the king's secretaries were summoned, and a writ exactly as Mordecai directed was issued to the Jews, and to the satraps, the governors, and the rulers of the hundred and twenty-seven provinces from India to Ethiopia; it was issued for each province in its own script and for each people in their own language, and also for the Jews in their script and language. The writ was drawn up in the name of King Ahasuerus and sealed with the royal signet, and dispatches were sent by couriers mounted on horses from the royal stables. By these dispatches the king granted permission to the Jews in each and every city to assemble in self-defence, and to destroy, slay, and exterminate every man, woman, and child, of any people or province which might attack them, and to treat their goods as spoil, throughout all the provinces of King Ahasuerus, in one day, the thirteenth day of Adar, the twelfth month. A copy of the writ was to be issued as a decree in every province and published to all peoples, and the Jews were to be ready for that day, the day of vengeance on their enemies. Couriers, mounted on horses from the royal stables, set off post-haste at the king's urgent command; and the decree was proclaimed also in Susa the capital.

When Mordecai left the king's presence in a royal robe of violet and white, wearing an imposing gold crown and a cloak of fine linen with purple thread, the city of Susa shouted for joy. All was light and joy, gladness and honour for the Jews; in every province and city reached by the royal command and decree there was joy and gladness for the Jews, feasting and holiday. And many of the peoples of the world professed Judaism, because fear of the Jews had fallen on them.

On the thirteenth day of Adar, the twelfth month, the time came for the king's command and decree to be carried out. That very day on which the enemies of the Jews had hoped to triumph over them was to become the day when the Jews should triumph over those who hated them. Throughout all the provinces of King Ahasuerus, the Jews assembled in their cities to attack those who had sought to bring disaster on them. None could offer resistance, because fear of them had fallen on all the peoples. The rulers of the provinces, the satraps and the governors, and the royal officials all aided the Jews, out of fear of Mordecai, for he had become a person of great power in the royal palace, and as the power of the man increased, his fame spread throughout every province. The Jews put all their enemies to the sword. There was great slaughter and destruction, and they worked their will on those who hated them.

In Susa the capital the Jews slaughtered five hundred men; and they also put to death Parshandatha, Dalphon, Aspatha, Poratha, Adalia, Aridatha, Parmashta, Arisai, Aridai, and Vaizatha, the ten sons of Haman son of Hammedatha, the persecutor of the Jews; but they took no plunder.

That day when the number of those killed in Susa was reported to the king, he said to Queen Esther, 'In Susa the capital the Jews have slaughtered five hundred men; they have killed the ten sons of Haman; what will they have done in the rest of the provinces of the kingdom? Whatever you ask will be given you; whatever further request you have, it will be granted.' Esther replied, 'If it please your majesty, let the Jews in Susa be permitted tomorrow also to take action according to this day's decree; and let the bodies of Haman's ten sons be hung up on the gallows.' The king gave orders for this to be done; the decree was issued in Susa, and Haman's ten sons were hung up on the gallows. The Jews in Susa assembled again on the fourteenth day of the month of Adar and killed there three hundred men; but they took no plunder.

The rest of the Jews throughout the king's provinces rallied in self-defence and so had respite from their enemies; they slaughtered seventy-five thousand of those who hated them, but they took no plunder. That was on the thirteenth day of the month of Adar; on the fourteenth day they rested and made it a day of feasting and joy. The Jews in Susa had assembled on both the thirteenth and fourteenth days of the month; they rested on the fifteenth day and made that a day of feasting and joy. This explains why Jews in the countryside who live in remote villages observe the fourteenth day of Adar with joy and feasting as a holiday, sending presents of food to one another.

## THE FEAST OF PURIM
### Esther 9:20–32

Mordecai put these things on record, and he sent letters to all the Jews throughout the provinces of King Ahasuerus, both near and far, requiring them to observe annually the fourteenth and fifteenth days of the month of Adar as the days on which the Jews had respite from their enemies; that was the month which was changed for them from sorrow into joy, from a time of mourning to a holiday. They were to observe them as days of feasting and joy, days for sending presents of food to one another and gifts to the poor.

The Jews undertook to continue the practice that they had begun in accordance with Mordecai's letter. This they did because Haman son of Hammedatha the Agagite, the enemy of all the Jews, had plotted to destroy them and had cast lots – Pur as it is called – with intent to crush and destroy them. But when the matter came before the king, he issued written orders that the wicked plot which Haman had devised against the Jews should recoil on his own head, and that he and his sons should be hanged on the gallows. This is why these days were named Purim, from the word Pur. Accordingly, because of all that was written in this letter, because of all they had seen and experienced in this affair, the Jews resolved and undertook, on behalf of themselves, their descendants, and all who might join them, to observe without fail these two days as a yearly festival in the prescribed manner and at the appointed time; further, that these days were to be remembered and celebrated throughout all generations, in every family, province, and city, so that the observance of the days of Purim should never lapse among the Jews, and the commemoration of them should never cease among their descendants.

Queen Esther daughter of Abihail gave full authority in writing to Mordecai the Jew, to confirm this second letter about Purim. Letters to ensure peace and security were sent to all the Jews in the one hundred and twenty-seven provinces of King Ahasuerus, requiring the observance of these days of Purim at their appointed time, as Mordecai the Jew and Queen Esther had prescribed for them, and in the same way as regulations for fasts and lamentations were prescribed for themselves and for their descendants. By the command of Esther these regulations for Purim were confirmed and put in writing.

## THE GREATNESS OF MORDECAI
### Esther 10

King Ahasuerus exacted tribute from the land and the coasts and islands. All his acts of might and power, and the high dignities which he conferred on Mordecai, are recorded in the annals of the kings of Media and Persia. Mordecai the Jew ranked second only to King Ahasuerus himself; he was a great man among the Jews and popular with all his many countrymen, for he sought the good of his people and promoted the welfare of all their descendants.

# Index of Primary Sources